Core Actors in America

Core Actors in America

A Vital View of Human Moral Nature And Political Change

Stephen Terhune Smith

LEXINGTON BOOKS

A division of
ROWMAN & LITTLEFIELD PUBLISHERS, INC.
Lanham • Boulder • New York • Toronto • Plymouth, UK

LEXINGTON BOOKS

A division of Rowman & Littlefield Publishers, Inc.
A wholly owned subsidiary of The Rowman & Littlefield Publishing Group, Inc.
4501 Forbes Boulevard, Suite 200
Lanham, MD 20706

Estover Road
Plymouth PL6 7PY
United Kingdom

British Library Cataloguing in Publication Information Available

Library of Congress Cataloging-in-Publication Data

Smith, Stephen Terhune, 1943–
   Core actors in America : a vital view of human moral nature and political change /
Stephen Terhune Smith.
      p. cm.
   Includes bibliographical references and index.
   ISBN-13: 978-0-7391-1766-8 (cloth : alk. paper)
   ISBN-10: 0-7391-1766-1 (cloth : alk. paper)
   1. Political science—United States. 2. Political science—United States—Philosophy.
I. Title.
   JA84.U5S572 2007
   320.97301—dc22

                                                                                    2007016400

To my wife, Nancy, whose encouragement has kept me moving forward, and who has taught me what it means to care.

Contents

Acknowledgments

This project began almost eight years ago with a suggestion from my then dissertation advisor, Jeffrey Leigh Sedgwick, that I interview some social and political activists in the University of Massachusetts, Amherst region and attempt to learn what it is that informs them and motivates them to act. My initial reaction to his suggestion was disappointment. Although I had a brief history as an activist during the mid-1960s, I had long-since rejoined the mainstream, gradually and reluctantly accepting the conventional view that peace and social justice activism was largely peripheral to America's political and social development. As the pages that follow will confirm, that is no longer my belief.

Somewhat skeptically at first, I decided to follow Jeffrey Sedgwick's advice. I soon discovered that his suggestion was not only intellectually challenging, but, for me, intuitively right. I cannot thank him enough for his advice, encouragement, helpful critique, and keen insight. The other members of my committee, Lewis C. Mainzer and Julius Lester, were the perfect complement. Professor Mainzer, who had recently retired from the university, donated extensive time and thought to each chapter, together with much encouragement. Professor Lester was gracious as well as generous in his willingness to serve not only as the outside member, but also in his thorough preparation, helpful questions, and valuable suggestions for the original structuring and final editing of the dissertation. Since then, each of them has further encouraged me to develop the dissertation into a book manuscript.

In all, twenty-six persons volunteered their time to participate in interviews, all of them lengthy and often inconveniencing. My thanks to each of them for their invaluable help and their patient toleration of my efforts to have them not simply "tell their stories," but to search deeply and critically within themselves for their motive resources. To those participants whose stories and self-insights I was not able to directly utilize, please understand that this occurred for reasons having only to do with space and time constraints. Each interviewee was an authentic, willing source of knowledge and insight, and as such, each has been included. Thanks also to Judy Rohan for moonlighting from her job at the DuBois Library and taking time from her family to transcribe the interviews, especially under the trying conditions of poor quality tape-recordings and my frugal budget.

Special thanks is owed to the late Wilson Carey McWilliams who offered me the precious gift of encouragement and the reinforcement of professional compliment in his generous response to the early chapters that he was kind enough to read. His book, *The Idea of Fraternity in America*, was a primary source of inspiration throughout this endeavor.

Finally, my appreciation and apologies to friends, family, and colleagues who endured my incessant efforts to try out the ideas that ultimately formed the core of this endeavor. This is especially the case with my wife, and also my dear friend, Hassan Gebel, both of whom read along as I wrote, offering their encouragement and suggestions, from the first chapter to the last.

Chapter One

Introduction

[I]t would seem that we have nowadays broken the natural link between
. . . acts and beliefs; that harmony which has been observed throughout history between the feelings and ideas of men seems to have been destroyed,
and one might suppose that all laws of moral analogy had been abolished.

—Alexis de Tocqueville[1]

A common view of the world, based on values and conceptions, constitutes
the essential unity between men who must necessarily see the world
through different eyes.

—Wilson Carey McWilliams[2]

Groups are formed for a great variety of reasons, but one of the chief reasons is to advocate or act out . . . a new conception of the highest good, a
conception at which the state does not aim, and perhaps cannot.

—Michael Walzer[3]

There is a strong dynamic that has long been at work in the development of
America. It consists of a particular coterie of individual and small group actors
who, in each generation, play critical roles in the process of political change.
They are the first to call for some fundamental alteration in our social and political structure and the first to demonstrate that such change is at least possible. By definition, the reforms that these "core actors" initiate are, along with
the actors themselves, highly unpopular in the early going. Their words and
deeds challenge prevailing norms and practices that are powerfully institutionalized and widely accepted. Slavery and the legal subordination of women
are good examples. Core actors contested these institutions, both here and

abroad, likely from their earliest inceptions. The nature, context, and consequences of their acts suggests that they did so on profoundly informed moral
grounds—certain belief that each practice was simply wrong, unjust, or evil.

Conceiving and acting both alone and in small groups, in venues of all
sizes, locales, and degrees of intimacy, core actors speak and act in conventionally foolish, at times risk-laden, nonconformity.[4] In doing so, they often
find themselves marginalized, suppressed, or expelled from the formative and
inevitably constraining embrace of our governing institutions. These forma-
tions, themselves often the partial products of earlier efforts to instantiate reform, now ironically serve as ramparts of a status quo that is both defined and
defended by other concrete actors. Many of the latter are powerfully armed
with prevailing philosophical wisdom, practical morality, collective symbols,
traditional faith, and, quite often, good intentions. As we look at the roster of
the guardian defenders, we should not be at all surprised to see many of our
names listed among them, at least in the early-to-middle stages of the campaign. Some of us may even be located at the outer bulwarks, earnestly seeking to avoid casualties by urging the challengers to be less confrontational,
less radical, and more patient—in short, more like ourselves. We see ourselves as peacemakers, realists, practical seekers of some middle ground—
important, yet inherently conservative tasks.

Despite our sincere advice and occasional willingness to condone outright
coercion by others, at least some of these challengers will persist, and, in a few
notable instances like the two mentioned above, their stubborn efforts will bear
substantial fruit. After several generations of sustained effort by the few who
were somehow able to live openly contradictory lives among us, our social and
political practices and supportive beliefs can be seen to have changed at least
somewhat in conformity with their views. Such results suggest that a sufficient
portion of us have been persuaded in some manner by the words and deeds of
former eccentrics, even as we isolate, attack, strive to ignore, or seek to dis-
suade others who serve as irritants in our contemporary midst.

Core actors are critical to the process of political and social change for two
reasons: *first*, as suggested above, because they are the first to act, to clearly, un-
equivocally identify some wrong in the presence of at least one other, and, by
their words and deeds, demonstrate that change is at least possible, if only in
the instance of their own visible behavior; *second*, when insufficient others
have been persuaded to either support or acquiesce in the change sought, either
in that generation or, more typically, those which follow, a few who have been
"converted," or who have arrived at the same belief of their own accord, somehow persist in their nonconformity and thereby maintain the possibility of future reform. Our profoundly informed ideals, we too often forget, have humble
origins. Moreover, they require the vitality of human embodiment not only for
their birth, but for their potential growth and eventual instantiation. As Isaiah

Berlin suggested, human ideals, such as political liberty, are not intrinsic to the notion of a human being. They represent "historical growth," attributable to the "conduct of *men*, who even according to Marx, make history. . . . "5

THE PROBLEM OF FINDING COMMON GROUND

Our failure to adequately acknowledge or even recognize the essential role of core actors in our past and, more commonly, in the present, or to discern the strong undercurrent that they set in motion both around and within us, involves more than our discomfort when confronted with their radical nonconformity. While gadflies are likely to disturb the members of any society, our particular unease is uniquely informed by two related, fundamental misapprehensions, both of which have been strongly influenced by our Enlightenment heritage. The first is that we lack a sufficient shared understanding of how our individual morality—our basic precepts concerning ourselves, others, and the world—is most strongly, deeply discerned and grounded. Under the influence of our Enlightenment philosophical legacy—dominant liberalism and subordinate communitarianism—we have narrowed both the scope and depth of what we are able to most profoundly learn and most powerfully share. The second, related misapprehension is that we fail in all but extraordinary times to detect the potential reach of our own moral capacity. Under the formative and legitimating sway of Enlightenment thought, we have come to think of ourselves—or at least of others—as less capable than we truly are.

PROFOUND LEARNING

Two frequently offered contemporary answers to the "how" and resulting "what" of our modern attempts at profound learning are the intimate, personal truths of subjectivism and the "that depends" of cultural relativism. Such responses, particularly when considered alongside the enervated rational and inherently divisive doctrinal rhetoric of our contemporary domestic moral discourse, are quite understandable. At the very least, they furnish logically soothing, even pragmatic retreats from our current inability to identify and publicly build upon deep, broadly supportive, common ground. As will be later explained in some detail, they are also part of our Enlightenment inheritance of liberalism and communitarian thought, respectively.

Among the variables in our moral formation, there is, to be sure, a wide range of human variety in our individual experiences, cultural traditions, and other inputs to our cognition and reflection. However, while our differences are considerable, and our uniqueness may approach the logic of infinity in the postmodern gossamer worlds of theoretical or aesthetic possibility, the record of our collective nonmaterial accomplishments at the urging, example, and persuasive insistence of morally informed core actors suggests that our fundamental differences in nature and perception are few and manageable by significantly noncoercive means.

Yet our diversity, including our major group distinctions, must be acknowledged. By doing so, we not only obtain a fuller composite of the human condition, including that which separates us, but also can begin to see ourselves, in part, as the product of the unifying efforts of some, in each generation, who disclose their vital, more inclusive world-view to us and to others. Such authentic, direct, intimate revelations, inseparable from the means of their communication, constitute a necessary part of the change dynamic—the above-noted ability of core actors, acting in imperfect concert, to draw enough of us in their direction to have a chance at practical social and political success. It takes a range of voices to reach and enlist the support of a critical mass within the broad polity that America increasingly represents.

The substance of what is called for and demonstrated by the words and actions that exemplify each core actor, however, must be essentially the same. Notwithstanding their diverse locales and origins, there must be some commonality not only in what they exhibit and seek, *but in what informs them.* Each voice, whatever its accent, requires for its moral vitality—its inner strength as well as its unifying social and political energy—that it be informed by some elemental, deeply affirming knowledge of its *intrinsic* connection to others and the world. As will be demonstrated in some detail, it is knowledge that is informed by momentary profound insights and more subtle awareness, each gained from repeated encounters that occur in the midst of unmediated relationships with the concrete particulars of life itself. To act persuasively and otherwise effectively against the comfort of conformity, the pressures of convention, and the fear induced by coercion requires no less.

These recurrent glimpses and more gradual awareness of fundamental truths inform, inspire, orient, and drive core actors across the broad spectrum of human achievement—from the intimacy of parenting to social and political involvement with the world-at-large. By their thus informed reactions to existing conditions and events, and their persuasive interactions with others in each generation, they furnish us with the fundamental parameters of justice and expanding content of the common good as part of the more inclusive, life-reverent world-view that they demonstrate and, in turn, concretely inspire.[6]

A combination of vital personality, strengthened by the passionate, active, demonstrative quality of their knowledge of the just, the unjust, and the good, stimulates in these core actors a pheromone-like attraction that draws at least a few of us into close, caring, common goal-seeking relationships with them.

Others, due to the constraints of proximity, time, and human capacity, must be content with more imaginative, physically distant, but still warm relationships of inspiration, common pursuits, and mutual support. As Wilson Carey McWilliams somewhat suggests, these shareable products of life encounter, insight, awareness, and more broadly informed reflection constitute the organic heart and mind bonds of fraternal and sororal association that nourish and sustain virtually all morally informed endeavors.[7]

SOME EXAMPLES OF PROFOUND INSIGHT

The inevitable variety in expressions of insight and awareness from these individuals mandates our return to the matter of surface confusion due to human diversity. Some core actors openly discuss their moral grounding, or at least the feelings and energy stimulated by their direct encounters with life. More commonly, however, they simply act, offering perhaps a simple reason or none at all. Those few who speak, write, and otherwise demonstrate in sight of a wide audience do so in ways that suggest a number of broad avenues, each leading to a common central locale. Hannah Arendt, for example, described the key insight of existentialism: our inability to know Being, except in the course of a life engaged with the world and with others. Even then, "[It] can be experienced only as something 'all-encompassing.'"[8] According to Jerome Kohn, Arendt described her reactions to such experiences as "'philosophic shock'—the sheer wonder at existence, which is to be sharply distinguished from mere curiosity."[9] For theoretical physicist Stephen Hawking, it was an accrued sense of underlying order, acquired by reflection on all manner of observations of the cosmos, which led him to posit a unified theory of the universe. He explains his noninstrumental quest as one instance of our common capacity for profoundly informed curiosity at work: "[E]ver since the beginning of history, people have not been content to see events as unconnected and inexplicable. They have craved an understanding of the underlying order in the world."[10]

In a more mystical manner, Jewish theologian and philosopher Martin Buber, described his brief, unmediated encounters with others and with the natural world that each offers a fleeting, encompassing awareness of a fundamental, intrinsic relationship between the observer and the observed. It is a moment where the instrumental "it" becomes "You," and the essential unity of the latter with ourselves—and of both within some irreducibly mysterious, encompassing whole—becomes apparent. [11]

Finally, on the evening before his assassination, Martin Luther King Jr. eloquently summarized his innumerable encounters with life as part of his spiritual

journey "to the mountain[top]. And I've looked over. And I've seen the promised land." As King made clear, however, the source of his broad vision was the
concrete world of America, in the places and with the people with whom he had
stood, acted, and come to directly know as *the sources* of his spiritual inspiration. "I may not get there with you," he continued, "[b]ut I want you to know
tonight that we, as a people will get to the promised land."[12] To detect only
metaphor or some ethereal destination in his remarks is to miss the vital epistemology of his life. His comprehension of the world as that of creation or Being
came to him directly from his many intrinsic engagements with life.

The most common form of profound life-awareness and resulting vitality
appears to come quietly, imperceptibly, cognitively, in the framework of otherwise ordinary existence. The "bush," we have long known, bursts forth into
flame only for some. For the rest of us, it briefly flickers or warmly glows,
most often in one's own back yard. Such awareness stems from daily routine
encounters with familiar others in authentic, caring relationships with oneself,
from observed like relationships among others, and from recurring encounters with life more broadly. Thus informed and nurtured, one is equipped to
act and to react, to the extent of one's other competencies, for justice and
against injustice, even to stand at times alone, armed only with a renewable
supply of fundamental insight and strength.[13] It is such knowledge that explains the vitality of the core actor.

The above expressions of moral learning suggest an understanding—some
elemental knowledge that informs a basic orientation to life—that is powerfully distinct from one that is informed most powerfully by fearful mortal
self-awareness, or one that is premised upon wisdom received under perceived conditions of social dependence, communal or otherwise. Yet, it is
these latter reference points that have furnished the ontological foundations
for our social and political development from their initial empirical discovery
on English soil to their fullest fruition in America. Neither of our corresponding public philosophies—liberalism or communitarianism—accords any
significant historical weight to the core actors just described. It is as though
they do not exist or are so exceptional that they do not much matter. As for
the truths that inform them, they are seen as private, unverifiable, and potentially dangerous due to the passion they arouse and their insufficient constraint within the safety of a mainstream institutional tradition.

OUR MORAL STRENGTH

Our second, related misapprehension, briefly mentioned earlier, is suggested
by the very attraction that core actors can sometimes stimulate in us: that we

fail in all but extraordinary times to detect the potential reach of our own moral capacity, to see its full contours displayed, our most profound aspirations expressed, either in our own actions, or in our typically private resonance with the words and deeds of these exemplars. Informed by what so pervasively surrounds and enfeebles us, they appear exceptional in their freedom—so wanton in their apparent detachment from mortal anxiety or the need for conventional levels of social standing and material comfort—that they stimulate in us a troubling mix of profound admiration and deep resentment.

This is not at all surprising. For over three hundred years we have become increasingly attuned to the modest moral expectations of both liberalism and communitarianism. Moreover, we have become so in a society whose laws, ethics, institutions, and major operating systems are so thoroughly constructed upon the former paradigm and its dispassionate methodology, Enlightenment rationalism, that they stimulate in many a myth-filled nostalgia for traditional versions of the latter. In the process, we have increasingly lost sight of our ability to discover, develop, and affirm our richer potential moral selves.

It is exactly as though we have escaped the grasp of premodern social, political and economic obligations dictated by arbitrary force, tradition, and otherworldly doctrines of faith, only to step into a world where rational design, professional expertise, and behavioral management—each lightly tethered by like-derived moral principles of toleration, civility, reciprocity, modest benevolence, and necessary obligation—are the highest capacities we can bring to bear on the otherwise pluralistic excesses of our enlightened freedom.[14] Occasionally, we sense that our twin public philosophies—our secular faiths as practiced in daily life—have failed to capture the essence and dynamic potential of who the core moral actor demonstrates we, at least in our potential, more fully are.

The consequences of this lack of robust self-understanding are unfortunate and mounting. As Michael Oakeshott trenchantly observed concerning the implications of our listless moral formation, ". . . what we ought to do is unavoidably connected with what in fact we are; and what we are is (in this connection) what we believe ourselves to be."[15] We need to redetermine "what we are" so that we can reformulate our obligations and arm them with the motive strength that emanates from awareness of a self that is more than materially robust and more than instrumentally connected to the world and those to whom we are not intimately attached within it. We must do so in order to move ourselves beyond the sterile soil of enlightened self-interest, prudence, and rational necessity that support modern liberalism, as well as the essential conformity and shallow-rooted affection that constitute so much of contemporary communitarianism. Properly understood, core actors demonstrate that such movement is possible.

The task before us is formidable, possibly more so today than at any time in our past, when our social arrangement and technological development rendered core actors more difficult to avoid. To the extent that the nature and capacity of the morally informed core actors is not captured by either of our public philosophies, and they must now act increasingly undetected in the stultifying outwash of our corporatized, stratified, systematized, behavioral republic, we lose precious opportunities to recognize them as both ordinary and extraordinary exemplars in the many locations where they remain at work—among us, but increasingly excluded from our shrinking public and intimate midst.

As with each preceding generation, we need to identify and acquaint ourselves with these mentors in order to discover or, more hopefully, confirm our own faint, private intimations of the above-sketched powerful, shareable moral grounding that stimulates and awakens capacities that we each possess. From their words and deeds, their expressed *and* demonstrated world-views and self-understandings, we are able to learn why and how they variously trouble our consciences, even as they educate, inspire, and draw us in their direction. They hopefully inform us that the key lesson of modernity—that we are each agents, unavoidable participants in evolution—need not be seen or accepted as a process without profound moral content, nor as one that is determined by external forces, complex systems, powerful concrete others, by an institutionally defined God, or by no one at all.[16] Each of us has the capacity to learn intimately, directly, profoundly from life, and to powerfully act on the strength of what we have learned. Each of us has the potential to become a core actor.

CORE ACTORS: A FURTHER INTRODUCTION

As first suggested, when seen through the combined insight of history and our own richly informed imaginations, a small number of actors emerge as the initiators and sustainers—as the critical agents—of profoundly informed change. They are *the first* to publicly label some practice wrong or unjust, or to otherwise call for fundamental alteration of our institutional pattern, whether by written and oral rhetoric, or by acts of protest and challenge. Acting both alone and in small fraternal and sororal groups, in venues that range from local to global, their actions and interactions also serve more simply as evidence of an actual alternative, of a better way to live. In doing so, they offer us an enhanced, more comprehensive definition of our personal selves, of ourselves in relation to each other, and to life itself.

Abolition and enhanced civil and social equality for African Americans, women, children, and others are a few of the more noteworthy products of their myriad initiatives where some plateau of accomplishment can be discerned in our formal and informal institutions. Other projects that target broader, more persistent and newly understood forms of injustice—poverty, war, and other forms of powerfully endorsed, socially supported violence or indifference directed at people, other life, or the planet—continue as endeavors, the life work of at least a few in each generation.

Taken together and over time, the above efforts suggest the presence of five moral perspectives—outlooks and beliefs shared by core moral actors that stand at variance not only with the conventional vantage points of their respective eras, but also with others acting under claims of injustice or some other foundation of moral reform. The first is a world-view of greater inclusion and expanded democratic participation, each informed by profound knowledge of our common humanity. The second is a reverence or respect for life that is most notably inherent in the self-assumed risks of public, nonviolent nonconformity. Often, this reverence extends to virtually all life forms and the world that sustains them, connecting human life with nature and the cosmos, but not of necessity in ways that deny the inevitable, powerful role of human agency in either realm.[17] The third is a palpable, seemingly reflexive sense of offense, hurt, even anger or outrage, when confronted with injustice—some painful incongruity between the humanly achievable and the actual. Characteristically, these passions are directed more at the offense, or at the institutions and systems that reinforce and legitimate the wrong, rather than at the offenders.[18] The fourth is a persistent, durable optimism, directly fueled by profound knowledge. This hopeful attitude is reflected in part by a predisposition to friendship and other forms of caring relationship that include, and extend far beyond, the local warmth of fraternity, sorority, community, and the particularity of loved ones and kin. It is further evident in their persistence despite their awareness that the changes they seek to instantiate are neither inevitable nor likely to occur in their lifetimes.

As will be demonstrated, this sanguine perspective does not indicate a naïveté when it comes to a practical assessment of our ability to take part in or condone massive injustice. To the contrary, it is accompanied by an uncommonly frank, personal and social appraisal of our universal capacity for good and evil. This essential knowledge, however, is accepted alongside a belief derived most vitally from authentic engagement with others: many, likely most of us, share an inherent preference for good, and a potentially robust ability to discern both its core content and its shifting, more diversely informed implications.

Finally, there is a keen sense of obligation, a duty to act that extends beyond any coherent definition of self-interest, attachment to loved ones, kindred, and community, or rationally informed will. Its motive force is care,

the profound valuing of life as it is most vitally known through direct encounter and unmediated awareness. Like the knowledge that informs it, the
scope of care is enhanced by formal and other indirect learning, by experience that falls short of encounter, by experience-informed imagination, and
by other forms of reflection. Its strength is afforded by knowledge that is received as profound, simple truth—certain beliefs that remain attached to
their concrete and relational origins, and upon which they depend for their
profound veracity.

A common set of perspectives, to the extent that they inform action of the
type suggested above, is evidence of a powerful combination of extant human
capacities. As just mentioned, it is the core actors' varied detection of some
profound truth about life—which is accepted as such—that most vitally informs them. They have each discovered something that we have been encouraged to avoid looking for or taught not to recognize as substance: a
morally informing awareness—some glimpse at or encounter with the profound nature of "what is" and what is therefore congruent and possible. In the
process, they have found themselves able to develop and reinforce by ongoing active, direct, and intimate engagement with others, and with the myriad
concrete particulars of life more broadly, a recurring, deepening, more complete awareness of the nature, relationship, and intrinsic significance of each
and of all. They have developed to an uncommon degree our *common* capacity for profound moral learning, caring, and informed action that both liberalism and communitarianism, in their mainstream permutations, have either
failed to detect or seriously entertain.

A FEW CONCRETE EXAMPLES

At this point, a brief introduction to a few of the contemporary core actors relied upon in this project is overdue. Jean Grossholtz, a gifted academic and
one of those interviewed for this project, has expanded her early, formative
insights from her hardscrabble childhood during the Great Depression in a
wide reach of formal learning and experience that includes a lifetime of extensive, often civilly disobedient, peace and social justice activism.

As a young child growing up in a large rural family, she was tutored and
otherwise equipped to see the common humanity of other, even poorer families driving and walking through town "with their full possessions" on their
back[s]." Her father would often bring them home for a meal or a short stay.
There was one family she vividly recalled: "I remember my father saying,
'you have to give these kids your socks' . . . and we didn't have any socks either. I mean, our socks had holes in them, but we gave them just the same."

Jean also has a broader sense of life congruence that it is perhaps most deeply derived from her habitual, daily encounters with nature:

[I] walk in the woods every day with my dog. And I see . . . the way nature is, you know? I see foxes out there, these beautiful foxes, and they live there in some kind of respectful way with nature. They put up with us coming into their space, and it just seems to me that it's natural for people to live in harmony.

For some core actors, part of their awareness of profound truth is negative.

Another of the interviewees, Ira H., attributes much of the motive-strength for his extensive antiwar, antinuclear, prodisarmament activism, to his coming of age in America in the 1950s and 1960s as the son of a holocaust survivor. His father imparted to him ". . . a tremendous sense, not just of the barbarism of the Nazis, but of the [complicity of] good Germans." His activism, which started when he was a freshman at Harvard during the Vietnam War,

. . . was not [motivated by] a fear of the draft . . . . [I]t was a fear of being a good German. What was happening in Vietnam was palpably wrong. My government was doing it, and if I did not do everything I possibly could to stop this evil, I was no better than the Germans who allowed the Nazis to carry out the final solution

As he reflected back on his twenty-two years of extensive nuclear disarmament work with Physicians for Social Responsibility, a group he helped revitalize in 1978 with noted activist Dr. Helen Caldicott and a few others, he identifies the simple belief that further informs his above fear: "[F]or me the notion that human life is good is a core value. It is *the* core value. That's what this is all about."[19] Clearly, Ira H. also began to learn this value from the same intimate, affectionate source that could so effectively expose him to the nature and consequences of evil.

Core actors come in a typical cross-section of American variety. There is, for example, Lucille, a frail white grandmother from Arkansas, interviewed by political psychologist Kristen Renwick Monroe around 1990.[20] Monroe recounts that "[t]he idea of defending others, fighting against injustice, taking personal responsibility for others, and loving all humanity ran like leitmotifs throughout Lucille's narrative."

Beginning with the story of her most recent, heroic intervention, the physical rescue of a neighborhood African American teenage girl she only barely knew from a vicious rapist, Monroe describes Lucille's history of civil rights activism dating from her Arkansas childhood. She credits her world-view largely to her grandmother, herself a life-long, somewhat well known suffrage and temperance activist. "[She] always told us that we were not allowed to destroy anything in nature *unless* it was harming something else . . . . Grandmother taught me that everything is dependent on everything else. . . ."[21]

One of Lucille's earliest memories of direct action occurred as a child in the late 1930s or early 1940s, while traveling on a streetcar in Little Rock, Arkansas, with her grandmother. On that occasion, at her grandmother's urging, she boldly intervened on behalf of a younger black child who was being harassed by the white conductor. During the 1950s, when Little Rock was the locus of some of the most nationally visible resistance to integration, Lucille marched and protested for civil rights for black Americans while running a repertory theater with an integrated cast.[22] In doing so, she ignored warnings from Governor Faubus, the Ku Klux Klan, and the local White Citizen's Council, as well as episodes of violence and numerous threats. The theater was closed only after she was ousted as director by the nonprofit's board of directors, who had also been subjected to warnings and repeated threats.[23]

Lucille's most recent act of individual heroism is easy to relate to and admire, especially upon learning that she was then an octogenarian with a cane and a heart condition. David and Goliath tales readily inspire us under conditions where we need not confront the possibility of some Goliath within us, or the humiliation of standing by while the assailant either prevails or is exposed by someone like the frail, diminutive Lucille as a coward. Space and time serve a similar function, allowing the majority of us, for example, to dismiss any obvious personal connection to the racial cowardice and bigotry that characterized the South—and the North—during the era of Rosa Parks, Dr. Martin Luther King Jr.—and Lucille. Contemporary core moral actors do not afford us that luxury.

Given the nature of her work, it is unlikely, yet entirely possible, that the name and story of Kathy Kelly, another of the persons interviewed for this project, will one day join Lucille and Lucille's better known counterparts in the American civil rights movement as moral icons and sources of broad or local inspiration. Few would argue that she is a core moral activist. To those familiar with the life of Dorothy Day and the Catholic Worker Movement, it is apparent that Kelly has been strongly influenced by both.[24] She acknowledges having been inspired and mentored by many from within that lineage, including her former husband and ongoing colleague. He, in turn, was a protégé of Day and A. J. Muste, one of the elder statesmen of American peace, labor, and social justice activism in the twentieth century.[25]

Consistent with her education as a teacher and lay theologian, Kelly describes her vocation since 1978, using Day's words, as an effort to "create a world wherein it is easier to be good."[26] Her methods, which she describes in Gandhi's words as "the further invention of nonviolence," have been anything but conventional, passive, or popular.[27] In addition to her ongoing work with the poor in Chicago, in the early and mid-1990s she took part in several "peace teams"—groups of nonviolent protestors—who placed themselves in open encampments, between opposing forces, both at the outset of the Persian Gulf Conflict and during the brutal siege of ethnic violence in Sarajevo, in the former Republic of Yugoslavia.

From 1996, continuing through the invasion of Iraq in March 2003, Kathy made numerous trips to Iraq with members of her aptly named group, Voices in the Wilderness. The early trips, which openly challenged the previous official U.S. policy of broad economic sanctions, including basic food and medicine, were undertaken for two purposes: first, to gather public health and other data on food scarcity, unmet medical needs, and living conditions; second, to distribute donated medical supplies, toys, and other life necessities to Iraqi families who were suffering and dying in great numbers under the combined effects of American-led Western and Iraqi official intransigence. In the months leading up to the invasion, her group tried desperately to build support for a peaceful resolution. Between visits, which have continued unabated, she and her colleagues travel in this country, speaking to small groups and larger audiences wherever possible. They do so in order to raise funds, broaden awareness, and build support for a change in what is increasingly seen as a morally bankrupt American policy.[28]

In the face of ample cause for harsh judgment of great swaths of our species, she clearly, demonstrably views humankind—locally and broadly—with warmth and a predisposition to friendship. It is equally apparent that it is her profound world-view, drawn from her intimate knowledge of life's particulars, which generates her optimism, just as it informs and sustains her remarkable, conventionally quixotic quest for peace and social justice. Each of us, she believes, possesses the capacity for good and evil, with an inherent preference for the former. Like Ira H. and Jean Grossholtz, however, she readily recognizes the relative purity of evil in major actors like Saddam Hussein, although she and they are concerned with our tendency to personify evil in others and thereby avoid implicating ourselves. To Kelly, life and the world as she has come to know it are precious, wondrous gifts. Her ability to access this knowledge explains why she still sees the possibility of moral political change through human agency, some twenty-six years, and many frustrations, following her activist conversion.

It is certainly possible to quarrel on a number of levels with the moral understanding, goals, and strategies of contemporary activists like Kathy Kelly. The last of these certainly locates her outside the periphery of the culturally and politically acceptable in our society. She and her colleagues have initiated, for our generation, moral claims in ways which are radical and discomfiting to most of us, yet they are not at all unlike those asserted by Lucille and her activist cohort in the American South many years earlier. They bear an even stronger resemblance to those pursued by abolitionist and women's rights advocates such as Frederick Douglass and Elizabeth Cady Stanton, two of the historical core actors who will be discussed herein at some length, and by others during the antebellum era of slavery and chattel womanhood. With the persuasive means available in their generation, each has strived to accomplish the most difficult moral task: to call to our attention some prevalent, profound wrong in our midst, a wrong in which we are at least thereafter implicated if we do nothing to end it.

CORE ACTIVISM IN THE AMERICAN SETTING

Many, perhaps most, of the specific projects—individual and small group "ventures into the public realm"[29]—that are begun by the core actors in our midst are failures from the vantage points of empirical verifiability or of unrealistic expectations.[30] Yet it is their undertakings and the achievements that sometimes follow which ultimately constitute the most profoundly unifying sense of moral direction or coherence in our history. This record of accomplishment also affords the only generally accessible external evidence of our ultimately congruent reactions to their efforts. They should be seen, in effect, as the latest efforts to build upon the enhanced, broadened, often unforeseen possibilities for individual and small group moral challenges to the social, economic, and political status quo that significantly drove the Reformation, the Enlightenment, and our founding in their respective times and settings.[31]

Individual and small group acts that can ultimately lead to change on the scale just suggested and their place in its outward rippling wave of initiation and reaction are an essential part of the human social mix of intended events and contingent outcomes. America, like many other prosperous liberal societies, is adequately supplied with tolerators, soft sympathizers, and those who are inclined to support or acquiesce in a wide array of results. Private, anonymous supporters—political, social, and philanthropic, elite and nonelite—can also usually be found. Core actors and those prepared to actively, publicly support their work at its earliest stages are, however, in chronic short supply.

Although it may later appear otherwise, our public philosophies—liberalism and communitarianism—are not offered herein as full-bodied actors to be held responsible for our current, morally enervated social and political state. To the extent, however, which ideas serve as interpreters of human nature, and are further accepted as both common and empirically validated wisdom, they are historically potent. There are also ample reasons to be grateful to both traditions for the platform and framework that their adherents have each helped construct and support, in part by the somewhat oppositional tension of their debate. Surely, liberal republican logic and structure have enhanced our supply of tolerance. Likewise, republican virtue, as understood, practiced, and transmitted by both traditional and newer social and political elites, has been instrumental in forming our various responses to external threats and internal crises by broadening self-interest and by softening its harsh impacts with philanthropy.[32] Moreover, our locally democratic communities and religious communal institutions have furnished significant support for core moral activism—as well as fierce opposition and subtle resistance. The fact remains, however, that their largely shared, incomplete understanding of who we are can no longer be ignored.

In addition to the growing consequences of the failure of both public philosophies to take in the full nature of our selves and the world, there is a further practical problem, namely, the justification that they afford to those in each generation who are powerfully, actively opposed to any fundamental alteration of our shared understanding of life and the institutional changes that such knowledge can inspire. The world-view of liberalism has shielded the pursuit of private interest and substantially preserved its largest fruit in private orchards by equating both with immutable human nature, hence, as moral necessities. It has further afforded a legitimate cover for the increasing numbers who, given their mortal personal perspective and their belief that spiritual immortality is a false promise offered to the irrational, regard their own gain as a high order good. As one result, progress beyond formal political equality and minimal democratic process has been subordinated to the unequal distribution of power that is the predictable progeny of the flawed ontological beliefs of so many who wield it.

Communitarianism has more subtly legitimized the same outcomes in our society by grounding human nature not only in an uncertain mix of creation, nature, and evolution, but in social institutions upon which we, by our very nature, are seen as dependent for our moral knowledge, identity, and strength. Given the subordinate institutional relationship of so much of American society along with democratic governance to our liberal economic regime, it is evident that neither philosophy has been grounded deeply or broadly enough to support the promise once offered within their respective, largely complementary edifices of civil society and liberal pluralistic state.

RATIONALISM AND MORAL KNOWLEDGE

If we are to enjoy a politics and society that reflects and supports our vital engagement in intimate human relationships and other unmediated processes of self- and world discovery, we must not only reconstruct the ontological foundation of our public philosophies, we also must expand our selection of epistemological tools rather than accept the limits of those now employed. Both liberalism and communitarianism have relied from the outset on exclusively rational methodologies to determine who we are and what we are capable of achieving individually, socially, and politically. Like-derived understandings have informed not only the actual development of our social and political structures, but also their subordination to our complex economy, a new form of systemic reality whose impersonal dictates are impossible to ignore—even as we participate in their creation.

This agency-stultifying, metastructural backdrop is unfortunately well illustrated by many contemporary critics, prophets, and other concerned observers—academics, policy experts, and other influential members of our two philosophical camps—both liberal and conservative. Over the past decade and longer, they have focused the debate on the relative importance of civic versus political, religious versus secular, and local versus national institutions to restore the moral health of America.[33] Individual, social, and political decline, anomie, and angst are variously depicted, along with actual injustice and real suffering, as the primary product of anemic, overweening, corrupt, or disappearing institutions, public and private. Institutions are the primary cause and the only significant locus of the cure.

Apart from the strong surge of religious moral revival on the right, and increasingly plaintive calls for political reform that emanate mainly from the left, remedies from the intellectual center consist largely of policy formulas, with the enfeebled heart of the debate focused on public versus private implementation. Some call for the restoration of local institutional wetlands where civic trust and good citizenship can grow. Others seek the reinvigoration of moral order via new prohibitions, enhanced penalties—or tax and spending incentives. Robert D. Putnam offers something of a liberal-communitarian synthesis of these approaches in a new millenium expansion of his "Bowling Alone" thesis:

> [S]ocial capitalists need to avoid false debates. One such debate is "top-down versus bottom-up." The roles of national and local institutions need to be complementary. . . . Another false debate is whether government is the problem or the solution. . . . [I]t can be both.[34]

Although he urges upon us the necessity of human agency, the call comes with implicitly modest expectations, at the very end:

> The final false debate to be avoided is whether what is needed to restore trust and community bonds in America is individual change or institutional change. Again the honest answer is "Both." America's major civic institutions, both pub-

lic and private, are somewhat antiquated . . . and they need to be reformed in ways that invite more active participation . . . . In the end . . . institutional reform will not work—indeed, it will not happen—unless you and I, along with our fellow citizens, resolve to become reconnected with our friends and neighbors. Henry Ward Beecher's advice a century ago . . . to "multiply picnics" is not entirely ridiculous today.[35]

The effective reforming power of individual and small group human moral agency is seen, from our enlightenment-derived, social-science-informed perspective, as limited to those with high intellectual rational capacity, who hold key positions in existing institutions or have access to those that do. To these requisites some would add, with modest expectations, character or virtue imparted by high-secular institutional imparted learning, traditional religious belief, or both.[36] The rest of America is left in the bovine pasture of pluralistic passivity—dependent on associational empowerment and mass market information, targeted and counted in one or more demographic sub-groups of an otherwise atomistic herd. Thanks, however, to ample material and other sensory satisfactions that constitute our up to deathbed pursuit, we are now less subject to manipulation by those who lack even modest enlightenment virtue and seek to stir radical emotive fevers. This group image, this national portrait, is emblematic of our present state of impoverished self and world understanding.

The foregoing is only suggestive—the tip of the contemporary iceberg—of our dilemma of rational over-reliance. America's development, if it is to be understood within a shared, profoundly moral perspective, must include significantly more than behavioral patterns, structures, forces, mass movements, conventional elite leadership, and other *exclusively* rationally conceived notions of change. We are not able, by empirical observation, behavioral experiment, life-detached theory, or other solely intellectual means, to adequately understand our actual and potential selves, let alone affirmatively, boldly, meaningfully seek to order our life together. It is this impossibility that lies at the center of our twin philosophical dilemma.

Our rational faculty, notwithstanding its importance, constitutes only a portion of our extant and developable capacity to discern the shape, order, content, and potential meaning of the world around us and ourselves within it. Reason and its product, intellectual knowledge, require the essential complement of demonstrated vital belief, itself the product of cognitive, intuitive, *and* rational learning, together with reflection, imagination, and deductive insight that can lead to, but which do not fully inform, profound moral knowledge. The essential, foundational source of such knowledge is direct, intimate, relational experience or encounter with actual others, with other life, and with the physical world. From the wellspring of such knowledge, further precipitated, informed, and enriched by other learning, there arises the motive force of deep and broad caring, a state of mind and heart that stirs us to act on what we have come to know with certainty about life.

Such elemental knowledge, by virtue of its simple yet profound content, ubiquitous source material, and varied means of acquisition, is widely obtainable, and shareable with others by means of demonstration and persuasion. In the context of social and political action, the certainty of profound knowing and the strength afforded by deeply informed caring, can subdue, even transform, the fear—unbounded self-serving, delusion—and avoidance that our rationally informed mortal self-awareness so often provokes. Such knowledge imparts a vital, life-affirming foundation for inferred principles of justice or morality, and the motive energy to seek out, plan, and act in concert with those who see the same world in a similar light. Core actors afford us with both a model and the opportunity for such learning and all that it portends.

MORAL PROGRESS: REVITALIZING AN AMERICAN NOSTRUM

To further frame this project, it is important to offer at the outset a reconceived version of a formerly widely accepted idea—progress. After its general introduction in the nineteenth century as a powerful new idea linked to technological and scientific development, as well as the popularization of evolution, it quickly came to signify boundless material prosperity and American national destiny. In the turbulent, disillusioned, reactionary aftermath of World War I, however, progress began to lose its intellectual and spiritual luster to the extent that it also included the possibility of moral growth leading to the betterment of either society or government.[37]

Notwithstanding its past association with various forms of hubris and its mendacious appropriations, the idea of progress as the possible product of morally informed, purposive, sustained individual and group social and political action must be reintroduced in America if morality is to be rightly conceived and integrated in our political and social lives. Thus defined, progress serves not only as a reminder of the essential role of human agency in the initiation of change, but also as a framework for authentic debate and public action.[38] Most important, the idea of progress reinforces a view of a human nature that is capable of personal, social, and political growth beyond the limits suggested by reason attached to self-service or existing community, by static received faith, or by the behavioral parameters of enhanced rational design.

The fact that the twentieth century has powerfully reminded us that words can be appropriated and redefined, or that the consequences of collective human action undertaken under any symbol or ideological banner can be horrific, does not obviate the necessity for concerted, morally informed human agency to move us in the direction of worthy goals. "Progress," as intended herein, has always been contested in its definition. It is also a contingent outcome, a product of our varied, often imperfect, yet common individual potential to comprehend simple, profound truths about life, to care deeply about what we learn, and to act congruently, as well as collectively, to implement justice and other social and political goods on the strength of both. The realization that morally informed agency is actual and powerful, and that by its means major, life-enhancing change has occurred in our social and political landscape, is to comprehend the full reach of human nature—its potential and ours—to learn and grow, not simply mutate and survive.

As a practical concept, the idea of progress must apply broadly, deeply, and personally. To accomplish this, we must come to appreciate and value the vital *informative* role of core moral actors in our past and in our midst. We must learn from them how we are variously able to drink from the same informing, inspiring well, and act with them to enhance our lives together, sustained in part by the future promise of what we can know with certainty and act upon in the present.

MAKING THE CASE

The primary goal thus far has been to provoke interest, to stimulate a conversation, and thereby encourage the reader to keep on reading. In legal parlance, this particular effort is analogous to making a jury opening in what is conceded at the outset to be a difficult, uphill case. To have a chance at success, the jurors—who are free in this instance to simply close the cover and move on—must be convinced they should not only continue, but also actively engage the evidence with an open mind. The last task is especially difficult. Each of us across the American sociopolitical spectrum has been raised and tutored, to some extent at least, in the Enlightenment tradition. Moreover, although many of us dispute key aspects of our two public philosophies, we have likely employed similar rational methodologies to arrive at our conclusions. Finally, there is the apparently considerable evidential weight of over two hundred years of relatively stable, liberal republican governance, as well as local communitarian experience within liberalism's comparatively tolerant framework.

Accordingly, the selection of an impartial jury is impossible. However, this is typically the case, unless one equates ignorance or disinterest with the absence of potential bias. An open mind is not an empty one, but one that is willing — motivated to entertain new evidence and unconventional methods that may lead to an alternate arrangement and interpretation of existing facts. Ideally, this willingness is informed, at a minimum, by unease or dissatisfaction with the current state of our society and its politics, and our largely passive, ineffective roles within them. The perfect juror for this imperfect text already senses that something is seriously wrong, and that neither satisfactory explanations nor effective remedies have been forthcoming.

Finally, this endeavor, if it is to be at all successful, should not be construed as another attempt to deconstruct the Enlightenment project or diminish its achievements. Rather, it is an effort to *expand* our existing understanding of why and how profound change has occurred in America and to suggest why further such change has become so difficult in our era.

The next two chapters consist of selected expert testimony, primarily from scholars of both the liberal and communitarian schools. Many are partisans, both secular and religious, and some are not. Cross-examination will be by analysis, comparison, and critique, pitting alleged hostile witnesses against each other to test not only the validity of their views, but also the actual depth of their claimed antagonisms. The primary focus throughout is on human moral nature — its content and grounding. This necessitates some further consideration of what each philosophy explains — and fails to explain — about our personal, social, and national development.

Enlightenment rationalism is the focus of further attention in each chapter. This special attention is, as already suggested, important. With few exceptions, rationalism of one sort or another has been assigned an exclusive role by adherents of both philosophies in the "discovery" of all shareable knowledge accepted as truth, or as a sound working hypothesis. Thus, rational technique is the perceived means of discovery of enlightenment and enlightenment-derived theories of our moral nature and, based on these suppositions, the method by which both the structure and most of the content of our social, environmental, economic, and political relationships have been created and understood. Hopefully, the effort will be enough to at least convince the reader of the inadequacy of rationalism as the sole means of fundamental moral comprehension or ethical design.

Chapters 4 through 6 involve testimony of a different sort. Two tasks are attempted in this part. The first is to restore the role of nonelite agency to its rightful place in our understanding of how fundamental change has occurred in America. All of the major changes that we have undergone as a society and a polity have had concrete, particular beginnings. In the midst of mass society and modern complexity, too many of us have forgotten that actors create and alter systems, structures, and events more than the obverse. Apart from the direct impact of natural calamity, all social change, regardless of scale or moral content, has its origins in action by one or a few, which stand in initial contrast with existing norms and practices. Private thoughts have led to intimate and local conversations, to more visible public action and reaction, and to some durable alteration in the social and political fabric of America. The first task, then, is to understand the full nature and dynamics of morally informed action in America, in contrast to the limited, Enlightenment-derived explanations of our social and political development.

The second assignment is to attempt understand the nature and capacity of those who initiate and sustain such action. Given the critical nature of their action, it is important to undertake that process by introducing several core actors and becoming familiar with each of them. Two groups are utilized for both tasks. The first consists of four historical activists: Elizabeth Cady Stanton (1815–1897), Frederick Douglass (c. 1817–1895), Jane Addams (1860–1935), and Eugene V. Debs (1855–1926). Each was chosen principally because of their well-known, early, and protracted association with notably unpopular causes. At least in part through their efforts, a few of the many specific reforms sought by them were achieved in their lifetimes, while other items on their broad agendas have either been achieved since their deaths or remain as unfinished business for others in our era and beyond.

These actors are chronologically paired in distinct, semi-contiguous eras. Stanton and Douglass were most prominent in the antebellum period, although each wrote, worked, and spoke out most frequently on their respective *primary* concerns for women's rights and African American equality until their deaths at the end of the nineteenth century. As will become evident, they knew each other well, and with one notable exception at the end of the Civil War, enthusiastically supported each other's work, almost from the beginning of their careers.

Jane Addams, a radical social reformer and peace activist, and Eugene Debs, a labor organizer, socialist political leader, and antiwar activist, began their careers early in the Progressive Era as the first pair's life work was ending. While Addams and Debs were undoubtedly aware of the others' accomplishments, and of the prior efforts of Stanton and Douglass, no claim of direct tutelage, substantial support for the other's work, or other concrete intergenerational linkage can be directly sustained. All four, however, should be accepted as constitutive of their era, which, in itself, is a form of mentorship for those who follow.

There are other criteria that warrant the selection of these actors. Their backgrounds vary by race, gender, region, and, somewhat, by class and circumstance. Although such a small sample is hardly representative, they are offered as emblematic of the many equally prominent, and the presumably much greater number, of less known and unknown core moral actors of their respective times, outlooks, and reform agendas. Further, their racial and gender diversity is particularly important, where one of principal problems of the English-American Enlightenment view of human nature is the extremely narrow make-up of the original empirical sample, a problem that persists. Women and blacks were entirely excluded, along with the overwhelming majority of politically inchoate white males; in fact, it is likely entirely accurate to assume that our dominant social and political ontological assumptions were gleaned only from a small cadre of progressive aristocrats and other white males with middle and upper class standing and aspirations. For reasons that will be only somewhat addressed, these omissions are quite significant.[39]

In addition, all four wrote extensively, and all but Debs wrote at length about themselves, thus offering us some direct insight into their self and world understanding. Further, each has been written about from a reasonably wide range of perspectives. Finally, each of them corresponded extensively with intimates and others connected to their activist work. Accordingly, although the actors and their witnesses are dead, it should be possible within the limits of interpretation over time and setting to detect and compare the following: their formative development; the origins, nature, purpose, extent, and methodology of their activism; and their understanding of themselves as individuals, in relation to others, and in relation to the world.

The second group consists of twenty-six contemporary peace, social justice, and political reform activists. Their names were gleaned from a variety of sources—news articles, referrals by reporters, academic colleagues, other activists, and in one case, by a meeting poster on a downtown telephone pole. Each of them was informally "deposed"—encouraged to talk about themselves and their activism in a semi-structured conversational format—by one or more individual, in-depth taped interviews.[40]

The activist focus of this group was broad, including the following:

1. Peace and social justice concerns relating to American foreign, military, nuclear, global trade, and environmental policy;
2. Poverty, racial, ethnic, gender, and other justice issues directly affecting the two largest cities in the region where some of them lived and/or worked[41];
3. Concerns over claims of political corruption and needed democratic reforms at the state and national levels;
4. Attempts to persuade others to their sincerely held belief in the immorality of abortion.

It is interesting to note that only one of those contacted did not participate. Technically, he did not so much refuse as avoid. Ultimately, the number of interviewees directly used and quoted at length herein was narrowed to thirteen. The decision to do so was difficult but inevitable, given the overriding importance of presenting each actor to the reader in enough detail so that their moral formation could be adequately described, their actions depicted alongside their words, and their expressed as well as inferred understanding of themselves in relationship to others and the world presented as fully as possible. Hopefully the reader will accept that the selections were not made to conceal inconsistencies but to more adequately reveal the variety, as well as the commonalities, strength, and depth of their moral natures, and our own.

In the last two chapters, an effort is made to assemble from the historical and contemporary ensemble a coherent image of their moral formation—that which informs and stimulates their capacity to act in the manner that they evidence in the preceding chapters. Chapter 7 explores the motive strength—the state of mind—that propels these actors to initiate and sustain their nonconforming action. The last chapter is an attempt to discern the sources and methodologies of moral learning that these actors appear to possess, and which inform their state of mind or will to act. Finally, it offers a brief look at the content of the knowledge that informs them, simple yet certain truths that they demonstrate, and which thereby and otherwise are available to us all.

NOTES

1. Alexis de Tocqueville, trans. George Lawrence, *Democracy in America*, ed. J. P. Mayer (1966: New York: HarperPerennial-HarperCollins, 1988), 16.

2. Wilson Carey McWilliams, *The Idea of Fraternity in America* (Berkeley: University of California Press, 1973), 44.

3. Michael Walzer, *Obligations: Essays on Disobedience, War, and Citizenship* (Cambridge, MA: Harvard University Press, 1970), 20.

4. Hannah Arendt, "What Remains? The Language Remains: An Interview with Günter Gaus," in *Essays in Understanding: 1930–1954*, ed. Jerome Kohn (New York: Harcourt Brace, 1994), 22–23. She argues that our common humanity is formed in this manner, by what she refers to as "ventures into the public realm."

5. Isaiah Berlin, *Four Essays on Liberty* (New York: Oxford University Press, 1969), xxxiii.

6. I am not aware of the first noteworthy introduction of the concept of "worldview" to the world of either philosophy or political thought. I first encountered the term as a translation of the German word *weltanschauung* while a teenager, when early ripening life curiosity prompted me to buy a book by humanitarian, philosopher, and theologian Albert Schweitzer (1875–1965), *The Philosophy of Civilization*, trans. C. T. Campion (New York: Macmillan, 1950). Written between 1900 and 1923, in part during Schweitzer's years as a missionary in Africa, his discernment of "the basic ethical character of civilization" informed his *weltanschauung*. Campion advises that this

compound term may be translated as "theory of the universe," "world-theory," or "world-view." At the heart of Schweitzer's world-view is "Reverence for Life," an attitude so strong in him that he associated it with "will-to-life," a by-product of his conscious reflection ". . . about my life and about the world" (xv). My copy of the book has long-since vanished; however, if the loan record of the university library copy I obtained is representative, I am one of the fortunate few to have come upon it.

7. McWilliams, 5–8.

8. Hannah Arendt, "What is Existential Philosophy?," in *Essays*, Jerome Kohn, ed., 186.

9. Jerome Kohn, introduction, *Essays*, Jerome Kohn, ed., xi.

10. Stephen W. Hawking, *A Brief History of Time: From the Big Bang to Black Holes* (New York: Bantam Books, 1988), 12–13.

11. Martin Buber, *I and Thou*, trans. Walter Kaufmann (New York: Charles Scribner's Sons, 1970), 55–60. Buber identifies three spheres in which such relational encounters occur: "life with nature . . . life with men . . . [and] life with spiritual beings." (56–57). For those who are intellectually informed but open to insight in the first sphere, his description of encounter with a tree is illuminating (57–59).

12. Martin Luther King Jr., *A Testament of Hope: The Essential Writings and Speeches of Martin Luther King, Jr.*, ed. James M Washington (New York: Harper-Collins-HarperSanFrancisco, 1986), 286.

13. Such awareness is often not evident to oneself or to others until the happening of a catalytic event. Perhaps the most notable example of this is documented in the interviews of rescuers of Jews in Nazi-occupied Europe during World War II. The most extensive set of interviews and analysis was conducted by Samuel P. Oliner and Pearl M. Oliner, *The Altruistic Personality: Rescuers of Jews in Nazi Europe* (New York: The Free Press, 1988). The Oliners concluded that for the vast majority of these moral heroes, the common salient factor was the relative extensivity of their capacity for relationships (249–60). They attribute this primarily to their beneficent formative exposure, to demonstrated behavior by parents and other trusted intimates who encouraged them to see others as part of common humanity. See also Kristen Renwick Monroe's excellent, smaller sample, but more in-depth study of rescuers and others: *The Heart of Altruism: Perceptions of a Common Humanity* (Princeton, NJ: Princeton University Press, 1996). She identifies the inclusive world-view of rescuers as the key variable that distinguishes them from traditional heroes and philanthropists (197–98).

14. Joseph Tussman, *Obligation and the Body Politic* (New York: Oxford University Press, 1960). Tussman makes one of the most lucid contract-based arguments for rational obligation, recognizing that classical notions of duty cannot compete on the same playing field with self-interest (17–18).

15. Michael Oakeshott, *Rationalism in Politics, and Other Essays* (New York: Basic Books, 1962), 248.

16. Matthew Fox, former Catholic Priest and Dominican theologian, offers a controversial Christian alternate perspective in which man has an unavoidable role as an agent in ongoing creation—a unitary realm in which God is immanent. His position stands in sharp contrast with fall-redemption theology, where man must depend on an

external God for earthly guidance, forgiving grace, and post-temporal salvation. Matthew Fox, *Original Blessing* (Santa Fe: Bear & Company, 1983). The concept of "co-creator" as used herein is less radically intended to acknowledge our formidable capacity to alter, destroy, and build from nature—something that Arendt so effectively describes in her description of *homo faber*. Hannah Arendt, *The Human Condition*, 1958 (New York: Doubleday Anchor, 1959) 119–53.

The use of the term "evolution" is intended to convey agreement with the notion that "knowledge development is evolution carried on by other means." Further as some evolutionary biologists have concluded, somewhat to the same effect as Fox, we are active agents in our own evolution. Finally, they argue that human evolution should be seen as *both* an individual and group process. See Kai Hahlweg and C. A. Hooker, "Evolutionary Epistemology and Philosophy of Science," in *Issues in Evolutionary Epistemology*, Kai Hahlweg and C. A. Hooker, eds. (Albany, NY: State University of New York Press, 1989), 21–44.

17. Physician, humanitarian, medical missionary, and philosopher Albert Schweitzer exemplifies this perspective. See note 6, above.

18. What is intended here is more than an inherent, behavioral response, such as is suggested by early cognitive dissonance theory. Leon Festinger, *A Theory of Cognitive Dissonance* (Evanston, IL: Row, Peterson, 1957). The perspective is an attempt to describe the powerful connection of a world-view formed by unmediated encounters with life with the particular state of mind that the knowledge thus derived stimulates in the core actors studied herein.

19. Italicized emphasis, unless otherwise noted, is that of the person quoted. In this instance, it is my interpretation, based on spoken emphasis by the interviewee. Physicians for Social Responsibility (PSR) was originally founded in 1961 by Bernard Lown, an eminent Boston cardiologist. The focal issue was nuclear atmospheric testing. Benjamin Spock, noted pediatrician and peace activist, was another of many well-known early members. Following the signing of the Comprehensive Nuclear Test Ban Treaty in 1963, however, PSR support waned. In 1978, Ira H., Eric Shivian, a Boston psychiatrist, and eight or so other doctors, including Ira. H., met at the Boston-area home of Dr. Helen Caldicott, a native Australian global peace activist. PSR, then dormant, was revived by these doctors due to renewed concerns about nuclear war and the consequences of U.S. nuclear energy proliferation. Although membership in PSR peaked in 1987 at around 48,000 American physicians, its current 20,000 membership remains involved in a variety of peace and social justice concerns. For further information see www.psrus.org.

20. Monroe, 63–90.

21. Monroe, 69; 73. According to Monroe, Lucille's grandmother worked with suffrage and temperance activist Carrie Nation, and had become sufficiently prominent herself to have intervened directly with Franklin and Eleanor Roosevelt to obtain wartime employment for Lucille in the Pentagon.

22. In 1958 Governor Orval Faubus defied a federal court order to admit nine negro students to Central High School in Little Rock. He deployed National Guard troops around the school, forcing Eisenhower to nationalize the Arkansas National Guard and dispatch regular army paratroopers to the scene. Stephen B. Oates, *Let the*

Trumpet Sound: A Life of Martin Luther King, Jr., 1982, (New York: Harper Collins-Harper Perennial, 1994), 124–25.

23. Monroe, 75–77.

24. Staughton Lynd and Alice Lynd, *Nonviolence in America: A Documentary History* (Maryknoll, NY: Orbis Books, 1995), 309–24.

25. Staughton Lynd and Alice Lynd, 529; Robert Cooney and Helen Michalowski, eds., *The Power of the People: Active Nonviolence in the United States* (Culver City, CA: Peace Press, 1977) 138–39; 237. According to Cooney and Michalowski, Muste (1885–1967) began his career as a labor activist by leading the famous nonviolent strike by the Lawrence textile workers in 1919, and ended it as a unifying elder statesman leader of the antiwar movement in the 1960s.

26. Dorothy Day, *On Pilgrimage: The Sixties* (New York: HarperCollins, 1972), 206.

27. I have been unable to locate this quote, attributed by Kelly to Gandhi. It does, however, clearly reflect his thought, which identifies nonviolence with Truth (knowledge of God), something one can briefly, imperfectly glimpse in the course of a life well-lived in terms of one's relations with others and the world. It is on the basis of such insights that one conducts one's life work, described by Gandhi in the title of his autobiography as humble "Experiments with Truth." Mohandas K. Gandhi, *An Autobiography: The Story of My Experiments with Truth*, trans. Mahadev Desai (Boston: Beacon Press, 1957).

28. I met Kathy Kelly at the very beginning of my research for this book, when she spoke at the All Souls Unitarian Universalist Church in Greenfield, Massachusetts on July 4, 1999. A few days later she appeared on the Lehrer News Hour on the PBS network. I have since spoken to her by phone and kept track of her via occasional news accounts and through her group's web site, http://vitw.org.

29. Jerome Kohn, introduction, Arendt, *Essays*, Jerome Kohn, ed., 22.

30. McWilliams, *The Idea of Fraternity*, 44. He analogously observes that "Unity among men can never be discovered empirically. The diversity of the species is united by the idea of 'man,' and that unity becomes important only as 'mankind' is valued among the lesser kindreds of men" (44).

31. This project assumes human variety and complexity in the motives of key thinkers and core actors—two non-distinct categories—of the above periods of social and economic change, as well as political reform and reforms in self and world understanding. It is further assumed that morally informed core actors were at work in each period in the manner suggested herein. In other words, what may have been unintended or unforeseen consequences for some Enlightenment actors, such as in the area of political equality, were already discerned, deeply valued, and striven for by others.

32. McWilliams, 170–74. See also Thomas L. Pangle, *The Enobling of Democracy: The Challenge of the Postmodern Age* (Baltimore: Johns Hopkins University Press, 1992); Alasdair C. MacIntyre, *After Virtue: A Study in Moral Theory* (1981; Notre Dame Press, 1984).

33. There is a plethora to choose from in the arena of contemporary rational moral analysis. The following are recent standouts: Robert D. Putnam, *Bowling Alone: The*

Collapse and Revival of American Community (New York: Simon & Schuster, 2000); Stephen L. Carter, *Civility: Manners, Morals, and the Etiquette of Democracy* (New York: HarperPerenial-HarperCollins, 1998). For an insightful critique of the social capital and civility approach, see Benjamin DeMott, "Seduced by Civility: Political Manners and the Crisis of Democratic Values," *The Nation* Dec. 9, 1996: 11–19.

34. Putnam, 413.

35. Putnam, 414.

36. Again, Carter stands out in both categories. Stephen L. Carter, *The Culture of Disbelief: How American Law and Politics Trivialize Religious Devotion*, 1993 (New York: Anchor Books-Doubleday, 1994). See also William John Bennett, John J. DiUlio Jr., and John P. Walters, *Body Count: Moral Poverty—and How to Win America's War Against Crime and Drugs* (New York: Simon & Schuster, 1996).

37. Reinhold Niebuhr, *Moral Man, Immoral Society: A Study in Ethics and Politics* (1932; New York: Scribner, 1960). Niebuhr was perhaps the pre-eminent twentieth century voice of Enlightenment theological "realism." Locke, in his view, had captured the essence of fallen human nature, characterized by "predatory self-interest" that manifests itself most powerfully in group conflicts that inevitably require a politics of power for their resolution (Introduction, xii–xxiv).

38. This is precisely what Herbert Croly attempted at the beginning of the last century in *The Promise of American Life* (1909; New York: Capricorn Books, 1964). He offered to America what he saw as its original national promise—democracy, something he saw "as a process and [moral] ideal" (7).

39. The omission of women and blacks, along with the men who comprised the balance of the then transitioning urban and rural underclasses, indicates more than a flawed empirical sample. To the extent, for example, that role and characters are important in both personal and social moral formation, as Alasdair MacIntyre (see note 32, above) believes, enlightenment theorists and several generations of their lineage are guilty of some incredible omissions in the cast of moral actors. Moreover, the omission of values historically associated with women in our culture, and the dynamic by which they are conceived and transmitted, has seriously narrowed our understanding of the *content* and *comprehension* of social and political morality.

40. The structure of the interviews was informed by the following: I. E. Siedman, *Interviewing as Qualitative Research* (New York: Teachers College Press, 1991); James A. Holstein and Jaber B. Gubrium, *The Active Interview*, Qualitative Research Methods Series, vol. 37 (Thousand Oaks, CA: Sage Publications, 1995). Holstein and Gubrium are admirers of the "Studs Terkel" approach, noting that we typically fail to appreciate that "both parties to the interview are necessarily and unavoidably *active*. Each is involved in meaning-making work" (4).

41. The cities are Holyoke and Springfield, Massachusetts.

Chapter Two

Our Enlightenment Misapprehensions

Egoism sterilizes the seeds of every virtue; individualism at first only dams the spring of public virtues, but in the long run it attacks and destroys all the others too and finally merges into egoism.

—Alexis de Tocqueville[1]

No doubt the view that there exist objective moral or social values, eternal and universal . . . accessible to the mind of any rational man if he chooses to direct his gaze on them, is open to every sort of question. Yet the possibility of understanding men in one's own or any other time, indeed of communication between human beings, depends on the existence of some common values, and not on a common "factual" world alone.

—Isaiah Berlin[2]

One of the most persistent trends in modern philosophy since Descartes . . . has been an exclusive concern with the self, as distinguished from the soul or person or man in general . . . . The greatness of Max Weber's discovery about the origins of capitalism lay precisely in demonstration that an enormous, strictly mundane activity is possible without any care for or enjoyment of the world whatever, an activity whose deepest motivation . . . is worry and care about the self.

—Hannah Arendt[3]

Whenever there is an ascendant class, a large portion of the morality of the country emanates from its class interests and its feelings of class superiority . . . . Another grand determining principle of the rules of conduct, both in act and forbearance . . . enforced by law or opinion, has been

29

the servility of mankind toward the supposed preferences of their temporal masters or of their gods.

—John Stuart Mill[4]

INTRODUCTION

We have each been "inescapably molded by a distinctive political culture that
emerged out of the great historical watershed of the seventeenth and eighteenth centuries called 'The Enlightenment.'"[5] Its concepts and underlying
beliefs, embraced in the public philosophy of liberalism, are nowhere more
dominant than in America. Accordingly, it is not at all surprising that the evidence of its essential foundational flaw—a partial, overly limited portrayal
of human nature and the corresponding moral capacity of social and political
actors—should be most prominent here as well.

Our republic has been largely premised from its founding on the liberal republican self-understanding, social perspective, and world-view. Taken together, they furnish a group portrait of a dramatically new model of elite actor—Enlightenment Man.[6] Although his construction herein is abstract, he is
offered not only as the embodiment of a particular philosophy, but also as the
representative face of actual actors, both powerful and ordinary, in our past
and present. As suggested above, he was first presented as the product of revolutionary philosophical thought, discovered and since reaffirmed by empirical observation, theoretical construction, history as structural development
most suitable for his subspecie, and ongoing behavioral research.

Enlightenment Man's origins, however, are best understood as concrete
and particular. As Thomas Pangle notes with respect to the contribution of
English political philosophers to his initial discovery, "We must also try to see
how their mighty, and often competing, intellectual beams were refracted and
disbursed through the medium of the statesmen—the men of action and practical wisdom."[7] Significantly, Pangle does not mention other initial refractors.
This hint, together with modest knowledge of the history of the era of his discovery, suggests something of great importance to the rest of us: that the dis-
coverers of the original model and their backers, the philosophers and their
political patrons, were related not only by race and gender, but also by class-
expanding commercial economic interests—including, in at least one instance, actual joint venture.[8] Accordingly, one can surmise that Enlightenment Man was conceived from the corresponding world-views and
self-understandings of a narrow class of actors known to the philosopher,
likely starting with observation of his close associates and his own mirrored
reflection.[9]

Since Enlightenment Man's early arrival in colonial America, he has acquired the broad support of those who see him as a moral, political, and social ideal—the best that man can make of himself—and those who assert from the conventional strength of realist insight and complementary theology that he is flawed, but factual and fundamentally immutable.[10] From his narrow but powerfully sponsored intellectual beginnings, stripped of his religious and ideological veneers, he has emerged from his former pragmatic modesty to offer himself as the cultural exemplar of our dominant public philosophy.[11] Today he lives among us, often within us, in apparently large numbers, flexing his increasingly pervasive, organized and systematized, economic and political strength as never before. It is therefore surprising to learn how insecure, how needy, how profoundly frightened and alone he has believed himself to be from the moment of his first published discoveries to date.

A SOMEWHAT COMPETING MODEL

In actuality there are two Americanized models that correspond with our prevailing public philosophies. Enlightenment Man, the dominant ideal, originated in England as modern capitalism was emerging and was constructed early on by John Locke and others. The second, Communitarian Man, is a more diffuse conception. Shaped somewhat by the Scottish branch of Enlightenment thought, it is also influenced by selective nostalgia for, and arguments grounded in, the ideals and practices of traditional society, including classical republicanism and Puritanism.[12] The contemporary model, however, is most indebted to a more recent, sociological understanding of society and of human nature within it. Democratic theorists have attempted to shape both models, often seeking to reconcile them, but with notably less success.[13] In part, this is because they so often ground their calls for enhanced democratic practices in views of human nature and moral capacity that closely mirror those whose models they seek to reform.

Although the communitarian model will be discussed in some detail in the next chapter, a brief account of his relationship with his Lockean rival is important for our understanding of both. Communitarian Man's presence was at first localized in America, as elsewhere, by the physical realities of place, the relative dearth of connective technology, and the logic of distinct traditions. He has since been subjected to the instrumental processes unleashed by the projects of his rationally self-enlightened competitor, namely, to the burgeoning of economic organization, specialization, the commodification of labor at the hands of its purchasers and managers, and mandated human mobility. This subservience to economic "necessity," greatly aided by material comfort and individual allure of liberal ideals, has led to the amorphous softening and out-right dissipation of traditional social institutions. In the process, freedom has been reconceived, leaving us with the right to choose, subject to the means within our uneven grasp, among the plethora of instrumental and private goods offered within the climate-controlled envelope of mass society. Reduced to an optional lifestyle evident in the production and distribution of alternative magazines, catalogues, and seminars, one wonders if proponents of the contemporary communitarian model fully sense the irony of their dilemma.

The foregoing only somewhat explains the quiet, reasoned tone of the communitarian critique and the puzzling lack of fervor, as well as action, behind its proponents' calls for incremental economic and political institutional reforms that would promote a national community capable of identifying and pursuing common goods. Trapped by their rationally grounded belief in our fundamental reliance on a society that is now seen as overwhelmingly individualistic in its values and so thoroughly constrained by the magnitude and complexity of its structural interactions, communitarians appear to have concluded that reform, triggered like all purposive change by individual and small group agency—even that of a social scientific elite—is not at all likely.

This notable lack of communitarian passion is also attributable to the basic compatibility between the pluralistic, multicultural variety of America that is valued by mainstream communitarians and our liberal republican political framework. Community as like kind, locale, or other association of belief and practice has, after all, been part of our liberal, federal, pluralist scheme from the beginning. All that has been insisted upon consistently by those at the helm of liberal republican governance is that community practices not pose a threat to overarching liberal republican social, political, and economic order. Polygamy, syndicalism, industrial unionism, and other potentially disruptive or contagious radical social and political grassroots projects are good examples of the limits imposed on community—often by other communities—within our liberal republican state. Lifestyle enclaves and other zones of status, personal moral preference, or comfort and nurture can be maintained and replicated, depending on one's ability to pay and one's willingness to accept the above over-riding constraints.

Under this subordinate relationship, the fact that Communitarian Man's proponents see us as the product of social formation only completes our political enervation. We do not exist as humans, even in theory, *apart* from society—understood in its current pluralistic form as a "community of communities."[14] Our moral content and our capacity as moral actors are each critically dependent on the vitality of families, communities, and the other institutions that comprise society. If society is disintegrating or changing too rapidly, if communities are disappearing, we become anomic, anemic, underdeveloped, dangerously radical, or otherwise dysfunctional. Lacking the virtues that can change society, qualities that society itself possesses and therefore must impart, we will continue to produce, consume, and remain quiescent within the liberal republican framework, likely past the point where it has ceased to be either liberal or even virtually republican. Communitarian Man is no threat to Enlightenment Man, who at least understands his emancipation from society, even if he is unwilling to acknowledge the destructive implications of the freedom he has chosen.

Upon closer examination in the next chapter, we should not be surprised to see actual others, and at least something of ourselves, in the communitarian model as well as in the Enlightenment individual construct. Further, as suggested above, we should acknowledge the possibility that both models are not only compatible, but have been potentially so from the moment of their original conceptions of who we are, how we are formed, and what we are capable of both socially and politically. Finally, most critically, we need to ask ourselves how *completely* these models, considered either separately or together, describe either ourselves or others whom we believe we know well. This is especially important for those groups—women, African Americans, and others—who were excluded from the dominant Enlightenment model, or who were assigned separate, subordinate functional roles in the American communitarian scheme that have lingered to the present.

GENDER AND OTHER OMISSIONS

The omission of women from our public philosophical self-understanding, at least until recently, has been unique in its moral consequences. It has been accompanied by the gendered segregation and subordinate ranking of virtues, such as compassion, cooperation, affection, nonviolence, nurture, and self-sacrifice without glory, all of which women are said to possess either uniquely or in greater quantity and noninstrumental purity than men.[15] The historical location of such behaviors, still actively discouraged in men, in the safe, non-political comfort of women's hands and domains, has left the larger playing fields of society, economy, and state largely cleared and organized for enlightened, pragmatic pursuits.

To the extent that the above values have persisted, notwithstanding the increasing but still limited social and political weight of women and those men able to withstand or recover from conventional moral nurture, we must further question the universality of the human ontological claims that are made by the proponents of each philosophical model. It is not enough to simply acknowledge the gradual admission of women within each paradigm and to thereby assume that their presence has thereby altered the models, inoculating them with gender neutrality.[16] The foundations, the "who we are" claims of both, must be re-examined. The point is not to state a case for either a sex- or gender-specific human nature, but rather to support a claim that human virtue—our personal moral capacity in action—is much broader, more routinely other-regarding, and more powerful in its potential than either liberal republicanism or communitarianism provides. Accordingly, both public philosophical models are described herein as masculine, both to reflect their origins and to remind us that much of their current content retains a distinctly male, as well as racial and ethnic, cultural bias. This reminder further helps to explain the contrast of the Enlightenment and communitarian models with core actors introduced in the first chapter and the moral dynamic they represent. The ultimate collective impact of morally informed action depends on the shared, yet varied, capacities of women *and* men of all hues, ethnicities, cultures, and circumstances.

ENLIGHTENMENT MAN AT CONCEPTION

The writings of John Locke afford a good place to study Enlightenment Man's gestation and birth where, as Thomas Pangle argues, he offers "the most completely worked out presentation of that current in political philosophy which exerted the strongest pull on the Framers as they struggled to formulate an adequate understanding of themselves and their ultimate goals."[17]

Locke presents man as a unique product of his tense, dynamic relation with the state of nature. Lockean scholars Thomas Pangle and Leo Strauss are in agreement that the state of nature that Locke describes "is not so much an historical condition that men dwelt in at some time in the past" as it is a "mixed mode"—a reality inferred from the "natural bent of the passions."[18] As such, it not only existed at some point in our prehistory, but can develop at any time, in any number of locations, "wherever there are any number of Men, however associated, that have no . . . decisive power to appeal to . . . ."[19] In sum, the state of nature is both the physical world of nature and the nature of unenlightened humans within it.

Prior to discussing the passions Locke is referring to, it is important to note his view that man differs in three remarkable capacities from those who are otherwise his brethren in the animal kingdom:

First, he is self-conscious, aware of his own existence, and able to identify his needs and drives, his underlying fears and longings, the sole possessor among creatures of a true "Self";

Second, he is capable of this task by virtue of his ability to reason, which not only enables him to understand himself, but also to study others, to comprehend the rest of the world around him, and devise sound strategies to deal with at least some of his existential dilemma;

Third, he is strongly motivated by his fears, needs, and drives and therefore possesses the necessary will to act in his rationally informed self-interest.[20]

Locke begins the construction of Enlightenment Man, then, from the premise of an inherently, unalterably isolated inner self, a personal identity that, once discovered, creates a fundamentally unbridgeable temporal divide between himself and everyone, everything else. He shares with animals and other humans a strong, primal instinct for survival, together with other needs and drives that he seeks to satisfy in a natural world of scarcity. His most "unremitting and powerful uneasiness is the fear of death and of the physical suffering that attends or intimates death."[21] This fear is not to be confused with our animal nature alone. It is much more powerful than primal instinct, informed as it is by self-awareness and rational world-understanding. We know that we are alive, that life as we know it will unpredictably end, and this prospect bothers us greatly. It is this fear, greater than any other, and the corresponding strength of the passion it triggers, which grounds—and limits—our moral nature.

In an associated manner, Enlightenment Man, until death forces its final, inevitable awareness upon him, is engaged in an unceasing quest to satisfy his bodily needs and drives and thereby obtain pleasure, or, more important, minimize or avoid pain. The conditions necessary to satisfy his fear and need driven nature—life, liberty, and the pursuit of happiness—are his fundamental, natural, or divinely ordained rights, inferred from the logic of his nature. Property, the possession of which affords most storable, lasting, effective means of producing pleasure or reducing pain, is what most comforts him. It is the source of his greatest joy, a ". . . delight of the Mind [which comes] from the consideration of the present or assured approaching possession of a Good [and the knowledge] that we can use it when we please."[22] According to Pangle's analysis of Locke, "this shows us why the practically limitless drive for power, hence property, but also dominion, prestige and triumph is so natural to man."[23]

Individual efforts to allay mortal fear and satisfy needs in the social and physical environment stimulate competition and a taxing awareness of constant potential danger. Being rational, Enlightenment Man is instrumentally social—others are necessary for one's own survival, comfort, and prosperity. He is also drawn into social relationships by unpredictable, disorderly, "impulsive passions of tenderness and lust, envy and triumph, fear and dominion."[24] Clearly, Locke does not trust unmediated affection of any sort to form a durable social adhesive. It seems that Enlightenment Man is able to remove himself from the constant potential anarchy of life in nature "only with the power of the passionate fear it induces, and by the human capacity to reason."[25]

His social and political morality is grounded in inherent isolation, mortal fear, and other drives or passions—and in his belief that others are similarly informed. Its precepts are derived by the instrumental use of reason, the same tool by which he has made his ontological discoveries. Only reason is available to tame passion, subdue nature, and construct a stable order. It is Enlightenment Man's only implement to aid him in the search for modest, unromantic, maximally durable social, political, and economic truths. Given the premises of his inner nature, his reason also has the unfortunate consequence of objectifying the world and everyone else within it.[26]

Enlightenment Man is also instrumentally political and educable, at least to the extent of common sense, in the acquisition of knowledge and its connections to self-interest. Accordingly, he is willing to consent to a regime that affords him the following:

First, a liberal personal sphere of property and other secured negative rights that safeguard his personhood and his ability to participate in the other two spheres;

Second, a voluntary sphere or civil society of social, economic, and political association;

Third, a carefully crafted republican governmental sphere to act as a neutral referee—or as an arena for constrained conflict—on behalf of an aggregate sovereign of nominal, juridical, or theoretical equals[27];

Fourth, the right of revolt if the contract is materially breached by the state or others in civil society.

These are Enlightenment Man's political conceptual gifts to himself and, by reciprocal obligation, to like-minded others. Each feature empirically reflects and is instrumental to his nature—to his separate self, his chronic, primary mortal anxiety and his need to assuage it, as well as to satisfy his less complex needs, drives, tastes, goals, and other pursuits that constitute his unique composite of happiness.[28]

THE AMERICAN MODEL

Whether roaming the corridors of our increasingly private social, political, and economic institutions, or receiving a membership renewal notice at home, Enlightenment Man—the current public version of the above original model of the rational self-seeker, the possessive pursuer of interest—increasingly reigns.[29] As a result, the search for, and the instantiation of, common good in

America—some deeply unifying sense of a living, vital, shared purpose and common enterprise that extends beyond aggregated projects of self-preservation and material enhancement—has been increasingly foreclosed. With Enlightenment Man at the helm of governance, the twin screws of utilitarian aggregation and the selective employment of absolute autonomous rights, each forged by a politics of economically biased, structurally and organizationally enhanced pluralism, have moved us in this direction.[30] It is the second prop that makes our pluralism liberal and occasionally tucks in the sheets around such strange bedmates as socially conservative libertarians, amoral privateers such as Larry Flynt, and Kantian purists in the ACLU.[31]

Our constitutional framework has operated as the device into which the fittings for these screws were installed at the outset. As Pangle and others have detailed, the Founders were well, although indirectly, imbued with the Enlightenment model of human nature.[32] They accepted the view of political actors as described at their abstract conception: individuals—men—who were unreliably social, virtuous, or altruistic outside of their respective private circles of family and intimate friends.

Experience on the challenging yet fertile, abundant soil of America modified the implicitly elite model only slightly at first, primarily by rewarding the long-standing constant of hard work and patient, risk-tolerant investment with the early elimination of frequent scarcity and the provision of somewhat broader rough economic parity.[33] These conditions, however, contributed to the imbuing of Enlightenment Man with a passion for liberty as autonomy. Nature, as Massachusetts Bay Colony Governor Winthrop discovered, could not be relied upon to ". . . compel men into the political community, they must be induced to enter it."[34] They also helped to equip him with a broadened sense of nonaristocratic elite equality, and an enthusiasm for economic self-fulfillment, which in an existing, growing commercial society, was potentially boundless in its scope.

Property only gained in importance in our dominant Protestant culture. It continued to serve as the guarantor of security for the fundamentally needful, isolated self, even as its unequal acquisition increasingly offered tangible evidence of Enlightenment-influenced religious virtue and possible salvation.[35] Later, as access to heaven became more democratic and less real to the most rationally enlightened, property still furnished the purchase price of philanthropic immortality. As always, wealth remained instrumental to power, but only to the extent that it could be pursued, enlarged, rendered more mobile, and protected in the realm of private freedom. If Enlightenment Man was optimistic concerning his own future, his mood was at least somewhat grounded in his assessment of the rational commonsense potential of others, informed

by practical wisdom and other modest virtues, such as tolerance and civic obligation.

At the Founding

Early evolutionary and other emerging technical and scientific learning acquired by Enlightenment Man at the founding confirmed his Lockean nature
in a process that, in turn, was seen as reflecting the prevailing component of
human moral capacity—reason itself.[36] It is this faculty, as Locke had already
informed us, which enables us to act with volition, and which constitutes our
freedom.[37] It also provides the means to design a system of limited governance and laws that are congruent with his nature. Reason, then, is Enlightenment Man's ". . . infallible guide to political activity."[38]

Rationality, in all its fact-seeking permutations, remained Enlightenment
Man's sole resource for detecting his moral nature, while instrumental rationality enabled him to construct moral principles, ethical rules, and laws to
govern his public (social, economic, and political) interactions. By this
means, he comes to acquire Locke's understanding of himself, and of the importance of prudent, practical virtue. He is able to be fair, even modestly generous, in his dealings, because reputation is useful and because reciprocity occasionally requires someone to open the bidding. He is also able to be ruthless
and deceitful when forced to contend with the unenlightened. He does, however, tolerate some degree of difference in religion or elsewhere in private
life, because a stable order is, above all, rationally preferable. He is frugal,
hard working, and modest in displays of wealth for similar reasons of enlightened self-interest.[39] Finally, he is willing to voluntarily consent to a system of limited republican government and positive law, where his capacity for
rational calculus leads him to conclude that his fears will be maximally reduced and his wants optimally secured. His consent, however, is conditioned
upon his personal inclusion in the actual embrace of its guarantees of political equality, maximum liberty, and, above all, secure property. Moreover,
with the assist of more recent enlightenment political expertise, he is able to
improve upon the Lockean political design.

Montesquieu, the only Enlightenment social and political theorist referred
to by name at the Philadelphia Convention, was a prime architect for our
unique version of the political structure of Enlightenment Man.[40] He expressed even greater confidence than Locke over the contribution to political
stability of the new, more modest and egalitarian, self-indulgent forms of
virtue, above-described.[41] He saw the grounding for this virtue in shallower,
narrower waters, however, identifying only the "spirit of commerce" as the
animating force of what he saw as a new, expanding political elite. He does

not appear to have agreed with Locke that Enlightenment Man reflected our universal human nature; however, he concluded that the commercial elites that were selected by Locke in crafting his model were the best hope for a stable republican order.[42] His institutional design was intended to harness this new vitality, and to reinforce it by "favorable laws" so that it would *replace* the older forms of civic and patriotic virtue, excepting only the lighter armor of fame and honor, and thereby make either monarchy or an aristocratic republic unnecessary.[43]

To accomplish this novel task, Montesquieu sought to institutionalize and privilege the spirit of commercial self-interest as the engine of regime stability. This special preference, he hoped would constrain the rationally unenlightened in both the lower and upper social strata from pursuing any exclusive, fanatical, divisive claims or obligations of a higher moral nature in the political realm. In other words, man would relinquish any hope that he might have of seizing control of government either to instantiate "pure" morality, or to engage in unbounded sensual or material pursuit.[44] Enlightened actors, men of modest virtue, and a republican governmental design of divided power, further safeguarded with checks and balances, would secure society from *either* democratic or aristocratic excess. Those who were powerfully motivated by a Machiavellian passion for fame would still be drawn to the flame of political leadership, but in a "form of government" that would constrain their ambition, while giving them ". . . a share in its honors and distinctions."[45]

Classical republican virtue, although evident among many of America's founding political leaders, was seen by Montesquieu and the Founders alike as occasional, prone to fanaticism, and therefore unreliable; competitive self-interest and ego rewards, within rational constraints, were more dependable constants.[46]

In sum, our constitutional design was masterful, brilliantly conceived, and based on a human model that was informed by a still narrow sample: a slowly diversifying, virtually all male, white, commercially savvy economic elite. How much the Founders felt that they, individually, had in common with the model is hard to assess; however, the historical record during the period leading up to the founding, including the Philadelphia Convention, suggests that they were much more complexly driven—often less self-interested, more fraternal, and less determined by mortal fear or bodily needs than the group model assumed. What is clear, however, was their general distrust of virtuous, fraternal men to reliably combine over time and distance in order to trump the organized self-interest of either a democratic majority or an elite faction. According to John P. Diggins, the classical notion of politics as a regenerative activity was overwhelmingly rejected by the Founders in favor of a design that assumed man's fallen nature and *their* enlightened rational capacity to create an architecture for politics that could withstand both mobs and factions.[47]

By the end of the founding era, our nonelite understanding of human moral nature and moral capacity was presumably also under the increasing influence of Enlightenment Man. The idea of a liberal republican state run by a propertied elite at the national level, for example, was already evident at the state and local levels. Yet there was evidence of internal dissension in the conflicts over democratic issues of sovereignty, participation, and representative accountability apparent not only during the ratification debates, but at least as early as the Andros Controversy in Boston between 1689 and 1691.[48]

Such episodes are early evidence of belief in an individual *and* social human nature that was more vigorous, broadly distributed, other-regarding, and capable of democratic self-governance than Locke, Montesquieu, or the vast majority of the Founders were willing to accept.[49] As social historian Gary B. Nash, Howard Zinn, and a few others have noted, part of the reason for their reluctance was the still common tendency in reporting or analyzing our history or current events, to ignore, over-aggregate, or mischaracterize the nature, behavior, motivation, and capacity of nonelite actors.[50] Another reason has been and remains a marked reluctance by those who hold or value elite status in our culture to share or entrust substantial power to those who are unwilling to incur the risks and costs—including moral compromise—of its pursuit, its use, or its maintenance.[51]

Achieving Dominance without Universality

During the nineteenth and twentieth centuries, Enlightenment Man has greatly strengthened his upper hand in American politics and society. On the surface, he seems to have overcome his fearful preoccupation with death. This was not due to any new transcendental discovery, although for the vast majority of us who still consider religion "somewhat important, important, or very important," the possibility of an easily accessible divine hereafter still dampens mortal fear and assuages guilt in present.[52] In the 1830s, Tocqueville linked the future of democratic self-government to the strength of individual afterlife-focused religion in an America that he saw as populated by enlightened men. Such a faith served to satisfy our "longing for immortality, equally tormenting every heart," without unduly burdening the liberal republican state with either religious zealotry or church supported moral activism.[53] Even the enlightened nonbeliever "still considers it [religion] useful. . . . He understands [its] power to lead men to live in peace and gently to prepare them for death."[54]

Thanks to scientific advance, death in America, although still greatly affected by race and class, has increased its average distance from birth. While most of us are still aware that, in the words of an anonymous Maine gravedigger, the base line rate remains at "about one per person," it is an event that has receded from the forefront of consciousness.[55] There are subtle signs, however, that mortal anxiety still retains the power to drive self-interest. Our apparently soft support for universal health care, for example, reveals the fears of some of those fortunate to have private coverage that universality may impair the quality of care they now receive and their future ability to stave off the inevitable. As the "Harry and Louise" campaign by the health insurance lobby in 1994 demonstrated, our fears are not hard to provoke.[56] Once aroused, they seem to easily overcome our residual belief in rough equality, much as Tocqueville had predicted.[57] What remains difficult to detect, in the absence of true democratic opportunities to inform, discuss, persuade, and decide, is the social prevalence and individual motive weight of such fears. Enlightenment Man's progeny may not be as numerous as they often seem when such issues are identified and framed in the overwhelmingly privatized, corporatized venues that pass as our vehicles and fora of public discourse.

As for supposed ubiquity and primacy of Enlightenment Man's acquisitive, entrepreneurial nature, McCloskey and Zaller offer some evidence that, for some of us, other concerns may matter more.[58] In their study of opinion surveys conducted in the late 1950s and the late 1970s, they detected a curious elite-mass disparity in the results. In a 1958 survey, for example, seventy percent of a large national sample from the general public (distinguished in the survey data from political influentials) thought that personal economic security for them was more important than advancement. For influentials, however, the figures were the mirror reverse. Further, only forty-two percent of the general public and fifty percent of political influentials, separately tallied in a 1978–1979 survey, thought that everyone would profit in the long run ". . . if businesses were allowed to make as much money as they [could]."[59] Finally, there was a significant negative correlation found by McCloskey and Zaller between the strength of one's commitment to democratic, as compared to capitalist, values, with members of the general public *and* opinion leaders, to some extent, clustered at each priority.[60] While the range of debate among both groups was—and continues to be—constrained by a wary acceptance of capitalism by strong democracy advocates and an equivalent ambivalence toward political democracy by the most enthusiastic supporters of capitalism, the differences were too wide to support the notion of general American conformity to the Lockean model of human nature and political structure.

The above findings, although somewhat aged, and certainly subject to shift over time, suggests that significant numbers of the American polity implicitly understand themselves and see others quite differently than the liberal republican account provides. McCloskey and Zaller, drawing upon a much wider range of social and political opinion data than indicated above, concluded:

> People who are convinced of the need for social change, who are strongly motivated to alleviate distress [in others], and who take an optimistic view of human nature, tend to be enthusiastic about democracy and wary of capitalism. In contrast, people who value order and stability, who are tough-minded about the prospects for alleviating social distress, and who take an essentially pessimistic view of human nature tend to be strongly pro-capitalist and cautiously democratic.[61]

Tocqueville's Insights

At the time of his travels in America, it was apparent to Tocqueville that the individual pursuit of material comfort beyond necessity had become an increasingly popular mortal distraction, facilitated by natural resource abundance. Apart from the modest restraint prompted by the doctrines of our institutional individual faiths, it was our republican "mores"—his term for the modest social and political virtues of Enlightenment Man—that supported the promise of stable democratic governance into the future, more so than our laws and republican framework.[62] Our sense of yeoman equality, our acceptance of majority rule, our belief in popular sovereignty—these "moral and intellectual dispositions" owed most of their observed strength to our practical experience with self-government, reinforced by public education that emphasized "the history of his country and the main features of its Constitution."[63] However, he also detected a general "restlessness amid prosperity," evident in the perpetual movement and commercial zeal of the population. He saw both as a reflection of Enlightenment Man's "perhaps most natural" drive for physical comfort, and as a potential threat to instrumental virtue.[64]

While Tocqueville admired the concept of "self-interest, rightly understood," he acknowledged the limits of its use in defining common goods and detected its centrifugal effects already at work. "One must expect that private interest will more than ever become the chief if not the only driving force behind all behavior, [b]ut we have yet to see how each man will interpret his private interest."[65] Even with the rational and religious constraints, along with the sense of rough democratic equality that Tocqueville detected, he concluded that even the kind of "decent materialism" that Enlightenment Man first offered in America would "soften and imperceptibly loosen the springs of [collective] action."[66]

He also commented on the evidence of indecent materialism he detected among America's small manufacturing elite. He thought this new "aristocracy" to be "one of the hardest that have appeared on earth [but] at the same time one of the most restrained and least dangerous."[67] Although he was prescient in many areas of American life, his gift did not enable him to discern the organizational and technological dynamic then gathering momentum. That energy, along with straightforward corruption, would soon combine to sweep away the external restraints he had noted.[68]

Fostering Certain Establishments

By the end of the nineteenth century, institutional religious faith, operating as Tocqueville had observed from its comfortable restricted sphere, was seen by some to have failed miserably in reigning in Enlightenment Man's then obvious excesses. In the space of only several decades, rough equality had given way to rampant inequality, liberty had become economic license for a few, and republican government had failed to maintain even a semblance of pluralistic balance. Moreover, new variants of Enlightenment rationalism—scientific, social scientific, and philosophical—justified the inevitability, even the overall desirability of the results. Tacitly acknowledging what many had known all along—namely, that Enlightenment Man was a model for dominant elite behavior in a new era—his most avid proponents offered Social Darwinism to explain the inevitable costs of progress to an audience that largely benefited from the changed economic landscape.[69]

At the same time, historically underrated changes in the organization and comprehension of economic pluralism were also underway. Enlightenment Man's admirers in our legislatures and courts, with professional supporters in the law and academia, developed, improved upon, and legitimated organizational and conceptual innovations that greatly strengthened the broad social, economic, and political reach of those whom the model best describes. Perhaps the most remarkable among many examples was the development of the modern business corporation. It entered the nineteenth century as a limited duration, licensed legal fiction, created to rationalize and facilitate the production, accumulation, and protection of capital for the benefit of private investors and the congruent public development needs of the liberal republican state. Public goods, in other words, were created by the harnessing of the tidal power of private accumulative desire in a "win-win" scenario that was rife with temptation to abandon civic virtue and go for the gold.[70]

By the end of the century, the prime investors in corporate business and financial entities had secured their divorce from public service, having already obtained an unconscionable property settlement of public land and natural wealth in the process. They had also acquired for their soulless fictions legal personhood, temporal immortality, constitutionally secured political liberties and civil rights, and the beginnings of virtual personality as well as faceless agency.[71] They further generated unprecedented wealth at greatly reduced individual risk, as well as astonishing political capital for their insider owners. All that was left in order to fully consolidate these organizational and political accomplishments, to complete the disguise of the de facto individual and joint ventured interlocking corporate accomplishment, was to anoint them with new concepts of historical, developmental inevitability.[72] Scholars from our newly secularized academia, equipped with an Enlightenment view of individual moral nature and armed with new forms of positivist rational expertise, were up to the task. No where was this more evident than in the field of economics.

The small "manufacturing aristocracy which we have seen rising before our eyes," Tocqueville wrote around 1836, was discovered in retrospect to have been evidence of the emergence of a powerful new historical force.[73] New technologies of mass production and transportation, innovative organizational methods to finance and direct their energy, the connection of these components, together with labor and other commodities in vast, interconnected market networks of supply and demand—all this was now comprehended as vast new system. What had begun as concrete projects of individual and joint-ventured business endeavor was now conceived as having necessitated a new level of economic abstraction, an understanding of something distinct from the sum of its entrepreneurial parts. Its actions could only be explained, interpreted by experts as interactions and signals, expansions and contractions, patterns and dislocations. In short, we had witnessed the birth and maturation of a new, autonomous realm of existence.

From the perspective of Enlightenment Man's exemplars, the elevation of the economy to a complex, interactive, systemic dominion was a delightful artifice or, more accurately, a series of them. Conceived of as a domain whose size and impersonal dynamics are detectable only via quantities and formulae, it is seen today by admirer and foe alike as an effective barrier to democratic governance. As political theorist John Dryzek observes, the dictates of "free trade, market liberal ideology, economic rationalism, and aggressive individualism" have combined "to obstruct any deeper democratization and to erode existing democratic achievements."[74]

Accepted as something greater—more powerful, *yet more delicate*—than any one of its complexly interdependent institutions and subsystems, the economic system has moved beyond direct safe or intelligent control by one of its larger subsystems, the nation-state. Its essential energy and fragile balance wheel are the key expressions of our professed common nature: rational self-interest expressed in markets for production and consumption of all manner of invention and enterprise; increasingly abstract, diluted, remote, and contingent forms of ownership as our new security; mortal anxiety expressed as a level of confidence upon which the whole system is said to depend; and the critical dependence of the whole enterprise upon constant bottom line growth fueled by endless, exponential growth in atomistic demand. In other words, even if Locke was wrong, it no longer much matters.

This reification of what had been—and still is—created or initiated by individual and small group invention, replication, and refinement, including propagation of the notion of inevitable progress by its critical means, has further dampened our sense of democratic equality, of sovereign citizen power, of human moral agency itself. The American model that Tocqueville described, a nation of small citizen freeholders able to variously pursue individual security and modest dreams, was retained as a growing popular myth, while servile wage labor and social, communal uprooting emerged on an increasing scale as mass reality. As Isaiah Berlin noted:

> To try to frighten human beings by suggesting to them that they are in the grip of impersonal forces over which they have little or no control is to breed myths. . . . It is to invent entities, to propagate faith in unalterable patterns of events . . . which by relieving individuals of the burden of personal responsibility, breeds irrational passivity in some, and no less irrational fanatical activity in others. . . . [75]

Countervailing Views

As the twentieth century arrived, Enlightenment Man's alienation from nature, from any sense of unified being, was approaching completion in practice, although not in his professions of faith.[76] Walter Rauchenbusch, a leading theologian of the Social Gospel Movement, derided Christian churches in America for their continuing focus on individual afterlife and for their silence on action against growing social and economic injustice in the present. Using Old Testament prophecy as his model, he chided the morality of individual Christian piety, noting that the lack of immortal self-assurance in Judaism, combined with a belief in divine justice, had once lent religious sanction to the demand for social and economic justice in the world.[77] He saw that the "virility and humaneness of the prophets and that capacity for growth which stir our enthusiasm were largely due to the breadth and inclusiveness of their religious sympathy and faith."[78]

There were many in academia and elsewhere who also were not enamored with the excesses and social consequences of the new rational economy. Muckraker journalists—Ida Tarbell, Upton Sinclair, and others—investigated corporate abuse, peered through organizational obfuscation, and named names. Setting the tone for the century, however, much of the political reform debate was internecine, an argument among proponents of liberal republicanism over how to best accommodate what they saw as the constant nature and undeniable economic benefits of the enhanced Enlightenment model. Accordingly, much of the Progressive Movement, while often critical of the primarily commercial republic conceived by the Founders, was a largely rational discussion among experts concerning the best means to reduce or offset harmful, socially destabilizing consequences of capitalism—while allowing large-scale self-interested pursuit to further organize, systematize, and flourish. Virtually all of them realized, with Woodrow Wilson, that they were "in the presence of a new organization of society . . . .[that] life has broken away from the past."[79]

Those who had benefited most from the faux laissez-faire frontier period of American development were seen as immoderate and greedy, but undeniably successful and ultimately philanthropic. In fact, those that had amassed great fortunes were and remain largely understood as having played a critical role in the development of a powerful new nation. At issue was the restoration of rational moderation, of self-interest rightly understood. Both the democratic and republican factions of the Progressive Movement called for the strengthening of government to regulate the new forms of highly organized self-interest, as well as to soften of some of "its" harsh human consequences. While they quarreled over the best means to control trust monopolies, both saw the necessity of a stronger, less corrupt, more competent republican government—one that emulated the efficiency of business structure and management, but which restored some mix of direct democratic and republican accountability. The call was for new rational public designs, institutions, and technical expertise that would offset the power of the private sector with the countervailing power of government.

Capable governance, understood as a separate system of skilled professionals able to counteract or regulate the excesses of private power, would restore the public's faith in American ideals.[80] Enlightened men could and did agree to progressive taxation and redistribution, as well as sound administration to regulate and ameliorate the new corporate-structured, mass-production, mass-consumption national order. Capitalism, seen by most elites as a legitimate reflection of human nature and the engine of material progress, was to be left in private hands, watched and regulated insofar as individual excess could still be detected and restrained without risking the whole enterprise.[81]

The fact that the new economic order had left labor without Lockean autonomy was acknowledged by many mainstream reformers; however, the inevitability of progress seemed to mandate that labor co-operate in the new order and look to the state to ensure health and safety in the workplace. When Progressivism's early principal spokesman, Herbert Croly, subsequently departed from mainstream reform orthodoxy with a call for workplace democracy that suggested at least a partial rejection of the American Enlightenment model, he was largely ignored.[82] Croly's realization that genuine political liberty could only be secured by eliminating the private political governance inherent in a corporatized, private economy and pluralistic political framework was drowned out by the arguments of others, such as Frederick Winslow Taylor, calling for the "enforced cooperation" of manufacturing workers mandated by the dictates of rational management.[83]

As the Progressives still saw it, the contents of our social and political morality were still deduced from a moral nature that remained constant in its mortal insecurity and boundless need for temporal satisfactions. In the heady, newly abundant, opportunistic environment spawned by a huge, powerful industrial republic, rational self-moderation required greater reinforcement than at the founding. New institutions and policies grafted on to the existing regime, each enhanced by new scientific knowledge and technical expertise, were essential for America to collectively manage its way into the future. In the analysis of new experts, the direction of that future would thereafter be understood as *the product* of organized and aggregated self-interests, mass-assessed individual needs and preferences, the defeat of oppositional ideologies, the adroit steering of systemic forces, and planning for unforeseen events.

Further Rational Obfuscation

Parallel with the development of economic rationalism, scientific rationalism, with its own claim of factual, moral neutrality, assisted greatly in the masking of human moral agency by its conceptual conversion of American politics and social relations into a framework of systems and processes. It also facilitated the reduction of moral values expressed as common public goods to the level of subjective individual and group interests that can only be aggregated and compromised within government. Its advocates accomplished this first by reducing shareable truth to facts that are verifiable only by empirical observation or experimental replication. Such knowledge is, in itself, virtuous and its pursuit noble, or, at any rate, significant. More important, it is only by theories developed and tested by these means that our knowledge of what is and what can be, based on the trends of past results and current data, becomes comprehensive, more complete. This is not to suggest that everyone concerned with politics or with science agreed then or now that science has emancipated fact from value, only that the partisans of this dichotomy have come to dominate our expert culture.

Our individual thinking about politics, society, and the self has also been increasingly informed by scientific rationalism. Those components of En-lightenment Man that are amenable to observation and experiment have been tested, and his Lockean human nature largely confirmed.[84] We are, few now doubt, most predictably motivated by individual, typically economic self-interest, as well as by the drives associated with pleasure and the avoidance of pain. There are, however, three problems with this behavioral assertion that remain either ignored or inadequately addressed:

First, an explanation of current behavior, even behavior carefully observed over time, does not explain how it developed. For such answers, science, like all other disciplines, must resort to history, individual experience, imagination, and conjecture.

Second, those who rely upon observational and experimental methods can only theorize from conflicting factual inferences, along with the rest of us, concerning the primacy of self-interest and the resulting priority it occupies in our lives. We know, for example, that war, depression, natural disaster, rapid socio-economic change, and other exigent events have markedly changed the content of our customary attitudes. There have been periods of reactive individual and collective mean-spiritedness, alongside intervals of widespread heroism and al-truism, with belief in greed's necessity in obvious decline.[85] It would be only amusing to read the tortured attempts of rational choice theorists to fit such be-haviors into a Lockean mold if they were not taken so seriously by so many.[86]

Perhaps, however, such extremes as meanness, greed, and sacrificial gen-erosity are more exceptional than typical, and this possibility, together with our observable tendency to focus on personal gain and pleasure in "ordinary times" each confirm Locke's theory. We are, to credit his insight with our own candid, inner confirmation, isolated from each other in fundamental ways, and it may be our existential insecurity that both brings us together *and* di-vides us into hostile groups.

It can further be argued that we act from mortal fear, except where peace and prosperity dull our awareness of our still immutable, factually known des-tiny of cellular breakdown and physical demise. Either is possible, given our fear-based passion, and our varying capacity for enlightened rational judg-ment. As already noted, if this is what we feel, *what we believe about ourselves* at such moments of "real" existential despair, then that is who we are at least becoming in the narrowing range of intimate relationship to each other.

In any event, due to the persistent limits of scientific rationalism in prov-ing motive, the answer we give to ourselves remains private unless or until we are seen in action upon its premises. Even our public demonstrations must be carefully assessed, however. Our words and behaviors are often intended to dissimulate, to mask the nonconformity of our at least occasional inner dialogue from the disparaging eyes and potentially adverse reactions of those who so clearly embrace the apparently dominant alternative.

The *third* problem, related to the second, is the primary reliance of social science on statistical methods to aggregate behaviors and determine our nature as a collective probability. As Hannah Arendt noted concerning the use of this method to explain history and politics:

> The laws of statistics are valid only where large numbers and long periods are involved, and acts or events can appear only as deviations or fluctuations. The justification is that deeds and events are rare occurrences in everyday life and in history. Yet the meaningfulness of everyday relationships is not disclosed in everyday life but in rare deeds, just as the significance of a historical period shows itself only in the few events that illuminate it. The application of the law of large numbers and long periods to politics or history signifies nothing less than the willful obliteration of their very subject matter. . . . [87]

The shape of society and government, including their moral content, are the product of human agency, of actors and actions that operate beyond the standard deviation from the norm, in either direction. Knowledge of common behaviors or prevailing opinion may be useful, practical, even determining at times; however, as Berlin reminds us, "At root, history deals with human motives and intentions and choices." He does not suggest that the search for cause and effect should be abandoned, or that nonhuman factors, institutional constraints, and unintended consequences from complex interactions should be ignored:

> But to try to reduce the behavior of individuals to that of impersonal "social forces," not further analysable [sic] into the conduct of men, who even according to Marx, make history, is a reification of statistics, a form of "false consciousness" [of those] who close their eyes to all that proves incapable of quantification. . . . [88]

Enlightenment Man may explain less of who we are than what many of us have become—at least in our observable conformity. Our current period of detectable unease, amid prosperity with record levels of income and wealth disparity, may be attributable to chronic mortal anxiety, to an enhanced awareness that life is isolated and fragile. Another possibility is that we are at least somewhat aware that life with or as Enlightenment Man in America is distractingly loud, enervatingly shallow, dangerously misinformed, and, in the absence of major crisis or other inescapable moral challenge, devoid of substance and meaning.

NOTES

1. Tocqueville, 507.
2. Isaiah Berlin, *Four Essays on Liberty* (New York: Oxford University Press, 1969), xxxi.
3. Arendt, *The Human Condition*, 253–54.
4. John Stuart Mill, *On Liberty*, ed. Elizabeth Rapaport (Indianapolis: Hackett Publishing, 1978), 6.
5. Thomas L. Pangle, *The Spirit of Modern Republicanism: The Moral Vision of the American Founders and the Philosophy of John Locke* (1988; Chicago: University of Chicago Press, 1990), 1.
6. The name is intentionally gendered. As mentioned in the introduction, there is no evidence that women were considered in the construction of the Enlightenment model; in fact, the undisputed evidence is that they were not. Further, while there is ample evidence that women are at least as capable as men of conforming to this model or any other design made by men or by themselves, it is fervently hoped that they will dramatically alter it for the better. Cf., note 16.
7. Pangle, *The Spirit*, 1.
8. The reference is to John Locke and his well-known relationship with the Earl of Shaftsbury. Locke followed his wealthy patron not only into politics, but into his investments. These included both the Africa Company, the exclusive crown franchisee of the lucrative English slave trade, and the Bank of England. Peter Laslett, introduction, John Locke, *Two Treatises on Government*, ed. Peter Laslett (New York: Mentor-New American Library, 1965), 56; cf. Richard S. Dunn, *Sugar and Slaves: The Rise of the Planter Class in the English Indies, 1624–1713* (New York: W. W. Norton, 1972), 112; 229–37.
9. It is assumed that Locke, given his background and his era, would approach philosophy both empirically, within the ranks of the politically influential, and self-reflectively, where philosophical thought typically begins. Arendt, "What is Existential Philosophy?," in *Essays*, ed. Jerome Kohn (New York: Harcourt Brace, 1994), 177–78.
10. Friedrich A. von Hayek, *The Road to Serfdom* (1944; Chicago: University of Chicago Press, 1994) serves as an articulate, ultra-libertarian exemplar. As noted in Chapter 1 (note 37), theologian Reinhold Niebuhr makes one of the most persuasive cases for the necessary marriage of liberal republicanism to man's fallen social nature.
11. Pangle, *The Enobling of Democracy*. Pangle reminds us that our political upbringing has occurred in a cave that is particular to America: "We all are necessarily brought up having our minds ordered and predisposed by terminologies, categories, beliefs, and prejudices that we, and most of our teachers, mistake for the natural or necessary ordering of human existence. . . . [Even] our skepticism hides a deeper dogmatism, upon which it is based—a dogmatism so deep that we are scarcely aware of it" (192).
12. The arguments of Alasdair C. MacIntyre in *After Virtue*, linking classical forms of virtue to particular forms of premodern community, are perhaps the most nuanced and eloquent. The use of the male gender to name the model is for the same reasons

mentioned at note 6. Occasional impersonal, neutral references are intended to acknowledge the greater sensitivity of contemporary communitarians to gender equality, as well to suggest other, troubling signs of impersonality. Overall, however, it is this writer's opinion that communitarianism retains enough of its masculine Enlightenment roots to justify the usage.

13. Carole Pateman, *The Problem of Political Obligation: A Critique of Liberal Theory* (Berkeley and Los Angeles: University California Press, 1985); Michael Walzer, *Spheres of Justice* (New York: Basic Books, 1983).

14. Amitai Etzioni, *The New Golden Rule: Community and Morality in a Democratic Society* (New York: Basic Books, 1996), 177.

15. Pateman, 188–90. She argues that our current problem of weak political and social cohesion stems not only from the artificial Enlightenment and founding focus on an isolated, abstract, possessive individual, but on the further identity of such persons as both masculine and entrepreneurial. She notes that contemporary liberalism, including its concepts of morality and moral capacity, are still hampered by gender exclusion, a defect derived from a particular, historical understanding of the male-female relationship, and the association of certain moral virtues with gender. Her latter claim is well supported by James Wilson, in his "Lectures on Law," given in Philadelphia in 1790 to an audience that included fellow Founders, their wives, and companions. Wilson interrupted his lecture, then focusing on the unique character of American virtue, ". . . distinguished by the love of liberty, and the love of law," to deliver a separate colloquy to the "female part of [his] audience." Adopting the presumed reaction of his distaff listeners, he asks, "What is all this to us? . . . Is everything made for your sex? Is our sex less honest or less virtuous, or less wise than yours?" He replies that women had demonstrated in history that they could possess and exercise these qualities, but only at the cost of adopting a masculine moral persona. At this dichotomous juncture he asks, "Would you wish to be judged by the qualities of *our* (emphasis added) sex? I will refer you to a more proper standard—that of your own." Wilson goes on to locate women within a distinct subrealm of the liberal private sphere where they (and their distinctive innocent virtues) are protected from the need to contend with men in their "fallen state," which is the inevitable, "necessary" task and human consequence of engaging in politics and government. Caring, compassion, and selfless devotion to others are thereby exiled from human nature at large and from politics conducted beyond the maximum visible feminine reach *within* the local community. James Wilson, *The Works of James Wilson*, ed. Robert Green McCloskey, 2 vols. (Cambridge, MA: Harvard University Press, 1967), I: 84–88.

16. One need only examine the gap between the legalized, social depiction of women in the in the late nineteenth century, and to contrast that subservient image with their roles in the vanguard of virtually all reform movements from the 1830s onward. As Theda Skocpol extensively documents, by 1870, women were already powerfully pursuing a national "maternalist" policy agenda from within a greatly expanded, although still separate, political sphere. Theda Skocpol, *Protecting Soldiers and Mothers: The Political Origins of Social Policy in the United States* (Cambridge, MA: Belknap Press, 1992), 351–72.

17. Pangle, *The Spirit*, 276.

18. Pangle, *The Spirit*, 246; Leo Strauss, *Natural Right and History* (Chicago: University of Chicago Press, 1953), 230–231; Thomas Hobbes, *Leviathan*, Ch. XIII, in *The English Philosophers from Bacon to Mill*, ed. Edwin A. Burt (New York: Random House, 1939), 159–62.

19. John Locke, *Two Treatises*, ed. Peter Laslett, 369 (II: 89).

20. Pangle, *The Spirit*, 186.

21. Pangle, *The Spirit*, 186.

22. John Locke, *An Essay Concerning Human Understanding*, II, xx, 7, quoted in Pangle, *The Spirit*, 185–86.

23. Pangle, *The Spirit*, 186.

24. Pangle, *The Spirit*, 244.

25. Pangle, *The Spirit*, 244.

26. Arendt, *Human Condition*, 292–94.

27. William E. Connolly, "The Challenge to Pluralist Theory," in William E. Connolly, ed., *The Bias of Pluralism* (New York: Atherton Press, 1969), 9–12.

28. Pangle, *The Spirit*, 188.

29. Michael J. Sandel, *Democracy's Discontent: America in Search of a Public Philosophy* (Cambridge, MA: Belknap/Harvard University Press, 1996), 3–5. Cf. C. B. Macpherson, *The Political Theory of Possessive Individualism: Hobbes to Locke* (Oxford: Oxford University Press, 1962).

30. Robert A. Dahl, *Dilemmas of Pluralist Democracy, Autonomy versus Control* (New Haven: Yale University Press, 1982); John S. Dryzek, *Democracy in Capitalist Times: Ideals, Limits, and Struggles* (New York and Oxford: Oxford University Press, 1996).

31. Mary Ann Glendon, *Rights Talk: The Impoverishment of Political Discourse* (New York: Free Press-Macmillan 1991). Flynt is the publisher of *Hustler* Magazine.

32. Pangle, *The Spirit*; John P. Diggins, *The Lost Soul of American Politics: Virtue, Self-Interest, and the Foundations of Liberalism* (1984; Chicago: University of Chicago Press, 1986); Bernard Bailyn, *The Ideological Origins of the American Revolution* (Cambridge, MA: Belknap-Harvard University Press, 1992).

33. McWilliams, 142–43.

34. McWilliams, 143–44.

35. Max Weber, *The Protestant Ethic and the Spirit of Capitalism*, trans. Talcott Parsons (New York: Charles Scribner's Sons, 1958). Weber greatly informs our understanding of how the modest virtues of rational morality, the moral evidentiary weight of material prosperity, and the perspective of the autonomous individual were powerfully influenced by Calvinism. Further, scholars such as Diggins, Stout, and Holifield explain how, in the context of the American colonial experience, rationalism, commercialism, and moderating Puritanism came to inform the shared experience of an increasingly unmediated, individual faith, and to separate the public affairs of state from both the institutional *and* private realms of faith and conscience. John P Diggins (see note 32); Harry S. Stout, *The New England Soul: Preaching and Religious Culture in Colonial New England* (New York and Oxford: Oxford University Press, 1986); E. Brooks Holifield, *Era of Persuasion: American Thought and Culture 1521–1680* (Boston: Twayne Publishers, 1989).

36. Oakeshott, 2–4.

37. Laslett, introduction, Locke, *Two Treatises*, 107–9.

38. Oakeshott, 3.

39. Pangle, *The Spirit*, 88–92.

40. He was referred to by Edmund Randolph and James Madison. See James Madison, *Notes of Debates in the Federal Convention of 1787* (New York: W. W. Norton, 1987), 224; 268; 311.

41. Pangle, *The Spirit*, 67–68.

42. Montesquieu recognized a greater human variety than Locke. He notes, for example, "[some] are poor only because they have . . . disdained the comforts of life, and these last can do great things because this poverty is part of their liberty." Montesquieu, *Spirit of the Laws*, trans. and ed. Anne M. Cohler et al. (Cambridge, United Kingdom: Cambridge University Press, 1989), Bk. 20, Ch. 3.

43. Montesquieu, Bk. 5, Ch. 1–8.

44. Pangle, *The Spirit*, 89–92.

45. James Madison, *The Federalist Papers*, No. 57, ed. Clinton Rossiter (New York: Mentor-Penguin Group, 1961), 352.

46. Montesquieu, Bk. 5, Ch. 2; Alexander Hamilton, *Federalist Papers*, No. 15, 105–13.

47. Diggins, 80–85.

48. According to McWilliams, Founder James Wilson argued that broad popular sovereignty and its necessary implication of actual consent was the necessary core of a legitimate regime. It was not only the ". . . best method of ensuring that government pursues legitimate ends, but also . . . it is the only 'radical cure' for disorder, depriving men of the most legitimate reasons for disobedience." *Idea of Fraternity*, 197–98. As regards the capacity for orderly popular democratic self-rule among average citizens the Andros controversy, where Massachusetts Bay Colony residents ejected the Crown governor and practiced self-rule for over two years, is illuminating. See Stout, 115–118; Gary B. Nash, *The Urban Crucible: The Northern Seaports and the Origins of the American Revolution* (Cambridge, MA: Harvard University Press, 1964), 19–24. While some are likely to counter with the take-over of the royal government in the port of New York by the Leislerians in 1689, and the ensuing factional violence, they should mention the role of New York's harshly competitive commercial elites and their virtually authoritarian domination of the rest of the populace. Nash, 24–28. Cf. David S. Lovejoy, *The Glorious Revolution in America* (New York: Harper and Row, 1972).

49. Pateman, 5.

50. Nash, intro., ix–xv; Howard Zinn, *Declarations of Independence: Cross-Examining American Ideology* (New York: HarperCollins, 1990), 7–8. Cf. George Rudé, *The Crowd in History: A Study of Popular Disturbances in France and England 1730–1848* (New York: John Wiley & Sons, 1964).

51. One suspects that it is this persistent ambivalence in our attitude toward those who hold political power that even today allows us to forgive elected leaders for their flagrant democratic lapses, so long as we do not see cash being exchanged and the official evidences a certain self-confidence, a self-interest that overlaps with ours, and

a style that is not overly dignified or self-righteous. We admire, or at least accept the necessity of Machiavellian skills and a certain moral "realism" in our leaders, a fact well reflected in our political scholarship. E.g., Diggins 345–46; Harvey C. Mansfield Jr., *Taming the Prince: The Ambivalence of Modern Executive Power* (1989; Baltimore: The Johns Hopkins University Press, 1993); Michael Walzer, "The Problem of Dirty Hands," *Philosophy and Public Affairs*, II (Winter 1973): 160–80.

52. Alan Wolfe, *One Nation After All* (New York: Penguin Group, 1998), 44 (and note 4, 329). Referring to a 1991 study, Wolfe reports that ninety-four percent of Americans report a personal belief in God, and other, more recent poll survey data indicates that eighty percent believe in an afterlife.

53. Tocqueville, 297.

54. Tocqueville, 299.

55. The story is one of many "down-east tales" recounted by Robert Bryan and Marshall Dodge in their recording series under the well-known heading of "Bert and I."

56. *Time*, 7 Mar. 1994: 41; Darrell M. West, Diane Heath, and Chris Goodwin, "Harry and Louise Go to Washington: Political Advertising and Health Care Reform," *Journal of Health Politics, Policy, and Law*, 21.1 (Spring 1996): 35–68.

57. Tocqueville, 510; 534.

58. Herbert McCloskey and John Zaller, *The American Ethos: Public Attitudes toward Capitalism and Democracy* (Cambridge, MA: Harvard University Press, 1984).

59. McCloskey and Zaller, 114–20.

60. McCloskey and Zaller, 173–84.

61. McCloskey and Zaller, 233.

62. Tocqueville, 305–8.

63. Tocqueville, 305; 302.

64. Tocqueville, 536; 531.

65. Tocqueville, 527.

66. Tocqueville, 534.

67. Tocqueville, 557–58.

68. Tocqueville, 555–58. He saw little potential for class solidarity among industrial elites. He believed that they would be not only alienated from their workers, but from each other by ever shifting, competing interests and disparities in wealth.

69. According to American legal historian, Peter Irons, Herbert Spencer's book, *Social Statics* (1851) which translated Darwin's theory of natural selection into "survival of the fittest," sold over 500,000 copies in the United States after it was first published here in 1865. According to Irons, lawyers and judges embraced its implicitly laissez-faire approach to business and government. Peter Irons, *A People's History of the Supreme Court* (New York: Penguin Putnam Inc., 1999), 237.

70. The use of public incentives to spur private development of Northern coastal cities, such as Boston, utilizing free public land, exclusive licensing, along with insider knowledge, was established as the pattern for national development well prior to the nineteenth century. See, e.g., Lawrence W. Kennedy, *Planning the City Upon a Hill: Boston Since 1630* (Amherst, MA: University of Massachusetts

Press (1992). By the end of the nineteenth century, the process had reached its logical extreme in Southern California where formerly public lands, furnished as incentives to railroad corporations, were sold back to the public at a handsome profit. Mike Davis, *City of Quartz: Excavating the Future in Los Angeles* (New York: Vintage Books, 1992).

71. One loud reaction to the so-called corporate revolution, from 1890 to 1912, which involved the merger "of the financial world of stocks and bonds [with the] remarkably abrupt proliferation of large manufacturing [and other business] corporations from virtually nothing to domination," was to denounce the new behemoths as "soulless." Corporate managers and other business spokesmen would endeavor to rebut this charge well into the 1940s. William G. Roy, *Socializing Capital: The Rise of the Large Industrial Corporation in America* (Princeton: Princeton University Press, 1997), 1–5; Roland Marchand, *Creating the Corporate Soul: The Rise of Public Relations and Corporate Imagery in American Big Business* (Berkeley and Los Angeles: University of California Press, 1998), 7–8. The related processes of corporate privatization and citizenship rights were begun in 1819 by Justice Marshall in *Dartmouth College v. Woodward*, 17 U.S. 518, followed shortly thereafter by the states' competitive adoption of general incorporation laws, and capped in 1886 by the Supreme Court's bestowal of Fourteenth Amendment "personhood" in *Santa Clara County v. Southern Pacific Railroad*, 118 U.S. 394. Cf. Jack Beatty, "The Case for and Against Incorporation," in Jack Beatty, ed., *Colossus: How the Business Corporation Changed America* (New York: Broadway Books, 2001), 45–53.

72. Roy, 10–20. In a thorough historical and quantitative analysis, sociologist Roy reminds us that corporate-organized power, greatly enhanced by the privatization of the corporate form and its conversion into a form of property that could be publicly held yet privately controlled, was determined not by efficiency or market forces, but by the dynamics of human agency that was both discrete and historically discernible.

73. Tocqueville, 558.

74. Dryzek, 3 (note 30).

75. Isaiah Berlin, intro, xxxiii–iv.

76. Arendt, "What is Existential Philosophy," in *Essays*, 168–72.

77. Douglas F. Ottati, foreword to Walter Rauschenbusch, *Christianity and the Social Crisis* (1907; Louisville, KY: Westminster/John Knox Press, 1991), 18.

78. Rauschenbusch, 27.

79. Woodrow Wilson, *The New Freedom: A Call for the Emancipation of the Generous Energies of a People* (1914; Englewood Cliffs, NJ: Prentice-Hall, 1961) 4.

80. This analysis follows somewhat the analysis of Eldon J. Eisenach, *The Lost Promise of Progressivism* (Lawrence, KS: University of Kansas Press, 1994), who detected an ideological motive force and coherence in a largely failed attempt at regime change among Progressive Era reformers. In some contrast, Morton Keller describes a more generally pluralistic process at work, with major change occurring rapidly, but in a continuum of institutional and ideological constancy. Morton Keller, *Regulating a New Economy: Public Policy and Economic Change, 1900–1933* (Cambridge: Harvard University Press, 1994). According to Keller, policy responses throughout the

Progressive Era "were deeply and inexorably conditioned by pre-existing values, interests, procedural and structural arrangements" (3).

81. Herbert Croly, *The Promise of American Life*; Cf. Claudio J. Katz, "Syndicalist Liberalism: The New Republic of Herbert Croly" (paper presented at the annual meeting of the American Association of Political Science, Boston, MA, August, 1998).

82. Herbert Croly, *Progressive Democracy* (1914; New Brunswick, NJ: Transaction Press, 1998).

83. Katz, 16 (quoting Taylor).

84. The intent here is not to suggest that the Lockean theory has been the acknowledged basis for all such studies; however, it is claimed that Lockean ontology is the operating assumption for most.

85. Samuel P. Huntington, *American Politics: The Promise of Disharmony* (Cambridge, MA: Belknap Press of Harvard University, 1981). Huntington attributes these swings in public sentiment to periods where we become more vitally aware of the gap between our political ideals and the realities of performance by those who operate our political institutions.

86. The benchmark critique of rational choice is by Amartya K. Sen, "Rational Fools: A Critique of the Behavioral Foundations of Economic Theory," *Philosophy and Public Affairs*, 6, no. 4 (Summer 1977): 317–44. For a detailed refutation as it relates to the field of political science, see Donald P. Green and Ian Shapiro, *Pathologies of Rational Choice Theory: A Critique of Applications in Political Science* (New Haven: Yale University Press, 1994).

87. Arendt, *Human Condition*, 42.

88. Berlin, intro., xxxiii.

Chapter Three

Enlightened Community

If terms like "populism" and "community" figure prominently in political discourse today, it is because the ideology of the Enlightenment, having come under attack from a variety of sources, has lost much of its appeal. . . . The Enlightenment's reason and morality are increasingly seen as a cover for power, and the prospect that the world can be governed by reason seems more remote than at any time since the eighteenth century.

—Christopher Lasch[1]

Whatever the future may have in store, one thing is certain. Unless local communal life can be restored, the public cannot adequately resolve its most urgent problem: to find and identify itself.

—John Dewey[2]

It is sad that men who feel a desperate need for communion have been so deeply affected by a society whose life and thought deny it, that they can conceive of community only as an "image," an illusion no less ephemeral for being willed.

—William Carey McWilliams[3]

DEFINING COMMUNITY

Communitarianism is one recent attempt to recover or recreate something that its proponents believe is injured and dying in America. There is no doubt that it has suffered under the onslaught of Enlightenment Man's dominant individualism and the highly organized, instrumentally rational structures he has

created to govern the territory and its inhabitants he has largely conquered—
the state, the economy, and society. That something is "community," a term
that today is most often used to capture a set of attributes that are associated
with traditional patterns of living together that many of us value deeply. One
of these characteristics, the one for which communitarian scholars and
philosophers in Aristotle's lineage is particularly long, is the capacity to identify and seek common goods.

In their broadest popular understanding, those traits associated with community are widely seen as forming at least part of the essence of the good life,
of connection with, participation in, and control over the content of family
and social life, local government, and at least some portion of the provision
of material and needs. Most important, communities are seen as essential locales and institutions for the nourishing of our moral, spiritual nature. They
function as moral anchors, as places where a shared outlook on the larger
world is, at a minimum, most effectively taught, observed, practiced, and preserved in an ongoing tradition.[4]

Conventional uses of the word community in America are good places to
seek a fuller understanding of its attributes and its status as a public philosophy in our culture. In routine references the concepts of place and belonging
are most evident. The brief phrase, "my community," when spoken by many
of us who live in rural areas and in some suburban and urban enclaves, means
much more than the place where we live, although that is included, along with
ownership of tangible, "real" property—an exclusive piece of a larger personally known space. It is more a statement about a place whose geographic,
legal, and political dimensions are further defined by a sense of attachment
and belonging. These comforts are also partly informed by experiencing that
one is among actual and potential family or friends, and others with whom we
share at least some deeply held values in common. It is a mode of living that
is closely associated with home and neighborhood, with being known, accepted, even appreciated for who one is rather than solely what one does.

We also use community to talk about certain activities and functions that
are important to us, in order to convey something about the qualities we want
each to possess. Schools, recreation, and policing are, for example, thought of
quite differently when community is their modifier. In addition to place and
belonging, other qualities, such as safety, order, exclusion, participation, cooperation, and control are more clearly present in the mix, although we often
vary widely on their respective priority and means of provision. This form of
usage further implies behavioral standards, criteria for our belonging that are,
to some extent at least, locally defined, imparted, and enforced.

Community, as Amitai Etzioni reminds us, denotes much more than a
"warm, fuzzy, comfortable" place.[5] It is a locus of obligations and other ex-

pectations made more enforceable by social ties and pressures. At this point, we—some of us more than others—are further reminded that community can also be a place of oppressive discomfort, involuntary exclusion, and physical violence for those who will not, or cannot, conform. These latter qualities are not mentioned to suggest that Etzioni and other communitarians admire them, particularly at their extremes; however, to the extent that community is connected with the inherent particularity of place, ownership, shared values, and belonging, the need for some form of exclusion and coercion must be taken into account.

Thus far, the selected uses of community have also carried with them, as first alluded to, an implicit connection with the past that is at peril in the present. For some, present experience or images from one's childhood are associated, while for others learned traditions and other images from other less direct, more distant sources are triggered by the word. Carried along with these connections is the identification of communities as places of relative equilibrium, stability, continuity, tradition, and status quo. Many of us value predictability, a steady rhythm in our daily lives, provided that the content is not stultifying or enslaving.[6]

Communities are also still understood in much of America as places that can mutually assure collective liberty against external threat and more subtle outside pressures, such as those imposed by our pervasive, market-driven, mass commercial society and culture. One suspects that there are few admirers of Tocqueville who do not share his appreciation for what he saw as the delicate communal liberty of the township:

> It is not by chance that I consider the township first. The township is the only association so well rooted in nature that whenever men assemble it forms itself. . . . But though townships are coeval with humanity, local freedom is a rare and fragile thing . . . . A civilized society finds it hard to tolerate attempts at [local] freedom . . . . However, the strength of free peoples resides in the local community.[7]

More recently, community has been widely employed to describe newer, less physical, more segmented places, from which one can confirm the continuing importance of the concept thus far discussed and parse out other attributes. For example, there is the "listening community" whose place is a particular FM radio frequency. If the signal is assigned to a typical commercial station, the phrase is lightly intended, largely as a component of a marketing package; however, where it is allocated to a public nonprofit station the usage may be apt.[8] Such a station, in principle at least, is one to which we can belong, not just as a listener, but as a formal member and by virtue of opportunities to volunteer and become a more active participant. In addition, the staff solicits and announces to other listeners our financial and volunteer support. They offer programs that we value and enjoy, and feel obligated to offer democratic or other satisfactory reasons when they do not. Between fund drives we listen, offer our praise and criticism, which they broadcast or report, with minimal editing and a serious attempt to be representative. The relationship is interactive, directly and vicariously affective, mutually informing, and voluntary. Because of the last quality, we are free to opt out, to move to a new place on the FM spectrum, or at least stop pledging and volunteering. We often do so when we come to feel that we no longer belong, that the community has become more virtual than actual, and it no longer represents or includes us.

Professionals, ethnic, gender, and racial groups, environmental, religious economic, and other segmented groups of all types are likewise frequently referred to as communities in ways that are considered legitimate by members and nonmembers alike.[9] The apparent purpose is to denote commonalties that are more than external characteristics, although, as with communities of place and belonging, external, readily detectable evidence of membership remains important. The use of community to modify or explain such groups implies a variety of things shared by a circumscribed group, which identify them to others, and promote their member identity. These include a common history or tradition, shared values and norms, conforming practices, a status rank among members and within the larger population, a shared language—in short, a distinct identity with a common subculture.[10]

Notably lacking in many of the above segmented group forms, however, are frequent, routine opportunities for the development of authentic, warm, affective relationships—or even existential tolerance—that stem from frequent contact around common, daily, generically human life activities, like raising, educating, and protecting children, and routine celebrations of life itself. In fact, the norms of such groups may actively discourage the combination of affectionate and intellectual interaction, either outside or within such communities, for the sake of the group's higher priorities. Professionalism, ideology, or some other form of group exclusivity hamper the formation of intrinsic relationships—often as the logical by-product of the individually instrumental nature of the group's shared goals. Collegiality, toleration, and other forms of civility may be encouraged, but those are less significant, evanescent matters, as most communitarians recognize.[11]

As is implied in each of the foregoing, the term community is invariably used in ways that connect it to the idea of shared values and practices. This is most evident in one of its largest applications, political community. America is still referred to on occasion as a national community, usually when someone seeks to evoke or promote themes of national unity, interdependence, loyalty, and solidarity. In our politics, it is often an attempt to capture America as a nation of varied peoples and interests, a pluralistic polity whose citizens share and exercise a common core of political ideals. It is also a reference to our history, to conscious efforts by the Founders, Lincoln, and numerous others to build a national society using these materials and means. We often forget, however, that the ideals, values, and practices that we share must themselves have unifying qualities. If, as has come to be the case in America, the former cohere foremost around the principles of personal liberty, instrumental pursuit, formal equality, and inviolable, antecedent individual rights, unity may be more apparent than actual, more circumstantial than durable. Similarly, if the practices—the acts we are called upon to perform to maintain government and support each other—are few in number, scant in substance, unevenly burdensome, overly bureaucratized, or performed in social isolation, our sense of community is neither enhanced nor further instantiated.

It is national community, as first suggested, which is a leading concern of mainstream communitarian scholars. Local community in America has been weakened under the impact of liberal values, no longer compensated for by republican virtue, no longer reinforced by our inadequate shared practices. As locales and regions compete for resources they require but no longer control, the losers watch as their most productive residents follow the resource trail, leaving those remaining out of attachment or decreased mobility to lie fallow. As a result, movement in the direction of national community has stalled, even reversed. We have failed, as Tocqueville urged, to integrate "communal freedom," a positive understanding of liberty, into our "national ideas and habits."[12]

CONTEMPORARY COMMUNITARIANISM

It is apparent from the above that community in both its traditional and modern usage is related to society. In fact, contemporary communitarians intend just that. They use community as a concept to capture in our society the attributes of place, belonging, and other affective comforts, as well as order, interdependence, shared purposes, volunteerism, and positive autonomy. Each is seen as a necessary, therefore moral, quality that should be present in the mix and balance of society—a social content that is appropriate to our time and setting. They share a *telos*, which is to move us in the direction of the "Good Society,"[13] an America that exists as a "community of communities . . . a set of attributes, not [just] a concrete place."[14] Unfortunately, however, their concept of society, and their corresponding views of community, human nature, and individual moral capacity within it—if we accept them as true— leave us without the individual and small group strength to directly seek, let alone generate movement in the direction they point toward.

Real Society; The Master Entity

The emphasis on community as a moral framework for our nation is based on the foundational communitarian belief that society itself, regardless of its configuration and moral content, plays a critical role in our individual and collective lives. For modern communitarians in particular, society is not employed simply as a useful meta-perspective from which to observe and categorize human interaction. It is also not enough to conceive of society as term used only to conceptually capture a set of institutions that relate to various aspects of human activity and which play a role in shaping and constraining our behavior. From a communtarian perspective, society is *a distinct realm of reality*, something that has evolved from humans interacting with each other and with the world within particular confines of place, time, and historic circumstance. Its institutions—community being only one type or form—encompass all forms and areas of human activity. They "mediate the relations between self and world," giving in the process a certain form or identity to the self and the world.[15]

American communitarians, as the foregoing suggests, have strong sociological roots. As social historian, Christopher Lasch observed:

> Communitarianism has its intellectual antecedents in a sociological tradition, initially a conservative tradition, that found the sources of social cohesion in shared assumptions so deeply ingrained in everyday life that they don't have to be articulated: in folkways, customs, prejudices, habits of the heart.[16]

According to Emile Durkheim, a principal founder of modern sociology—conceived by him as the parent social science—a legitimate government presupposes and, therefore, can only reflect a healthy, cohesive society. Societies are the fundamental, essential human context, the largest realm of shared understanding and practice. They possess a reality, a nature, a life of their own.[17] Each contains a distinctive set of functional institutions and their particular practices of living, working, and governing. In its fullest understanding, society is a comprehensive, interrelated, complex *entity*, the essential *master system* for all aspects of human life within its reach. At its most highly developed, robustly integrated, cohesive best, it is a vastly more powerful agent than any individual, group, or institution within its all-encompassing realm. Its agency exists primarily in the fact that it informs and therefore shapes virtually all human understanding. Society is what makes us both human and particular.

Society as Morality and Soul

In its most abstract conception, society is a particular "composition of ideas, beliefs and sentiments of all sorts, which realize themselves through individuals."[18] Chief among them are moral ideals, a set of core beliefs that are seen by a society's members as its (and their) *raison d'être*. Morality in its profound and mundane forms is part of the essence of a society, and its content reflects our state of social dependence.[19] However, while these ideals, beliefs, and associated feelings result from the interaction of individual conscious minds, and are dependent on them for their existence, *they are not reducible to them*.[20] Thus, although "sociology is defined as the science of societies, [and] human groups . . . are the immediate object of its investigation . . . society can only exist if it penetrates the consciousness of individuals and fashions [them] in its image and resemblance."[21]

Writing in 1914, Durkheim exuberantly—too much so for many contemporary sociologists—proclaimed the fullness of society's penetrative strength. It was the source of our sense of soul or transcendence, the higher voice of our inner-conflicted human nature.[22] With this positivist master stroke, he dissolved the conflict that Hawthorne and Emerson had debated in the nineteenth century—the attempt to reconcile mortal man with his desire for transcendence. He sided with Emerson's view of history as inevitable human progress, while locating the grand design of mankind—and the possibility of progress itself—in society, a place that Emerson, a robust individualist, would have detested[23]:

> The painful character of the dualism of human nature is explained by this hypothesis. There is no doubt that if society were only the natural and spontaneous development of the individual, these two parts [consciousness of self and of "something else"] would . . . adjust to each other without . . . friction. . . . In fact, however, society has its own nature, and . . . .. its requirements are quite different from those of our nature as individuals: the interests of the whole are not necessarily those of the part. Therefore society cannot be formed or maintained without our being required to make costly and perpetual sacrifices. Because society surpasses us, it obliges us to surpass ourselves . . . .[24]

Over time, society acts to separate, to filter out the dross—ideas and practices seen within its own frame of reference as base, trivial, or inferior. What remains is stored in its "collective consciousness," or more localized "communities of memory."[25] Both are accessible to all members through their involvement in its institutions—its functional patterns of belief and behavior, formed by our history of regularized interaction. In turn, they constitute our living and being framework, that which renders us as human and particular. Having accomplished our initial formation, our institutions guide us through life, accepting our modest discrete inputs as feedback in the above process of refinement and adjustment that is ideally continuous and accretive. The moral content of society is something we can only indirectly and secondarily affect.

To assist in the transmission of moral ideas and behaviors, society carries within its institutional memory models of individual human behavior in the form of characters and practices associated with roles, together with lesser group and an overarching collective identity, developed over multiple generations. Characters such as literary and historical heroes serve a broad societal moral educative purpose, furnishing us with the ideal contents of character or virtue. They are a society's "great men," its moral exemplars, those whose greatness depends on our approval even as it inspires our own.[26] Institutional roles impart a more specific, routine morality—that of family, community, work, and politics.[27] Taken together, they integrate us into the whole, demonstrating not only who we are, but also where and how we belong.

To summarize the communitarian claim thus far, societies, the communities and institutions *contained* within them, are an observable phenomenon in all human development: the geographically, historically, circumstantially varied expression and, most important, the formative force of our identity and our nature. Institutions are the essential intermediary links connecting us to each other and to the whole.[28] We *require* society to provide us with the vital information of who we are, what we are capable of achieving, together with the information—knowledge of methods and means—and the opportunity to go about doing it.

If a society is to perform these tasks well, if it is to become a "Good Society," it has, as Durkheim argued, functional needs that must be addressed. According to Etzioni, social order and individual autonomy are the twin requirements that are universal to all societies, to their successful, systemic operation—"the contributions of the parts to the needs of the whole."[29] From a "value neutral" viewpoint, there are alternative "responses" or methods for meeting these needs; however, if we are to move toward a good or communitarian society, "an order that is aligned with the moral commitments of [its] members," we need to be mindful that some responses are better than others.[30] The fundamental need at any given time and setting is to attain and maintain equilibrium between order and autonomy, a task that is best accomplished by methods that are consistent with the fundamental values of the particular society. In America, this requires *primary* recourse to voluntary compliance and to democratic practices as opposed to state coercion.[31]

Robert N. Bellah and colleagues are less comfortable with the communitarian label, due apparently to Etzioni's candid call to balance or condition freedom with the need for social order, and his implicit refusal to eschew coercion.[32] Instead, they seek to restore the "moral ecology" of American society through institutional reform.[33] They acknowledge our strong cultural resistance to the implications of their empirically based belief that we are socially, institutionally dependent, attributing it to the fact that "some of our institutions have indeed grown out of control and beyond our comprehension. But the only answer is to change them, for it is illusory to imagine that we can escape them."[34]

OUR SOCIAL HUMAN NATURE

As is implicit in the foregoing, the core ontological assumption underlying the sociological communitarian model is the *a priori* social nature of man. It is a nature that is a combination of fundamental needs and abilities that enable us to meet those needs. In sharp contrast to Enlightenment Man—to liberalism—the communitarian focal point for the development of human nature as a work-in-progress is the external locus of social relations and social formation, not the inner world of self-conscious isolation or the outer world of atomistic striving.

Democratic theorist Carole Pateman acknowledges with empirical integrity that the original order of human formation "cannot be known"; however, she responds to the liberal claims of natural autonomy by asserting that "individuals may be 'born free and born equal,' but they are neither born as full-fledged persons, nor are they born outside of a network of social relationships."[35] The composite, individual-social interactive formation of human nature that Pateman suggests, however, is not the stuff that Communitarian Man is made from. He is *inherently*, not just initially, dependent on others for the content of his life. His language and thought patterns, his relation to others and the physical world, his beliefs and values, his unique personal identity—all are furnished to him by family, community, and other social institutions. Each shapes man into who he is, and, in turn, informs him what he should do. In one of the strongest statements of the communitarian position, Etzioni states, "communitarians have shown that individuals do not exist outside particular social contexts . . . it is erroneous to depict individuals as free agents."[36]

In contrast, Pateman is keenly aware that individual and intentionally organized power affects the structure and moral content of society, and that Enlightenment Man is, if not in his theoretical origins, today as much a social product as is his communitarian counterpart. Mere socialization, in other words, is only a process that stems from our social nature. Its content, in the short-term at least, can be decidedly antisocial.[37]

If communitarians are correct, American Enlightenment Man now suffers from a major mental malady, the self-aware delusion of individual freedom. Thus misinformed, he is spurred on by his mortal unease—a feature common to both models—to boundless material and sensual striving. He seeks the impossible, to bypass society except for personal comfort and limited instrumental support. He turns to the false voice of inner-informed reason to define his virtue, establish government, and adopt laws to maintain order on a pluralist playing field of individual opportunity.

Under the communitarian model, our self-awareness is itself socially informed, the product of group life as institutionalized in a particular time and setting. Our freedom, as Socrates saw his life in the polis, depends on citizen support and is therefore bounded within its limits. Stable order exists not simply because of fear-informed prudence as Hobbes saw it, nor is it primarily a Lockean instrumental response to both fear and the drive to pursue personal happiness. Further, it is not the product of a rationally prescribed political regime—Hobbesean, Lockean, or any other. Social order develops from "deep-seated sociological and historical need."[38] It is durably achieved by the development of a system of beliefs and supporting sentiments in a cohesive society that set limits to what its members can do.[39] *Only* in such a society can common goods be identified and pursued. To be sure, such pursuit, if it is to be generally available, requires the practice of human virtue; however, virtue itself, along with the concepts of good and evil, right and wrong, is defined, reinforced, and transmitted by society. Conforming habits, patterns of behavior supported by the mind and the heart are the driving force of virtue.[40] They must be both taught and practiced with some constancy. Virtue, therefore, depends upon society and its institutions, just as society requires virtue and conforming habit for its vitality and cohesion.

OUR INHERENT MORAL NATURE

The social nature of Communitarian Man must be further examined if we are to understand his moral capacity. Clearly, to the extent that we intrinsically value rather than merely depend upon the many forms of social interaction, we are more comfortable with society and more inclined to acknowledge our dependence on its key institutions—and our moral duty to support them. Accordingly, it is important to discern the traits or abilities that motivate and enable us to enter into relationships and maintain them for their own sake. It also seems important to do so if we are garb the autocratic emperor that is society with rational dignity. It therefore seems essential to equip Communitarian Man with an inherently social nature, one that is at least strongly motivated to act socially, or at least conformably, as well as altruistically, based on genuine warmth toward others. We must do so unless we are to assume that society predates men living together, or that learned behaviors cannot be fairly readily unlearned.

David Hume

The insights of Scottish Enlightenment philosopher David Hume have been a substantial influence on the construction of the American communitarian model. His concept of our moral nature seems, at first, to differ substantially from that at the base of liberalism. His distinctive emphasis on the social dimension of human nature, not only in terms of the formation of human personality, but also in the development of moral capacity and the defining of morality itself, is certainly helpful. In doing so, Hume offers a social and political actor who is motivated by more than mortal fear and consequential self-interest. He discerns within us sympathy or fellow feeling and appears to strengthen—even ground—morality with this inherent sentiment. Moral principles and virtues are both received and derived from our social life by the placing of utility judgments upon human character and actions.[41] They are more than logical conclusions drawn from reason, yet Hume observes "that reason and sentiment concur in almost all moral determinations and conclusions. . . ."[42] He points in the following to an apparently essential role for sentiment or human feeling in determining the moral:

> Extinguish all the warm feelings and prepossessions in favor of virtue, and all disgust or aversion to vice; render men totally indifferent to these distinctions; and morality is no longer a practical study, nor has any tendency to regulate our lives and actions.[43]

It soon becomes apparent, however, that the sentiments that Hume has detected at work are little more that a rewarding complement to virtues that are themselves rather modest, akin to those called for in the contemporary discourse on civility.[44] They are feelings that are short-lived, impulsive, and ". . . geared to the ordinary life of humanity."[45] More substantial moral topics, such as the principles of justice, are as rational as Locke's formulations and similarly grounded.[46] Further, they are seen as lending utilitarian support to a liberal social and political order, which relies more significantly upon the devices of Hume's contemporary and colleague, Montesquieu, for its preservation.

Hume, as noted, does somewhat improve upon the exclusive rationality of Enlightenment Man by adding social feeling, supported by a moral intuition or instinct, to the rational mind as informants of morality. However, he rejoins other enlightened political thinkers, as Adam Smith would do a generation later, by concluding that the passion of acquisitiveness, as well as other "selfish" drives, strongly outweigh man's capacity to act virtuously.[47] In doing so, Hume ultimately places personal morality or virtue on weak inner-pleasure and social approval footing. Finding that ". . . [personal] morality is determined by sentiment," he relegates its content to "whatever mental action or quality gives to a spectator the pleasing sentiment of approbation"—in other words, to the equivalent of receiving an Academy Award for film-makers and actors, or the pleasure of attending a "feel-good" movie for a mass audience.[48]

Hume finally divorces us from any residual expectation that the moral instinct or social nature he has observed has any real breadth or depth by assigning the job of building support for the new, rationally determined liberal political order to a cadre of unsentimental rationally enlightened leaders. It would seem that both the virtues and supporting sentiments that are required in the enlightened social and political order must be inculcated, nurtured, and enforced in the populace.[49] The moral sentiment he detected may be grounded in man's inherent nature, and constitute an ineluctable component in his moral judgment; however, it is too weak to obligate man to act, except where ". . . an agreeable sentiment, a pleasing consciousness, a good reputation" will suffice.[50]

To construct Communitarian Man, particularly in our time, from insights such as Hume's is even more enervating than the Lockean alternative. Hume places the socially attached, moral sentimentalist under the thumb and Machiavellian tutelage of those from whom he has modeled his elite version of Enlightenment Man. The hearts of the populace must be educated along with their minds to support the liberal framework and to live in an atomistic, pluralistic society held together by rational virtue, soft affection, and a common love of individual freedom. Unfortunately, this elite-driven approach seems quite compatible with the calls for institutional reform that are favored by modern communitarians, just as they are with Durkheim's urging that we, in modern society, should defer to the "natural superiority" of our "great men."[51]

Contemporary Views

As indicated above, contemporary advocates of the popular communitarian model either share Hume's view of our moral nature and capacity or subscribe to a close functional equivalent. Robert N. Bellah and his colleagues, in their widely discussed study of American middle-class mores, *Habits of the Heart*, view human moral nature in terms of our inherent social need and our capacity to learn.[52] Thus armed, we are able to form good habits that "establish a web of interconnection by creating trust, joining people to family, friends, communities, and churches, and making each individual aware of his reliance on the larger society."[53] Civic virtue, or one's commitment to some larger public good, must be learned in concrete "communities of memory." This phrase is intended to softly convey their belief in the necessity for strong institutions, "real communities" that have a history—a "constitutive narrative" that is regularly retold.[54] In such communities—they mention churches, as well as ethnic and racial associations—we learn about who we are, acquire a collective sense of history, and, most important, we learn the "practices of commitment . . . the patterns of loyalty and obligation that keep the community alive."[55]

While Bellah et al. clearly favor certain institutions, primarily those that promote the classical and religious tradition of civic friendship, they are silent as to the nature of their (and presumably our) capacity to distinguish between "good" and "bad" communities of memory.[56] Further, although they place Dr. Martin Luther King Jr. firmly within the embrace of such communities, they fail to account for the either the manner or the narrow, often shallow extent of his inclusion. There were, for example, only a scant few white churches or denominations in either the South or the North that either opened their doors or emptied their coffers to support the southern civil rights movement, even at its zenith in the mid-1960s. African American churches in the South were also hardly uniform in their support, although their reluctance was certainly more justified. There were, however, individual clergy, church members and groups within such organizations who did commit their time, well-being, and money to King, often against the wishes of fellow members and the directives of church and denominational elders.[57] The same was even truer of mainstream civic institutions at the local, regional, and national levels.

It is of further importance to note that most of the formative influences gleaned by Bellah et al. from their interviews of social and political activists came from *individuals*—parents and other exemplars—who demonstrated virtues that were exceptional and frequently opposed within the communities and the larger institutional environments where they lived and worked.[58] They recognize a few such persons among their interviewees, but seem puzzled, unable to account for them other than as highly virtuous exceptions. In one instance, a woman, labeled by Bellah as a "professional activist," traces her initial sense of social responsibility to her grandfather, "a member of the socialist Wobblies (Industrial Workers of the World) and of the Catholic Worker Movement."[59] Both were fringe groups that he joined either at their founding or in their early stages. More important, each was organized in stark opposition to the prevalent social mood—and social structure—of their era.[60]

Another interviewee, an environmental activist who abandoned traditional Catholicism during her adulthood, is portrayed as "remarkable in the scope with which she defines her community: 'I feel very much a part of the whole—of history. I live in a spectrum that includes the whole world. . . .'" Bellah and colleagues expressed concern for the mental health of this woman—that her "adoption of the 'whole world' [as] a community of memory and hope" would adversely affect her emotional well-being. "In trying to give substance to what is as yet an aspiration by defining her community as the whole world, she runs the risk of becoming detached from any concrete community of memory."[61] One wonders if they are aware of the numbers of "communities of memory" that would never have come into being if their founders had not sought to persuade others toward their comprehension of reality, their "far out" vision of larger community. One also questions whether labeling such persons as exceptional does not have the effect of limiting the scope of our moral capacity to that which is consistent with the stable, incremental mode of traditional and institutional constraint.

Ultimately, Bellah et al. rely more on Hume's version of Enlightenment human nature and moral capacity than they appear willing to acknowledge.[62] Although their strong sociological perspective leads them to conclude that we are more fundamentally dependent on society for our moral content than Hume allowed, they suggest that we (some of us) are at least able to rationally discern this empirical fact for ourselves. Our rational faculty further informs us of the importance of civic association for the common good, although we might, at first, become engaged primarily for reasons of self-interest.[63] However, once we become involved, committed to the pursuit of larger goods, we experience the deeper forms of satisfaction and friendship that come from service to others.[64] As Hume suggested, psychic rewards reinforce our behavior, define it as virtuous, and encourage us to perform civic duties as a matter of preference and habit.

The communities of memory that Bellah and other more classically informed scholars conceive of still leave us with the inertial dilemma of liberalism: in this case, virtuous souls supported and nurtured in communities and societies separated by their own group-formed concept of the good, each vigorously engaged in efforts to oppose the common good sought by the other and to install its own version. Their struggle is unending because no deeply shared truth, nor any common virtue or capacity, exists to bring the communities together, except for the liberal rules of engagement and the occasional rational perception of some common crisis or other instrumental, precautionary need. Transient psychic rewards can result equally from service performed for the exclusive benefit of their member group, even service that is geared to deny those benefits to outsiders by any means deemed necessary.

To extend beyond the confines of group pluralism, Bellah et al. offer only the hope of a gradual, broadening "cognitive awareness" of our mutual dependence on one another, a sort of social intelligence that sounds quite like the rational capacity for enlightened self-interest relied upon by John Locke.[65] They hint at a further solution in their brief discussion of classical or civic friendship; however, they construe such friendship, with rare exceptions, as another learned virtue, dependent on the existence of "face-to-face" community, and other pluralist institutional supports whose demise in America they declaim.[66] It seems not to have occurred to them that friendship and fraternity might not *require* the intervention or mediation of institutions, but only their practice among individuals acting and responding from their own nature and initiative. They are able to do so on the strength of their inherent, nurturable disposition for affectionate relationship, their belief in inclusive ideals that are informed by life as they have come to directly know it, and their capacity to imagine the potential for such relationships among others whom they have not yet had the opportunity to befriend.

Etzioni and James Q. Wilson see the problems of agency and group moral relativism left unresolved by Bellah and associates in their exclusive reliance on social formation and institutional reform to properly constitute our moral nature and to furnish its content. Etzioni recognizes the fallacy of the implied assumption underlying much of our contemporary discussion about values, "that once people are brought up right, they will be good people, as if they have been equipped with an internal virtue rod that suffices to energize their good behavior." He further notes: "The sociological fact is that values do not fly on their own wings, that more . . . is required *for the values of a society to realized*, to be reflected in behavior, to guide a people's life.[67]

In what seems at first to be a successful effort to avoid the circularity of encompassing society that mainstream communitarians seem unable to escape, Etzioni balances the "external moral voice" of society with an "inner moral voice" of conscience.[68] It soon becomes apparent, however, that the purpose of the latter is to serve the former. "Most of us need not consult a sociological or psychological study to know what this inner voice is. . . . Typically [it] takes the form of statements that contain 'I ought to' as distinct from 'I would like to.'"[69] This voice fosters moral behavior in a manner that follows both Hume and Bellah et al. "by according a special sense of affirmation when a person adheres to his/her values" and a sense of unease when they are ignored.[70] For this process to occur most effectively, the moral content of the inner and outer voices must be the same. Society and the individual must be on the same page. This is most effectively the case at the level of the community where members are encouraged to abide by community values, and censured when they are not. The "moral voice [of the community] . . . is subtle, and highly incorporated into daily life. It often works through frowns, gentle snide comments (and some that are not so gentle), praise, censure, and approbation."[71]

Etzioni clearly has not afforded us with the means for either resistance or escape from society. It is not surprising that he finds the 1960s to have been the fulcrum of an episodic swing toward social anarchy, or that he takes comfort in his belief that, "beginning with the 1990s, a regeneration has begun to set in."[72] One is left wondering how he is able to reconcile the moral voice of community with life in the rural South, either during Jim Crow or its demise.

A Communitarian Realist

James Q. Wilson is comfortable with order and conformity, but not with society as it has evolved in America. He blames science and "intellectuals" for modern relativism, stating that "the spirit of the age has been one of skepticism [where] science has challenged common sense."[73] Morality is seen as mere opinion, as culture-specific custom, and man is portrayed as having no nature apart from that imparted through culture. Seeing his task as a continuation of the work begun in the seventeenth and eighteenth centuries by Francis Hutcheson, David Hume, Adam Smith, and others from the Scottish Enlightenment, he seeks "to add to this tradition . . . a knowledge about what the biological and social sciences have learned about what they were the first to call the moral sense."[74]

For Wilson, the moral sense is something that most of us possess. It is formed out of "the interaction of [our] innate dispositions with [our] earliest familial experiences."[75] He defines it as "an intuitive or directly felt belief about how one ought to act when one is free to act voluntarily."[76] Our moral sense has several aspects, each of which are detectable by observation of and inferences drawn from the universal social practice of judging others. Sympathy, fairness, self-control, and duty are four that he identifies and discusses.[77]

Average Americans, according to Wilson, are losing confidence in the sources and importance of their moral sense. He sees many causes for this shift (in addition to those above-noted), but attributes most of the blame to one, namely, "the collapse in legitimacy in what was once respectably called middle-class morality—but today is sneeringly referred to as 'middle-class values.'"[78] With this otherwise unexplained connection between the moral sense and a shared moral code that is particular to America, Wilson appears to join the communitarian camp and its project to replicate the moral stability of traditional society. In his effort, however, he reaches too far back even for those who seek to recapture time with social engineering and revamped institutional design. His membership is further brought into question by his emphasis on the role of family and kindred rather than society as the primary agents for the development of a child's moral sense through bonding and control.[79] Although he does look to local communities to assist families in order to furnish the necessary "group-centered" as opposed to "individualistic" child-rearing norms, he does not look to society to play a morally helpful role.[80]

Ultimately, Wilson finds himself uncomfortable with either the contemporary communitarian or Enlightenment models. Human nature is social, yet he

believes that kinship and small communities still set the outer limits of our social nature and largely determine the range in which we apply our moral sense.
Outside of family, friends, and other face-to-face intimates, destructive human
passions that are facilitated by our individualistic culture readily trump our inner motive power. In his final paragraph, he arrives at Hume's position:

> Mankind's moral sense is not a strong beacon light. . . . It is, rather, a small can-
> dle flame, casting vague and multiple shadows, flickering and sputtering in the
> strong winds of power and passions, greed and ideology. But brought close to the
> heart and cupped in one's hands, it dispels the darkness and warms the soul.[81]

Wilson somewhat resignedly accepts the liberal framework, with its embrace of civil society, as the best available system to safeguard against the
various tyrannies that are formulated either in the name of narrow community
or authoritarianism.[82] As did Reinhold Neibuhr, Wilson appears to conclude
that while society is real, it is hardly the locus of the soul or of immortality.
Man, within its intrusive, modern mass embrace, is irredeemably frail,
blessed only with individual grace and the rational capacity to give government the power to protect him from others—and from himself.

CONCLUDING THOUGHTS

Communitarianism leaves us in a state of "Catch-22," wondering how or to
what extent we can change something that we are so dependent on, that has
grown beyond our control or comprehension, and from which there is no escape. Fortunately, both society and its institutions are decidedly less real in
the sense of autonomy, coherence, and power than either Etzioni or Bellah et
al. portray them. Neither possesses the agency to maintain itself, except to the
extent that we furnish our leadership, our support, or our acquiescence.

A long, broad view of history informs us that society and its institutions are
both intentionally produced and—particularly at the intimate, familial level—
organic or spontaneous unions of human desire and need. Society and its
larger components are formed and changed by a wide variety of agency and
upheavals, and are maintained by power in its many forms, as well as by law,
habit, and conformity. Most important, its institutions can be radically, purposively altered as well as escaped from, either by those willing to accept the
potential consequences for their nonconformity, or by those with the means
to impose new behavioral standards on others.

Communitarian calls for the reform of institutions in order to foster moral
community, to instill an Aristotelian ethos of common pursuit, are weakly

framed, misdirected, and out of sequence. Those who occupy institutional seats of authority in our liberal regime, in the economy, and in supportive civil society are free to ignore such calls—or to warmly endorse them—largely without peril. Major institutional reforms of the type that foster a deeper, more inclusive community ethos in America are the last events of major social and political change. Social and political transformation begins with individual and small group actors acting directly for change, living while they do so as though society—and community—are something quite different than either past traditional forms or the sociological version that now prevails. Such actors will not succeed, however, to the extent that we accept the idea of socially determined human nature and congruent moral capacity as valid. It may be difficult to persuade each other authentically, given the intimate requirements of authenticity; however, it is misguided at best and mass manipulative at worst to focus our reform efforts on entities that depend for their existence on unreflective minds or fatalistically resigned consciousness. Given the communitarian view of human nature—not theirs, but ours—we are constrained to utilize the macro-institutional approach. Society must be manufactured, its components carefully crafted and repaired by experts capable of objective detachment, those with the rational expertise to detect its flaws. The fact that those who undertake this task largely do so with a strong desire for local democracy and a Humean heart offers only the faint comfort that their successors and less benevolent counterparts will continue to depend upon our happiness, to any significant extent, for their psychic rewards.

NOTES

1. Christopher Lasch, *The Revolt of the Elites and the Betrayal of Democracy* (New York: W.W. Norton, 1995), 93.

2. John Dewey, *The Public and its Problems* (1927; Athens, OH: Swallow Press-Ohio University Press, 1997), 216.

3. McWilliams, 621.

4. MacIntyre, 258.

5. Etzioni, 123.

6. Lasch, 27.

7. Tocqueville, 62–63.

8. In the case of WAMC, an Albany, New York, affiliate of National Public Radio, the usage is apt.

9. This use does not include the assignment or use of labels or classifications by one group to define or isolate another.

10. Etzioni, 127.

11. Robert N. Bellah et al., *The Good Society* (New York: Alfred A. Knopf, 1991), 12.

12. Tocqueville, 62.

13. Bellah et al. The title is taken from the title of Walter Lippmann's book, *The Good Society* (Boston: Little-Brown, 1937).

14. Etzioni, 177–78; 6.

15. Bellah et al., 287.

16. Lasch, 92.

17. Emile Durkheim, *On Morality and Society: Selected Writings*, ed. Robert N. Bellah (Chicago: University of Chicago Press, 1973), 16.

18. Robert N. Bellah, intro., Emile Durkheim, *On Morality and Society*, ed. Bellah, ix–x.

19. Bellah, intro., Durkheim, ix–x; Durkheim, *On Morality and Society*, 135.

20. Bellah, intro, Durkheim, xix–xx; Durkheim, *On Morality and Society*, 15–17; 128.

21. Durkheim, 149.

22. Durkheim, 149–63.

23. McWilliams, 280–89; 301–27.

24. Durkheim, 163.

25. Bellah, intro, Durkheim, xix; Bellah et al., 153.

26. Durkheim, 25–33. Cf. MacIntyre, 258.

27. MacIntyre, 27–28.

28. Bellah et al., 287–88.

29. Etzioni, 6.

30. Etzioni, 6–7; 12. Bellah et al. similarly define a good society as one that is engaged in "an open quest [for the common good] actively involving all its members." The common good has "no pattern . . . that we or anyone else can simply discern and then expect people to conform to. . . . [T]he common good is the pursuit of the good in common." Bellah et al., 9.

31. Etzioni, 12–13.

32. Bellah et al., 6.

33. Bellah et al., 5–6; 287–90.

34. Bellah et al., 6.

35. Pateman (ch. 2, note 13), 25.

36. Etzioni, 6.

37. Pateman, 177–78.

38. Etzioni, xvi. He does not explain either further. Presumably, he intends merely to restate that we are social by nature, that we prefer the company of others. The reference to history is likely to our progressive interdependence stemming from learned patterns of cooperation.

39. James Q. Wilson, *The Moral Sense* (New York: The Free Press/Macmillan, Inc., 1993), 14.

40. Robert N. Bellah, et al., *Habits of the Heart: Individualism and Commitment in American Life*, 1985 (Berkeley and Los Angeles: University of California Press, 1996).

41. David Hume, *An Inquiry Concerning the Principles of Morals*, Charles W. Hendel, ed. (1751; Indianapolis: Bobbs-Merrill, 1957), VI: Parts I–II, 58–73.

42. Hume, I: 6.

43. Hume, I: 6.
44. Carter, *Civility* (see Ch. 1, note 33).
45. Pangle, *Spirit* (see Ch. 2, note 5), 71.
46. MacIntyre, 229.
47. Pangle *Spirit*, 71.
48. Hume, *Inquiry*, Appendix I: 107. Cf. MacIntyre, 230–31.
49. Pangle, *Spirit*, 71–72.
50. Hume, IX: Part II, 102.
51. Durkheim, 32–33.
52. See note 40, above.
53. Bellah et al., *Habits of the Heart*, 251.
54. Bellah et al., *Habits of the Heart*, 152–55.
55. Bellah et al., *Habits of the Heart*, 154.
56. Bellah et al., *Habits of the Heart*, 114–116; 219; 237–43.
57. Charles Marsh, *God's Long, Hot Summer: Stories of Faith and Civil Rights* (Princeton, NJ: Princeton University Press, 1997), 3–9; Aldon D. Morris, *The Origins of the Civil Rights Movement: Black Communities Organizing for Change* (New York: Macmillan, Inc.-Free Press, 1984), 68–73. The intent here is not to devalue the role of institutional religion in the struggle for civil rights in the South, or in any of the major peace and social justice campaigns waged in America during the nineteenth and twentieth centuries. It is intended, however, as a reminder that, with few exceptions, our large-scale religious institutions have often been divided, if not outright opposed to the initiation of morally informed social and political change. Often their support has been dependent on the efforts of core actors to persuade members and church leaders to re-examine their teachings and redirect their resources and energies.
58. Bellah et al., *Habits of the Heart*, 158–61.
59. Bellah et al., *Habits of the Heart*, 193.
60. The IWW, a militant socialist industrial union, was founded in Chicago in January 1905. Wobblies were a primary target of the period of harsh political repression following World War I. Many of its leaders were arrested, jailed, and deported in the reactive aftermath of the November 1917 Russian Revolution. See Nick Salvatore, *Eugene V. Debs: Citizen and Socialist* (Urbana: University of Illinois Press, 1982), 205–6; 288.

The Catholic Worker Movement was founded by Peter Maurin and Dorothy Day in 1933 in New York's lower east side "to encourage Christian Pacifism, forthright defense of those who suffer [from] social injustice and dedication to 'personalist' social action." Never formally affiliated with the Roman Catholic Church, it has functioned to date as a highly decentralized, broadly ecumenical, grass roots radical movement. Cooney and Micalowski, eds., *The Power of the People: Active Nonviolence in the United States*, 85–87.
61. Bellah et al., *Habits of the Heart*, 158–59.
62. Bellah et al., *Habits of the Heart*, 80.
63. Bellah et al., *Habits of the Heart*, 167–69; 174.
64. Bellah et al., *Habits of the Heart*, 192–95.
65. Bellah et al., *Habits of the Heart*, 163–77.

66. Bellah et al., *Habits of the Heart*, 194–95.
67. Etzioni, 119–120. Emphasis added.
68. Etzioni, 120–22.
69. Etzioni, 121.
70. Etzioni, 121.
71. Etzioni, 123–24.
72. Etzioni, 73. Cf. 64–73.
73. Wilson, intro., vii–viii.
74. Wilson, intro., xiii.
75. Wilson, 1.
76. Wilson, intro., xii.
77. Wilson, intro., xiii.
78. Wilson, 10.
79. Wilson, 142–48.
80. Wilson, 148.
81. Wilson, 251.
82. Wilson, 245–46.

Chapter Four

The Nature of Action and Our Capacity to Act: A Pair of Nineteenth Century Core Actors

The doctrine must be understood through the deed. It is the only possible way not only to stir others into action, but to give the message itself a sense of reality.

—Jane Addams[1]

. . . [I]f I literally cannot make my character or behavior other than it is by an act of choice (or a whole pattern of such acts) which is itself not fully determined by causal antecedents, then I do not see in what normal sense a rational person could hold me morally responsible either for my character or for my conduct.

—Isaiah Berlin[2]

The fact that man is capable of action means that the unexpected can be expected from him, that he is able to perform what is infinitely improbable. And . . . this is possible only because each man is unique, so that with each birth something uniquely new comes into the world.

—Hannah Arendt[3]

THE IMPORTANCE OF INTENTIONAL ACTION

Nothing reveals the content and reach of human social and political nature more fully than our intended actions. Our habits, customs, and other unreflective behaviors, although more common and therefore more predictable, are incomplete indicators of who we are, both individually and collectively, and what we are capable of doing. When examined in their well-established forms, whether from the perspective of a society or a self, they are revealed as the acquired product of past purposive action, sometimes our own, but more often someone else's. As such, they serve as a pattern for living, a routine way of being in the world as it has been perceived and acted upon largely by others. Seen in this light, both Enlightenment and Communitarian Man are, to a significant extent, creatures of acquired habit.

Our shared habits, our routine enactments that comprise so much of our interactive selves and our social and political institutions, are always subject to change—or reinforcement—when their meaning, purpose, or utility is called into question, whether by reflection on individual experiences or our reactions to broader events. At such times, it is our individual and collective capacities to consciously—concretely *and* imaginatively—experience and encounter life, to learn variously and profoundly, and to act congruently with what we have most significantly learned. It is this dynamic ability to overcome our tendency to conform automatically to existing patterns of perception, conception, action, and reaction that constitutes our maximum mortal reach. These capacities, and others that they implicitly embrace, further constitute our sole potential for individual, social, and political growth—for generally discernible moral progress, as opposed to some aggregated shape of discernible development.

Our world, the context in which we act, is a "known" place of potentially infinite dimensions, in a constant state of being and becoming. Our experience of this world, including our interactions with each other, aided where necessary by personal reflection, imagination, and the sharing of learned results, moves us beyond the narrow realm of facts and stimulates in us our senses of mystery and beauty, horror and ugliness, to name only a few. These states of mind are evident in our profoundly felt need to learn, unlearn, and learn anew. In this process of living and learning, including learning about the past, we are able to sense and increasingly detect not only the matter and energy that constitute the reality of ongoing extra-human creation, but also our increasing capacity, for better and worse, to participate in that reality, to shape and alter both matter and events—including our own nature and existence— by intentional as well as habitual human action.

In such a world, our earnestly held ideas, beliefs, aspirations, needs, and feelings—whether inner and private or public, institutionalized, and iconic— lack vitality unless willed to life and sustained by congruent acts in some context where they can matter. It is our capacity to act purposefully, consistently, and persistently, both alone and together; it is our willingness, desire, and ability to implement that which we have powerfully learned with deeds and with words, which enables us to offer to others an actual, living model of the world, including our relationship to it, and to others within it.[4] The results, particularly of our initial efforts, may not resemble the world that we then inhabit, but the only possibility that they ever will consists of our intended actions and the possibility of a harmonious, strong, potentially durable response from others.

DEMONSTRATION AND INITIATION:
A MORAL DYNAMIC

By our purposeful deeds and explanations, we demonstrate as we enact something of our world-view to everyone and upon everything in our ambit. In doing so, we disclose to others our consciously held moral values and priorities, our most profound sense of who we are, what is most important to us, of what life for us is about. Part of that disclosure, a message embodied in the nature and quality of our acting much more than in our words, is our informing others what we think of and feel toward them.

The type of action that is the focus of this effort is initiatory or non-conforming social and political action, morally informed words and deeds by core actors who seek to fundamentally change prevailing law, practices, and other employed beliefs that they see as inadequate, unjust, inhumane, or simply wrong. It is the exceptional nature of their efforts, the fact that they are the first to act on their conception in some public setting—that they initiate, demonstrate, or lead, and thereby make *further*, congruent action more likely and possible—that necessitates our recognition of them as core actors.

This quality of action, while it sets core actors apart in the social and political context of their actions, should not elevate them from our midst or suggest our incapacity to join their ranks, whether as followers or as co-initiators of lesser or greater reach. It does, however, necessitate separate discussion and a corresponding, *potentially* misleading division into "us" and "them." This bifurcation is, however, artificial in the sense that the essential capacities for *some form* of sustained, morally informed action lie within each of us. Many of us, one suspects, are already uncomfortably aware that this is so.

THE RELATIONSHIP BETWEEN
MORAL INFORMATION AND ACTION

There are, of course, some core actors who do not want our company—except, perhaps, on terms that they determine. Just as some are by no means deeply informed in their social and political action, seeking only to increase or maintain some advantage or to satisfy some drive or need, those who act upon their moral beliefs initiate with some variety. Their action takes in the gamut of human interaction, ranging from broadly altruistic, affectionate, and sacrificial acts of inclusion, to dogmatically conceived acts of terror, forced conversion, categorical ranking, and exclusion. Many at both extremes are undoubtedly certain of their grasp of truth; however, only the doctrinaires act as though truth is somehow separate from and more important than life itself. Interestingly, the quality of their action, in terms of its effects upon others, is little different than action by those who find meaning only in themselves and their own mortality. In both cases, it is the exclusive nature of the truth each claims, and their irreducible ontologies of self and other, which informs their action, greatly broadening the range of means they are prepared to employ to achieve their essential ends.

The dominant characteristic of the initiatory acts of the core actors focused on herein is their use of methods, as a matter of intention and belief, which explain, demonstrate, and seek to persuade, rather than obfuscate, manipulate, coerce, or avenge. Their foundational beliefs are, as just suggested, firmly held—often remarkably so—but are typically not rigid, overly institutionalized, exclusive, or ideologically informed. The content and grounding of such beliefs, and the related question of how these actors come to possess them, are highly important and will be more fully addressed in the final chapter. The point at this juncture is that their methods are neither exclusively instrumental nor fully determined by the social and political logic of nonconformity in an effort to establish a self or group identity in a given oppressive setting. Rather, their choice of active means is animated by the same worldview and convictions—knowledge seen as profoundly simple truths—that inform their goals. This suggests, at a minimum, a strong optimism stemming from the nature and quality of the insights that have informed and motivated their action, and the related pleasure that they derive from their active engagement with life itself.

Their actions further convey their conviction that we—ultimately, most of us—are capable of achieving consensus on values and priorities, of arriving at a shared elemental perception that what they are demonstrating and calling for lies at the heart of what life, for each of us, is all about. Moreover, their chosen means reveals their belief that we are somehow intrinsic to their efforts, a highly desired and valued *part* of their world, and therefore worth the risks to self that are inherent in standing in the open, unarmed, outside conventional or acceptable standards of behavior.

Finally, their actions convey the belief that we, in our potential to learn, to know, and to act, are as capable as they of initiatory action in our respective domains, whether larger or smaller. At some point in their life ventures, they have become aware that the success of their efforts to achieve lasting social and political change depends upon a chain of initiation and response that has usually preceded and must extend well beyond the time and place of their action. They have learned from past accomplishments by others and their own experience that a great many of us are capable, at any given moment, of core activism and that enough of the rest us can at least be persuaded in the direction of reform.

It is from these common premises that core actors seek to convince us by nonviolent means, except perhaps where institutionalized and other violence, directed either against them or others who are unable to protect themselves, overwhelms freedom and thereby denies the substantial possibility of peaceful persuasion. At such moments, core actors evidence the existential moral conflict posed by opposing violence with violence, a dilemma that is most painful when one understands and values life more inclusively than one's opponents.

THE QUALITY OF AUTHENTICITY

If initiatory actions by core moral actors are to be deeply persuasive to those who witness or reliably learn about them, they must first be discernibly authentic. In most social and political settings, authenticity involves a consistent pattern of speech acts that disclose what the actor believes or intends, combined with some type of actual performance that confirms the earnest quality of the words.[5]

Nonconforming words that are merely uncomfortable to listeners, such as occasional calls for improved racial harmony made from the pulpit of a de facto segregated church, lack the ring of hard currency in all but the most hostile settings, unless accompanied by congruent acts that are substantial in their context. Where, as is so often the case with actors who occupy traditional institutional moral roles, significant action is neither taken nor attempted, their words are weighed accordingly and the moral dyspepsia of the congregation quickly, safely subsides. The discomfiting gap between the ideal and the actual has been dutifully acknowledged, reinforced, strengthened, and further legitimated by the message implicit in mere speech.

In a similar manner, words and deeds by social and political actors who disguise or hide themselves from the at least potentially intimate disclosure of public venues cannot be reliably judged for authenticity. To be discernibly genuine, to be a potentially durable as well as contagious expression of the beliefs and proposals of an individual or group, there has to be a willing and intimate disclosure of individual identity, along with a candid disclosure of belief, under conditions that assume some risk of social or political accountability. Those of us—most of us—who follow and build upon the moral social and political initiatives of others need the embodiment of new, presumptively unpopular ideas in personified action. We require the actors' self-disclosure, not necessarily to inform us that the change that they urge upon us is desirable—we may already know that—but to demonstrate that it is possible in the life of at least one other tangible actor. Someone has to speak and act first before some public, and, accordingly, at significant personal peril, before others will likely act at all. Upon close examination, the apparently spontaneous occurrence of major social change—the deposing of the Shah of Iran or the toppling of the Berlin Wall—is revealed as a close temporal culmination of initiation and response, the end game of a much longer, more locally interactive process.

Actions that meet the foregoing criteria may not possess all of the qualities necessary to persuade us to alter our existing, habitual thoughts and behaviors, but we at least know that the actors who demonstrate them are committed and capable of disclosing something new in our corner of the world. By their authenticity, they also inform us that they are seeking more than praise or distinction. With only minimal reflection, we are aware that there are many safer, more prosperous, and better-lit venues for such pursuits.

CONTEXT, HUMAN VARIETY, AND PERSPECTIVE

Morally informed nonconformists must, by the very nature of their action, initiate change under social, political, and material conditions that limit the impact, but not necessarily the authenticity or other disclosing and persuasive qualities, of their actions. As long as they are able to add their actions to some context, they alter it, even if only in the memory and conscience of a public that consists of one other potential core or supporting actor. No testimony better demonstrates the elemental truth of this proposition than that of those saved from the Holocaust by the actions of lay rescuers, many of them total strangers to those who sought their perilous help during the Nazi occupation of Europe. As students and survivors of that systemic horror have attested, it was virtually impossible to take such action in total secrecy. Just as there were collaborators with the Nazi regime, as with southern slavery, so there were active or at least acquiescent supporters of rescuers' efforts to save lives and preserve humanity when it was least valued in society.[6]

In every time and setting, from isolated local moments to national and transnational eras, it is the observed and recounted, authentic, morally informed initiatory acts of a few which demonstrate to the rest of us what we, as persons or a people, are actually and potentially capable of conceiving and doing in the world. We may not, at a given moment, be able to match the courage, strength, or particular talents that characterize the actions of the core moral actors whom we learn of or encounter; however, we can respond to their initiatives by emulating or supporting—or opposing—them in ways that retain the essential social and political qualities of morally informed authenticity.[7] This, after all, is the ordinary manner in which they began their initiatives, never knowing where their action would lead or who, if anyone, they might inspire.

CONGRUENCE AND CONSISTENCY

As suggested in the foregoing, inconstancy and variety are two further aspects of the human condition that we must take into account, for both core actors and ourselves. Our individual and collective records of all forms of action, our life narratives and our shared history, if honestly constructed, reflect both. Harmony between our core values and actions—our fundamental beliefs and our capacity to live them in the open—often yields in encounters with the immediate and particular. Yet action that is heroic, far-reaching, or otherwise exceptional in the self-comparisons of many is already ordinary for at least a few. As such, exceptional, nonconventional action should be seen as a possible harbinger of what will later, often much later, become ordinary for most.

For the above reasons and others, the consistency of all forms of morally informed individual and group action, including that of core actors, should be judged over lifetimes and its persuasive effect assessed over generations. Moreover, consistency should not be the sole criterion for moral strength or reach, particularly of a single life. A brief interval of exceptional courage or sacrifice may have a familial, social, or political impact far greater than that demonstrated in the vast remainder of a lifetime otherwise spent tending to self-focused need. Alternatively, a life that is consistently well-lived, discernibly authentic, and filled with daily initiatives, but which is only local or familial in scope, may profoundly affect others who then visibly add to the moral quality of their nation and beyond. Thus, as suggested, life narratives and longer, broader context historical accounts offer the best evidence of our capacity for initiatory moral action and its rippling persuasive effects. Again, when seen in this light, core actors become decidedly less exceptional, more ordinary or human—in fact, quite like ourselves.

EFFICACY AND POWER

It is unfortunate that it is necessary to set forth an argument for the social and political efficacy of morally informed agency and for the essential role of core actors in the process of profoundly conceived change. Few would argue that purposive action backed by power lacks such causal strength. When action utilizes power in any of its conventional, coercive, ultimately life-threatening forms, social and political conditions can change rapidly and dramatically.

It is equally apparent, however, that the greater efficiency of power, even when harnessed to some more inclusive moral purpose, has long-term repercussions that confirm its limited utility in the achievement of individual, social, and political gains. Having accomplished visible, external conformity by coercive means, its partisan wielders must now instantiate and otherwise defend their product against those who now are preoccupied with action to resist, reverse, or ameliorate its effects. Competing, newly invigorated ideas, purposes, and visions, each dependent for their vitality on motivated actors and various forms of action, will rekindle and emerge until the social, political, and physical landscapes are again detectably altered. It is only a question of time and circumstance, even where power is employed with moral reluctance, and accompanied by the extensive, authentic efforts at moral suasion.

The above process results in a frequently vicious, ongoing cycle where individual and group coercion is the dominant method of social and political action. As battle veterans, historians, and others familiar with action at the outermost margins of our universal capacity for good and evil can attest, death or total impairment are the only outcomes that preclude all opposing action—if our consensus is to move meaningfully forward.

Students of Machiavelli may admire the modern political aesthetic of skilled, technologically enhanced, swift suppression, preemption, and artful manipulation, even as they miss the larger point that has lingered in the Italian landscape ever since. In social and political action, all methods and means employed to promote change or preserve a status quo contain moral qualities that will invariably affect the content and viability of the resulting product.[8]

RATIONAL IDEALISM AND REALISM

The essential connection between means and purpose, the quality of action and the achievement of durable, morally progressive results is no less true in the contemporary era. In America, thanks to our prevailing liberal mindset, the overriding quality of most social and political action is now instrumental, whether to self-service, national and communal goals, or some conservative or liberal agenda. Even American political ideals, which, when authentically employed, have historically demonstrated their potential to ameliorate the cycle of conventional power-driven change, lack the necessary embodiment to end it.

Under the influence of enlightened rational thought and action, our lexicon of values—political equality, democratic participation, fairness, toleration, and justice under an impartial rule of law—have been defined in increasingly sterile, secular, theoretical and legalistic terms. Artificially detached at the outset from their historical origins as the blended, life-enhancing products of self-pursuit *and* sacrificial, morally informed action, they are now largely devoid of durable, cohesive substance in our official and social realms of speech and action. They precariously exist in the thin atmosphere of generic political rhetoric as amorphous, political-cultural buzzwords, or in the narrow juridical confines of individual rights.[9] Meanwhile, we largely fail to detect their profound substance in the actions of core actors in our midst.

Liberal realists, from Madison to Reinhold Neibuhr and E. E. Schattschneider, have long understood the inadequacy of rationally weighed or endorsed political ideals to achieve lasting moral consensus—to serve, in other words, as a platform for shared action.[10] In their enlightened, pragmatic world-view, our values are employed along with our interests in ongoing power struggles and negotiations among competing groups, coalitions, and communities, with their public moral content—the current status quo of rationally constrained and aggregated past action—at stake on the table of acceptable outcomes. Accordingly, persuasive pressure by core actors who are willing only to employ nonviolent means, but are not otherwise constrained in the quality of their action, is essential if the consensus is to more us meaningfully forward. Too many in the realist and American idealist camps, however, do not accept this contention.

The process of contained contest has worked only to the extent that competing group members have remained susceptible to rational structural constraints and instrumental norms that limited both the contagion of belief and the ability of a minority to deny all other competing claims. Unfortunately, the Madisonian version—our large republic and its "auxiliary precautions"—has been out-organized and largely overpowered by economic and political actors whose self-focused perspective is legitimated by the moral logic and ontological underpinnings of the institutional framework that they dominate.[11]

Neither the rational idealists' nor the realists' views are adequate. Before any *major* change in the concrete expression of our values is the subject of a final round of negotiation, it is first the objective of concerted action. If the action bears *only* the quality of rational persuasion premised upon ideals understood as self-entitlements, group enhancements, or the product of prior compromises, efforts to achieve reform will invariably fail, except at the margins. Such efforts on behalf of weak constituencies, as advocates for the poor and incarcerated can attest, will often not even get their proponents to the realists' bargaining table. Just as political goals must be more profoundly understood than as rational goods by those who support them, political methods and their underlying values must be the product of much deeper grounding than instrumental common sense if major change is to be possible.

The realist approach—action to mobilize, organize, realign, coerce, and manipulate by means of conventional political and governmental power—carries with it the same cyclical qualities that have threatened not only our capacity to deepen and expand our values, but also the viability of our liberal framework from the beginning. Those who are defeated in a process that equates all morally grounded assertions with interests know that they have lost to power, manipulation, and artifice (all rationally defensible moral strategies) in a contest where some coalition of private interests and traditional communal values typically enjoys the incumbent advantage.

Rare victories for rights claimants and idealists who act within the perspective, rules, and outcomes of rational persuasion or pluralist engagement are usually the first to be reversed. Rationally informed reform coalitions are quintessentially fragile, subject to easily formulated strategies of co-optation, division and defeat. Changes in conditions—unforeseen peace, escalating crime, a declining economy, some new external threat—inevitably alter the premises of instrumental accommodation and the practical toleration of dissent. Profoundly informed change can only succeed *and endure* when sought by actors whose willingness to work for and support reform is informed by more than rational individual and group interests, however benignly practiced, or by ideals that are accepted only as rational ideals.

Acting instrumentally from the ontological premises already discussed, the earnest promoters of our system—dominant liberals and complementary communitarians—have failed to institutionalize the ideas, values, and congruent practices that are necessary to fully engage us or to durably provide us with more than the modest, incremental reform proposals that either group supports. While our lives have become, "on average," remarkably better under this structure than some other, more predictably tyrannical option, we find ourselves, once again, profoundly dissatisfied over our inability to reliably construct and maintain a more just, unified, democratic, active, and purposive public life.

At no time in our recent history is this more evident than at the current moment. In the long-lingering wake of a brutal, massive terrorist attack, many of us look for ways to act on our tragically reinforced desire to become more deeply related to other citizens and the world. Meanwhile, our political leaders devote most of their attention to seeking the best combination of techniques to identify, locate, and destroy—perhaps even exploit—externalized evil and to providing the technologically enhanced vigilance, including domestic surveillance—as prophylactics against future attack.[12] In sum, we have returned to Machiavelli for strategies to avenge and protect us while we focus on the chimera of improving our security by the exclusive means of overwhelming power and enhanced rational designs.[13] Once again, it is a particularly difficult time to be a core moral actor and to initiate action intended to inform and redress the injustices that are so banally perpetrated in our national name and interest.

In order to move away from these and other perils of our conventional, pragmatic wisdom, we must learn to look *in the present* for the counterparts of those whom we have, at best, been taught were only somewhat significant in our past. We need to examine the lives of core moral actors for the type of social and political action that has originated and sustained profound, morally driven change in America.[14] By doing so, we can learn more about our own nature and capacity. Our deep, congruent reactions to their words and deeds—like our recent response to more conventional public safety heroes recently rediscovered in our midst—offer confirmation of our own actual and potential nature. Their initiatory actions and our varied yet resonant reactions are indispensable components in the dynamic of morally driven change that has significantly shaped our history.

LOOKING BACK AT A PAIR OF NINETEENTH CENTURY ACTORS

As suggested, it is easier to detect our potential deep resonance with core actors in the present by first examining the words and deeds of those who have acted in our past, and connecting their actions to our own moral framework, similar to theirs, in the present. This concurrence facilitates our ability to consider openly the nature and quality of their action, as well as the capacity and role of such actors, in the context of their respective eras. It also helps us to overcome our personal, culturally reinforced bias against the core actors in our midst. In large part, this is due to our propensity to either dismiss or mix admiration with ambivalence toward those contemporary actors who act in ways that express a moral outlook that we find discomforting. By looking first to the past, and finding moral comfort in the present, it is possible for us to at least identify some of those who were at the moral forefront of their place and time.

Accordingly, the task of persuasion begins in our past with a pair of actors who are generally accepted as connected to past moral achievements. Elizabeth Cady Stanton (1815–1902) and Frederick Douglass (c. 1817–1895) capture the essence of moral action—the "grand battle of individual liberty against unjust authority"—as framed in America in the heart of the nineteenth century.[15] As is characteristic of American peace and social justice activists in every generation, their lives intersect throughout their long activist careers, as mutual supporters, friends, and agonistic colleagues.[16] Each became widely visible during the 1840s, Stanton in the area of women's rights, Douglass in the cause of abolition. As is also evident for almost all the actors relied upon in this project, historic and contemporary, the scope of their activism and concern was much more encompassing than the causes with which we now associate them.[17]

Activism, in the sense of altruistic, justice-seeking, morally informed behavior, describes their lives, their persistent orientation to the world, not simply their public personae. Stanton and Douglass, for example, were active advocates of the other's primary cause and generous supporters of a wide variety of other reforms, ranging from temperance to penology and from child rearing to poverty and labor reform.[18] Stanton, a New York state native, became an ardent abolitionist during the 1830s, apparently influenced by her older cousin, Gerrit Smith, a prominent leader of the political wing of that movement.[19] She married an antislavery activist in 1840, and spent the first part of her honeymoon at the World Anti-Slavery Convention in London, the first of its kind. After Stanton and other women delegates elected by American antislavery societies were denied their seats by the male majority, they used the opportunity to become acquainted with each other and to focus on the issue of women's social and political status. Stanton met Quaker activists Lucretia Mott, Lydia Maria Child, the Grimké sisters, and other core actors with whom she would later work to organize the nineteenth century movement for women's rights in America.[20]

Radical Freedom

All core actors demonstrate with some regularity the radical freedom of self and societal transcendence. Frederick Douglass uniquely displayed this quality, having struggled for liberty almost from the moment that he first understood its meaning. He was born into slavery on the Wye River Plantation on Maryland's Eastern shore, "a secluded . . . place," largely out of the reach of "public opinion [which] is, indeed, an unfailing restraint upon the barbarity and cruelty of masters, overseers, and slave-drivers, whenever and wherever it can reach them."[21] He recalled the early questions of his youth, such as "Why am I a slave?" or "Why are some slaves and others masters?" together with his inability to accept the religious fatalism and simple resignation of many older slave children and adults.[22] Thanks to the confluence of early affectionate raising by his grandmother, a few brief, furtive visits from his mother, isolated caring and mentoring acts by others, a remarkably strong dose of the varied potential with which we are all born, the coura-geous action (for a slave) of self-improvement, and the circumstances of good luck, Douglass escaped some of the harshness of a plantation slave upbringing.[23] On the further strength of these gifts, he escaped to the North as a young man, asking for and receiving help on at least one occasion from a white stranger.[24]

Speech, Publication, and Organization as Action

It is difficult to comprehend the full extent of Douglass's activism. In the con-text of his era, however, there is little doubt as to its authenticity. Beginning in slavery, he not only acted to become educated against the dictates of harshly enforced law and convention, but also assumed the risk of educating other slaves under conditions where the risks of exposure were always con-siderable.[25] Less than three years after escaping to the contingent freedom of the North in 1838, he had already begun speaking publicly—under a pseudo-nym that he later kept as his surname, but totally without institutional sup-port—against slavery in New Bedford, Massachusetts, where he then lived and worked. A Unitarian clergyman from Nantucket, having heard him speak at a local African American church, invited him to address an antislavery con-vention to be held on the island. He did so and was promptly recruited as a full-time orator by the Massachusetts Anti-Slavery Society (the Garrisoni-ans).[26]

For the next twenty years, Douglass spoke, debated, and wrote for aboli-tion. In one early campaign in 1843, he traveled while still encumbered by runaway slave status, as far as Indiana, where, after speaking to an unusually hostile crowd, he and a fellow speaker were assaulted and almost killed.[27] In the first of three autobiographies, published in 1845, he assumed even greater risk in order to buttress his authenticity, furnishing the details of his life in slavery, including his birth name and that of his former master. As he ex-plained in his second autobiography, he did so because people doubted his stated "credentials" as a former slave. "They said I did not talk like a slave, look like a slave, nor act like a slave."[28]

To become publicly active in the social, legal, and political emancipation of women, actors like Stanton typically did not have to overcome the condi-tions of slavery, or, for that matter, poverty. They did, however, have to as-sume the burden of widespread public opposition from virtually every tier of society and government. To be a woman's rights activist—and a woman—was to invite widespread scorn and ridicule, from women as well as men.

In addition, many, including Stanton, had to contend with obdurate oppo-sition from family and other intimates.[29] Accordingly, one should not use eco-

nomic status or other summary means to lump Stanton and other radical reformers with utopians, romanticists, transcendentalists, religious revivalists,
and other idealists of the antebellum reform period.[30] While each reflected the
social, political, and intellectual ferment in American life that existed during
the two or so decades that preceded the Civil War, it was the ceaseless agitation and coordinated action of core actors such as Stanton and Douglass that
furnished the momentum in the direction of actual social and political reform.
Neither should we diminish their nonconforming, initiatory agency with explanations of newly possible leisure opportunities for an expanding middle
and upper class.[31] There were, one can readily imagine, many things that
someone with leisure and means could engage in that were less contentious
and more conventionally rewarding.

It is also difficult for us to imagine the key formative social and political
roles played by public speakers in nineteenth century America. "In a time
undistracted by television, the cinema, radio, or quick sound bites, audiences
were prepared and willing to listen. . . . [O]ratory was an important source of
education, information, inspiration, and entertainment. . . ."[32] For the same
reasons, people were also eager to read—to expand their local informative
reach—an appetite greatly stimulated during the antebellum period by the
new technology of mass publication. These circumstances, together with the
development of railroads and the telegraph, furnished actors like Douglass
and Stanton, who were skilled in both arenas, with access to a broad, cross-
sectional audience. Opportunities to increase the potential efficacy of nonconforming action, however, do not explain either the decision to act or its
contagion.[33] It is the actors themselves, the nature and quality of their ideas,
their willingness to convey them, and the manner in which they do so which
matter first, and therefore most.

Other forms of action are much easier to comprehend. Then as now,
"holding a meeting was a characteristic response among reformers," when
the fervor generated by injustice, perhaps further heightened by some recent
event, stirred core actors to gather and act.[34] It was that stimulus that had
cumulated in the World Anti-Slavery Convention that Stanton had attended
in London in 1840, which led to her mentoring friendship with Quaker activist Lucretia Mott, a Philadelphian resident some twenty years older than
Stanton.

A similar impetus, combined with the unadorned wish to strengthen a
friendship that had been maintained for over eight years by occasional letters,
prompted Mott in mid-1848 to invite Stanton to join her at a social gathering
with Mott's sister and two other Quaker friends in Waterloo, New York, near
Stanton's home in Seneca Falls. According to Stanton biographer Elizabeth
Griffith, the five women were not extraordinary in many respects. Most no-

tably, "[a]ll of them were married; all of them had children." Along with Stanton, most of them had probably attended temperance and various other reform meetings; however, only Mott had previous experience "as an organizer, delegate, or speaker. In terms of women's rights, [the organizers] of the first women's rights convention were all amateurs."[35]

In her autobiography written years later, Stanton recounted her state of mind when she and the other four women decided that day to organize the Seneca Falls convention:

> The general discontent I felt with woman's portion as wife, mother, physician, and spiritual guide, the chaotic conditions into which everything fell without my constant supervision, and the wearied, anxious look of the majority of women impressed me with a strong feeling that some active measures should be taken to remedy the wrongs of society in general, and of women in particular. . . . My experience at the World Anti-Slavery Convention, all I had read of the legal status of women, and the oppression I saw everywhere, together swept across my soul, intensified now by many personal experiences. . . .[36]

The Seneca Falls Convention was, by any definition, a radically nonconforming event. The Declaration of Rights and Sentiments, signed by just over one hundred of the three hundred or so attendees, was prepared in the tone and format of the Declaration of Independence, calling for the redress of grievances that encompassed virtually every aspect of women's social, legal, and political status. It was nothing less than a direct frontal assault on the "woman's sphere" mindset that dominated gender relations in America throughout the nineteenth century. The most contentious provision was the call for political suffrage, a demand insisted upon by Stanton. It was so controversial that Lucretia Mott, the rest of the organizing group, and Stanton's husband vigorously opposed it. Stanton refused to yield, however, and the measure was brought up for debate. With the notable rhetorical support of Frederick Douglass, who traveled from Rochester to attend, "the resolution barely passed."[37]

News of the convention and editorials on its Declaration confirm that the capacity of actors like Elizabeth Cady Stanton to "go public" with clear, authentic expressions of opposition to prevailing public moral wisdom defines the true prevalence of that wisdom. In this instance, it was almost immediately apparent that Stanton and her cohort had tapped into an artery of dormant, widespread discontent among hundreds, if not thousands, of women and sympathetic men. While "very few newspapers cheered the effort," most reported it, although from a common perspective of derision and ridicule.[38] At the time, most major papers were quasi-official arms of the major political parties, institutions that have not proved quick to lead in the direction of fundamental reform in America.

Two weeks after the Seneca Falls Convention, a similar forum was held in Rochester, where Douglass was then living. Over the next two years, women in Ohio, Massachusetts, and elsewhere organized women's rights groups and held conventions. From 1850 to 1861 (except in 1857), national woman's rights meetings with delegates from state and local groups were held annually in various locations. However, the demands of travel associated with organizing and speaking—combined with an equally sincere belief that domestic, maternal roles were critical tasks that they performed with unique competence—largely constrained women with young children, like Stanton, from acting beyond their communities or regions.[39] This is not to suggest that Stanton was not active or that all of her action was entirely local in contact or effect. She was, however, fiercely torn between two roles that she clearly enjoyed and deeply valued—that of mother and reformer.[40]

Like other core actors of her era, Stanton's home life was also filled with action. She corresponded widely, wrote letters to the editor, drafted speeches—many to be read at temperance and women's rights conventions that she was unable to attend—and wrote articles for reform journals on a wide range of social and legal reform topics. In 1852 she served as the President of the Woman's State Temperance Society, using that forum somewhat instrumentally to enlist supporters of women's rights.

In 1854, at age thirty-eight, she was the first woman to address a joint committee of the New York Legislature. Speaking in the Senate chamber, spoke eloquently, passionately, and candidly as she "described the legal position of women in American society—as woman, wife, widow, and mother," and called for broad, fundamental reforms in each venue.[41] Again adopting the rhetoric of the American Revolution, she continued:

> Gentlemen, in Republican America, in the nineteenth century, we, daughters of the revolutionary heroes of 1776, demand at your hands the redress of our grievances—a revision of your State Constitution—a new code of laws.

She assumed their shared opprobrium of plantation slavery, and used it to confront them with a powerful gender analogy:

> It is impossible to make the Southern planter believe that his slave feels and reasons just as he does—that injustice and subjection are as galling to him—that the degradation of living by the will of another . . . dependent on his caprice, at the mercy of his passions, is as keenly felt by him as [by] his master. If you can force on his unwilling vision a vivid picture of the negro's wrongs, and for a moment touch his soul, his logic brings him instant consolation. He says the slave does not feel this as I would. Here, gentlemen, is our difficulty: When we plead our case before the law-makers and savants of the republic, they can not take in

the idea that men and women are alike; and so long as the mass rest in this delusion, the public mind will not be so much startled by the revelations [of women's injustices] as by the fact that she should at length wake up to a sense of it. . . .[42]

As the following excerpt from an article in the *Albany Register*, commenting on her speech, confirms, Stanton's impeccable grasp of social reality had angered many:

While the feminine propagandists of women's rights confined themselves to the exhibition of short petticoats . . . and to the holding of conventions and speechmaking in concert rooms, the people were disposed to be amused by them, as they are by the wit of the clown in the circus. . . . But the joke is becoming stale . . . . disgust is taking the place of pleasurable sensations. . . . People are beginning to inquire how far public sentiment should sanction or tolerate these unsexed women, who would step out from the true sphere of the mother, the wife, and the daughter. . . .[43]

During the pre-Civil War era, Frederick Douglass, if anything, pulled fewer oratorical punches than Stanton in his efforts to persuade his white audiences of the equal competence and common humanity of African Americans and the corresponding moral evil of slavery. Having obtained his personal freedom with the help of English supporters in late 1846, he returned from an eighteen-month stay in the temporary safe-haven of England, where he had found himself "regarded and treated at every turn with the kindness and deference paid to white people."[44] Like Stanton, he was aware that the greatest barrier to the ending of slavery or any other system of subordination was neither political nor economic." It was "the low estimate . . . placed upon the negro as a man, that because of his assumed natural inferiority, people reconciled themselves to his enslavement and oppression as things inevitable, if not desirable."[45]

The content of initiatory action to end deeply institutionalized injustice was at least as well understood by Douglass as by Stanton. He was keenly aware that moral persuasion, to be effective, had to be authentic, truthful, discomforting, and unceasing. "'Agitation,' he constantly reiterated, 'is the life blood of all moral reforms.'"[46] In his famous 1852 Fourth of July speech in Rochester, New York—a public address he was invited to give in order to officially celebrate the holiday—he conveyed the intensity of that conviction:

At a time like this, scorching irony, not convincing argument, is needed. . . . For it is not light that is needed, but fire; it is not the gentle shower, but thunder. We need the storm, the whirlwind, the earthquake. The feeling of the nation must be quickened; the conscience of the nation must be roused; the propriety of the nation must be startled; the hypocrisy of the nation must be exposed.[47]

In one of many scathing passages, his identity and his oratorical genius combined, in a sudden shift from his, until then, common voice, with devastating, intended effect:

> Fellow Citizens! I will not enlarge further on your national inconsistencies. The existence of slavery in this country brands your republicanism as a sham, your humanity as base pretense, and your Christianity as a lie. It destroys your moral power abroad; it corrupts your politicians at home. It saps the foundation of religion; it makes your name a hissing and a by-word to a mocking earth. It is the antagonistic force in your government, the only thing that seriously . . . endangers your *Union*.[48]

In contrast with the Garrisonian abolitionists who had furnished him with his first organized support, Douglass understood from the outset that his activism, if it were to be maximally effective, would have demonstrate its own, free-standing human competence.[49] As Stanton had argued in her 1854 speech, it was not enough to evoke sympathy by detailing the horrors of slavery or the particulars of other injustice. The core actor had to refute, by the actuality of embodied words and deeds, the claim of racial or gender superiority upon which slavery and racial and gender paternalism were based. Toward that purpose, Douglass had moved his family to Rochester from Boston in 1847 and, with the further help of English supporters, expanded his activist reach beyond public lectures by publishing his newspaper, *The North Star*. While he continued to travel and speak incessantly, the paper was published weekly, with a subscription base of three thousand, from December 1847 until 1863, the year that Lincoln issued the Emancipation Proclamation.

For her part, Stanton had "long believed that [for women] 'radical reform must start in our homes, in our nurseries, in ourselves,' rather than in conventions."[50] Her reform philosophy mirrored her own experience as one who had struggled with the pleasures, challenges, and exigencies of attempting to balance marriage and parenting with her activism.[51]

Stanton's first extended speaking tour, undertaken in 1860, less than a year after the birth of her seventh (and last) child, was a several-week venture throughout upper New York State, as part of a campaign calling for immediate abolition and for Lincoln's election. Her effort, and that of her activist colleagues, took place at the height of the extreme national tension leading to the fall 1860 election and the outbreak of the Civil War shortly thereafter. As Stanton biographer and historian Lois W. Banner notes,

> the possibility of civil war created fear and dissension among Americans every where, and the abolitionist message, implicitly pro-war, elicited violent opposition. In Rochester and Buffalo, angry throngs made so much noise that her

speeches could not be heard. In Albany, the Mayor sat on the platform with them, holding a gun in plain view. Police lined the hall inside and out to maintain order.[52]

As the slavery-union crisis erupted in civil conflict in the months prior to Lincoln's election, Stanton and other women's rights activists were generally willing to subordinate the moral primacy of their claims to the higher moral priority of ending slavery. The Civil War, however, spent the momentum of women's reform—and of social and political reform more generally—that had been gathering since the 1820s. As a result, by the end of the 1860s, progress toward equality and political inclusion for African Americans and women stalled with the end of slavery and the formal recognition of citizenship and suffrage rights for black males only. Over three decades of extensive social agitation, organization, and political action by women such as Stanton seemed to have accomplished little for their cause.

By 1869, with her youngest child old enough to be left in the care of others, Stanton made speaking on behalf of suffrage and women's rights her primary mode of persuasive action. She saw doing so as part of the same reform philosophy—as, in effect, taking "woman's rights into the homes and lives of the American people."[53] She was also undoubtedly influenced in that direction by her utter frustration and anger over the partial reversal of state-level women's rights reforms during the Civil War; moreover, she was bitterly disappointed by the failure of most abolitionists, including Frederick Douglass, to join with female co-activists in insisting that women—African American and white—be enfranchised along with black males.[54]

The Quality of Persistence

At such historic junctures, the identity of core reformers is further revealed by their capacity to adjust and persist. For the next ten years, Stanton, now in her fifties and more radical in her feminism than the younger generation of women reformers, distanced herself somewhat from what was becoming a more mainstream political reform movement focused on suffrage. Announcing her plans in the final issue of *Revolution*, a publication started by her and Susan B. Anthony a few years earlier, Stanton declared her intention to "spend her future 'teaching woman her duties to herself.'"[55]

Taking advantage of the postwar-revived lyceum phenomenon and her unique talents as an orator, Stanton spent eight to ten months each year on paid speaking tours, mainly in the mid- and far West. "She usually spoke once a day and twice on Sundays."[56] Using the lecture circuit to frame her itinerary, help educate her children, and support her broad feminist reform agenda, she also "spoke before church congregations and reform societies [and] often scheduled afternoon lectures . . . [to which] only women were admitted" in order to "teach independence and avoid embarrassment." Her separate lectures "often lasted three hours or more 'and then they hunger still. The new gospel of fewer children and a healthy, happy maternity is gladly received.'"[57] Some might also have enjoyed her often expressed belief that married women had the ability and right both to enjoy sex and to refuse it at their discretion.[58]

Elizabeth Cady Stanton persevered into her eighties, continuing to demonstrate her primary strengths: those of a female exemplar, radical educator, and consciousness-raiser for women and men. When her age and health made frequent travel too difficult, she returned to writing as her next most effective means of moral reform. During the last two decades of the century, she wrote almost as prolifically as she had organized, lobbied, and spoken during the previous thirty plus years. As her co-authorship of *The Woman's Bible* in 1895 demonstrates, she never lost her capacity to challenge the fundamental issues of justice in America, and to call for changes in its most basic texts and institutions.

Frederick Douglass evidenced the same capacity for sustained authentic action that enable one to identify core moral actors over time and changing circumstance. It is difficult to imagine the deep personal frustration that Douglass experienced as he worked to build upon the hard won gains represented by the Civil War Amendments, only to witness them reduced to complete inefficacy with the collapse of Reconstruction marked by the Compromise of 1877. He had attained personal stature, a measure of respect, appointed federal office, and material comfort in the aftermath of the war. Notwithstanding his new comforts, however, he "continued to lash out at racial injustice. . . ."[59]

Speaking in 1876 as the featured orator at the dedication of the Freedman's Memorial Monument, intended to honor Lincoln, with President Grant and virtually all of Washington's officialdom in the audience, he criticized the statue for "show[ing] the Negro on his knees when a more manly attitude would have been indicative of freedom."[60] He then reminded the audience that Lincoln, whom he had come to know and respect during the Civil War, was nonetheless "in his interests, in his associations, in his habits of thought, and in his prejudices . . . a white man."[61] Conveying subtly, yet forcibly and with irony, his understanding of what was happening and what was to come for blacks in the South, he claimed the monument for not only Lincoln but "the black man as well," as he decried the resurgent power of racism:

> When now it shall be said that the colored man is soulless, that he has no appreciation of benefits or benefactors, when the first reproach of ingratitude is hurled at us, and it is attempted to scourge us beyond the beyond the range of human brotherhood, we may calmly point to the monument we have this day erected to the memory of Abraham Lincoln.[62]

The unfortunate truth of Douglass's remarks was confirmed a little over a year later when, shortly following his appointment by President Hayes as U. S. Marshall for the District of Columbia, he gave a speech lashing out at Jim Crow laws and practices in the Capital, declaring the city "a most disgraceful and scandalous contradiction to the march of civilization. . . ."[63] In response, the *New York Times,* after noting the accuracy of his published remarks, "which everybody knew to be true," took him to task, as might a parent with a disrespectful child, for criticizing the "conservative element" of Washington who had supposedly acquiesced in his controversial appointment as part of a political deal (The Compromise of 1877) that Douglass was assumed to have agreed to. The editorialist archly observed:

> When a class of men consent to let bygones be bygones, every consideration should be shown their tender feelings. If they have consented to receive a colored office-holder, after due protest, as a man *and a brother*, it stands to reason that he ought to walk very softly before them. He is, in a manner, on probation. But the conduct of this dark-skinned official was simply monstrous. . . . It was clear that he did not realize his position as an olive branch and a token of reconciliation.[64]

As with Elizabeth Cady Stanton, Douglass continued to act by writing, speaking out, and demonstrating his superb competence under the vastly changed circumstances of the post-reconstruction era in America, until the day of his death.[65] Each had acquired extraordinary stature and national visibility, a public status as elder exemplars created by their own protracted, authentic efforts to achieve change. More important and less fortuitous, each had helped to achieve some instantiation of moral progress against long conventional odds.

Although each would contribute to the process of morally driven change until their deaths, their place in the vanguard was inevitably altered, a transition not always performed with tact or accepted with dignity. Regardless of their respective moral strengths and the acknowledged reality, at least by the departing generation, of cumulative achievement where fundamental values are at stake, the imperfect accomplishments of one generation are passed on, like all human knowledge, imperfectly to the next.

NOTES

1. Jane Addams, "A Book that Changed my Life," in *Christian Century*, 44 (Oct. 13, 1927): 1196, cited by Anne Fior Scott in Forward, Jane Addams, *Democracy and Social Ethics* (Cambridge, MA: Belknap-Harvard University Press, 1964), xxi.

2. Isaiah Berlin, introduction, xvii.

3. Arendt, *Human Condition*, 158.

4. Arendt, *Human Condition*, 155–61. As Arendt notes, the distinction between words and action is somewhat artificial. Words can be a form of action and action can be expressive. Further, action without speech often loses "its revelatory character." Disembodied actions, like anonymous words, fail to answer the vital question "Who are you?" We need to know the author of both if we are to know one's intentions (158).

5. As mentioned in the preceding note, no attempt is made to artificially separate speech from other acts. As Arendt conceives of action, each of them often carries the quality of the other within it.

6. Oliner and Oliner, 81–112.

7. Those who oppose have a special burden if they are to demonstrate their authenticity. They must be willing to disarm themselves from the power and trappings of convention, to receive the concern over their nonconformity, and respond to it openly, on its merits. In politics, this is seen as a sign of weakness; however, it does occasionally happen discretely, often in the latter stages of a social movement campaign. The Civil War meetings of Frederick Douglass with Abraham Lincoln and the civil rights era contacts between Martin Luther King Jr. and Lyndon Johnson offer some evidence. Philip S. Foner, *Frederick Douglass: A Biography* (New York: Citadel Press, 1964), 197; 225; Frederick Douglass, *Life and Times of Frederick Douglass* (1892; London: Collier-Macmillan Ltd, 1962), 347–49; 357–58; Stephen B. Oates, *Let the Trumpet Sound: A Life of Martin Luther King, Jr.* (1982; New York: Harper-Perennial, 1994), 246; 272; 305.

8. Niccolò Machiavelli, *The Prince*, trans. Luigi Ricci, Ch. V–VI, in *The Prince and the Discourses*, ed. Max Lerner (New York: Random House-Modern Library, 1950), 18–23. This is somewhat the argument made by Robert Putnam in his well-known study of Italian civil society. His argument is confined to differences between Northern and Southern Italy; however, his study does not explain the political instability of the *entire country*, only the relative material prosperity and density of social capital and social trust in the civil society of the North compared to the South. Robert D. Putnam et al., *Making Democracy Work: Civic Traditions in Modern Italy* (Princeton, NJ: Princeton University Press, 1993).

9. Mary Ann Glendon amply illustrates the latter, in particular. *Rights Talk: The Impoverishment of Political Discourse* (New York: Free Press-Macmillan, Inc., 1991).

10. James Madison, Federalist 10, *The Federalist Papers*, Clinton Rossiter, ed, (New York: Penguin-Mentor, 1961); Reinhold Niebuhr, *The Children of Light and the Children of Darkness: A Vindication of Democracy and a Critique of its Traditional Defense* (1945; New York: Charles Scribner's Sons, 1960); E. E. Schattschneider, *The Semisovereign People: A Realist's View of Democracy in America* (Hinsdale, IL: Dryden Press, 1960). Madison makes this point perhaps most effectively in Federalist No. 38, wherein he alludes to the good faith major differences of opinion concerning the definition and priority of political ideals that characterized much of the ratification debate.

11. James Madison, *Federalist Papers*, No. 10.

12. The "War on Terror" has emerged as a policy mantra for our unilateral engagement with a host of actual and potential threats to American interests at home and abroad.

13. As Harvey Mansfield has observed, Machiavelli never really went away. He is most notably present in the ambivalence of modern executive power, where presidents know that they will be held accountable, "not forwards from their principle, but backwards from the effects of their actions." Mansfield, *Taming of the Prince*, 148.

14. Hannah Arendt, *Crisis of the Republic* (New York: Harcourt Brace Javonovich, 1972), 80.

15. Ellen Carol DuBois, Introduction, Elizabeth Cady Stanton, *Eighty Years and More: Reminiscences 1815–1897* (1898; Boston: Northeastern University Press, 1993), v.

16. Douglass and Stanton met in Boston, where Stanton lived from 1843 until 1847 with her husband, while he started practicing law and continued his abolitionist work. While there, they socialized with the moral reformers and other idealists of that era, and for which Boston was renowned. Douglass, who in 1838 at age twenty-one had escaped from slavery in Maryland, was "discovered" by the New England Anti-Slavery Society, founded by William Lloyd Garrison, at one of its conventions held in Nantucket in 1841. By 1843 Douglass was working full-time for the Society, headquartered in Boston, as a "slave-spokesman" for abolition, and had achieved considerable notoriety. In contrast, Stanton's public activism was still nascent when she met Douglass. In 1848, he was one of the approximately forty men out of the three hundred or so who attended the first public convention on women's rights, organized by Stanton, Quaker activist Lucretia Mott, and three other women. Douglass had relocated to Rochester, New York, in 1847, evidencing his split from the radical abolitionists. The convention, advertised only as a "meeting" in an area newspaper on July 14th, was held five days later in nearby Seneca Falls, New York, the sleepy upper-New York state town where Stanton then lived. Over the next four decades, they appeared on the same platform on many occasions. Although their relationship was affected by Douglass's pragmatic opposition in 1869 to the inclusion of women in the 15th Amendment, it survived. See James M'Cune Smith, introduction, *My Bondage and My Freedom*, by Frederick Douglass (1855; New York: Dover Publications, 1969), xxi–xxiv; Stanton 127; 144; 148–49; Lois W. Banner, *Elizabeth Cady Stanton: A Radical for Women's Rights*, ed. Oscar Handlin (Boston: Little, Brown and Company, 1980), 22–47; Mary Ann B. Oakley, *Elizabeth Cady Stanton* (Westbury, NY: Feminist Press-SUNY, 1972), 40–48.

17. As will be discussed, this was much less the case with Eugene V. Debs, whose singular activist focus was the oppression of the working class. It was also not the case with a few of the contemporary activists, whose action has been focused almost exclusively on their moral opposition to abortion.

18. Banner, 74–75; David B. Chesebrough, Frederick Douglass, *Oratory from Slavery* (Westport, CT: Greenwood Press, 1998), 48–49.

19. The Garrisonian or radical wing argued that the Constitution, due to its legitimization of slavery, was fundamentally flawed and, like the political union of North

and South, should be abolished. The political wing, briefly organized as the Liberty Party during the early1840s, did not share either opinion. Interestingly, it was the Garrisonians who had also insisted that women be full members in the American Anti-Slavery Society, an issue that contributed to the 1839 split of the movement into two groups. Garrison himself refused to participate at the London convention when it voted to exclude the American women delegates. Stanton's husband voted with Garrison, but remained. This dispute depicts the uncertain line between pragmatism and idealism that exists in virtually all reform groups, indeed virtually all political movements. It also suggests that the issue of women's rights, with its attendant social and personal impacts, was, in a sense, more radical in 1840 than even abolition. See Banner, 22–24.

20. Banner, 24–25. Quakers have been involved in virtually all of the peace and social justice reform initiatives undertaken in America, including the introduction of Quakerism itself to America in the late 1600s. To a significant extent, the same is also true of Unitarians. However, this is less due to the institutionalization of reform practices within either tradition, although this has occurred to a considerable extent, than it is attributable to their institutionally paradoxical shared belief in the supremacy of individual faith (the "inner light") and conscience over doctrine, and to their practices of radical, nonviolent freedom, fraternity, and sorority. Such believers could impress even Frederick Douglass. Speaking of his first encounter with Lucretia Mott, he wrote: "Great as this woman was in speech, and persuasive as she was in her writings, she was incomparably greater in her presence. She spoke to the world in every line of her countenance. In her there was no lack of symmetry—no contradiction between her thought and act." The Grimké sisters were born in Charleston, South Carolina. After converting to Quakerism, they emancipated the slaves whom they had inherited and moved to the North in 1828, where they became active in both the antislavery movement and the struggle for the general betterment of women. Frederick Douglass (1892), 469. See also Lynd and Lynd, ed., intro., xii–xvii; 1–12.

21. Frederick Douglass (1855), 61–62. It was still a secluded setting in July 2000, when it was used to host an unsuccessful attempt by the Clinton administration to revive the Middle East peace process by direct Israeli-Palestinian talks.

22. Douglass (1855), 88–89.

23. At around age ten, Douglass was sent to live with relatives of his owner in Baltimore. Thanks to his own resourcefulness and the brief initial assistance of his new owner's wife, he became literate. He learned about liberty both from its absence on the plantation and from his experience with highly constrained *de facto* freedom in the city. He learned about the Northern abolitionists from overheard conversations among Southern whites. Following the death of his owner, he was returned to the Eastern Shore in his mid teens, "to be valued and divided." Douglass (1855), 174. He again spent some time on the plantation of his original master, Thomas Auld, and again experienced starvation, this time at the hands of an owner who had "acquired religion" after attending a Methodist revival meeting. At age sixteen, after several months of rebellious behavior, he was sent to a small farm whose tenant-owner had a "reputation of being a first rate hand at breaking young negroes" (203). After some months of frequent whippings and other hardships, he recalls reaching the end of his

endurance and fighting back. "I had reached the point where I was not afraid to die" (247). According to Douglass, the overseer never reported the fight and shortly thereafter, he was returned to his owner. See generally Douglass (1855) 142–44; 151–69; 174–82; 202–48.

24. After arriving "homeless, shelterless, breadless, and moneyless" in New York City, "I kept my secret as long as I could, and at last was forced to go in search of an honest man—a man sufficiently human not to betray me into the hands of the slave-catchers. . . . I found my man in the person of one who said his name was Stewart. He was a sailor, warm-hearted and generous, and he listened to my story with a brother's interest." Douglass (1855), 340.

25. During his stay at the Friedland farm in 1835–36, he taught reading to over forty slaves at a secret "Sunday school." Chesebrough, 10–11.

26. Douglass (1892), 215–16.

27. Chesebrough, 24.

28. Chesebrough, 25–26; Douglass (1855) 362.

29. Stanton's father, a prominent lawyer, former Congressman, and judge, was a social and political conservative. He opposed her marriage to an abolitionist activist and, in general, never supported her positions on women's issues, although he apparently did not publicly oppose her. Her husband, although a political abolitionist and a supporter of increased legal rights for women, often found her positions on women's equality too radical. He refused to attend the Seneca Falls Convention, for example, when his wife refused to remove what everyone there considered to be the most radical plank in the proposed Declaration of Sentiments—the call for full voting rights for women. According to one account, Frederick Douglass spoke powerfully in support and the plank passed by a narrow majority in contrast to the others, which were adopted unanimously. Only one hundred men and women signed the Declaration. One of them was Stanton's sister Harriet, who, along with several others, retracted her signature under pressure from their father and her husband. Banner, 36–47.

30. McWilliams, 229–43.

31. Ronald G. Walters, *American Reformers, 1815–1860* (New York: Hill and Wang, 1978), 13–15.

32. Chesebrough, 104.

33. Historic openings and strategic opportunities are often offered by social movement theorists to explain why certain movements succeed and others fail. Too often, however, these accounts do not take into account either the role of core actors in the creation of such opportunities, or the necessary prior task of core actors in introducing and keeping new forms of justice alive so that unforeseen openings can be exploited. Cf. Sidney Tarrow, Foreword, *How Social Movements Matter: Social Movements, Protest, and Contention Series* (vol. 10), ed. Marco Guigni, Doug McAdam, and Charles Tilly (Minneapolis: University of Minnesota Press, 1999), xix.

34. Elizabeth Griffith, *In Her Own Right: The Life of Elizabeth Cady Stanton* (New York: Oxford University Press, 1984), 51.

35. Griffith, 51. Griffith would likely accept the qualification that these women shared much in common with others of similar, prosperous circumstances, who still accepted the traditional roles of wife and mother. Two of them, Stanton and Frances

Wright, were married to lawyers and each of them had seven children, something of a career in itself. Wright had an activist career in women's rights that paralleled Stanton's, becoming an officer in the National Woman Suffrage Association, a group that Stanton headed.

36. Stanton, 147–48.

37. Griffith, 57. Douglass and Stanton first became acquainted while she lived in Boston. Moreover, her cousin, abolitionist Gerrit Smith, was instrumental in persuading him to move to New York State.

38. Griffith, 57–58. Banner further informs us that the telegraph and the newly formed Associated Press, which picked up the convention story from the local paper that had carried its only advertisement, facilitated the rapid dissemination of the convention and its Declaration. Banner, 46–47. The most supportive (at that time) of the major paper editorialists, Horace Greeley, observed "It is easy to be smart, to be droll, to be facetious in opposition to the demands of these Female Reformers . . . [yet] however unwise and mistaken the demand [for full equality], it is but the assertion of a natural right, and as such must be conceded" (58).

39. Griffith, 60–61. The 1850 convention held in Worcester, Massachusetts, was attended by over one thousand (65).

40. Griffith, 86–107; Banner, 52–53.

41. Griffith, 83.

42. Ellen Carol DuBois, ed., *The Elizabeth Cady Stanton—Susan B. Anthony Reader* (Boston: Northeastern University Press, 1992), 50.

43. Stanton, 190–91. The reference to petticoats is an allusion to the introduction of bloomers as practical clothing for women, first by Stanton's cousin around 1851, and popularized by Amelia Bloomer, an assistant postmaster in Seneca Falls, New York, and founder of *Lilly*, a small woman's literary magazine which published a pattern in response to numerous requests from readers. Griffith, 71–72.

44. Douglass (1855), 370. He had gone to England after his autobiography was published, when he was at greatly increased risk of fugitive capture. From the perspective of self-interest, one must wonder why Douglass, already famous and experiencing for the first time the relative absence of discrimination and the heady atmosphere of elite and mass admiration during his nineteen months in Great Britain, would return to a country where constant physical risk and denigration would be constants in his pursuit of change. The same question pertains to all core actors.

45. Douglass (1855), 389.

46. Waldo E. Martin, *The Mind of Frederick Douglass* (Chapel Hill, NC: University of North Carolina Press, 1984), 174.

47. Martin, 147. The entire speech, a jeremiad worthy of its name, "What to a Slave is the 4th of July?" can be found in Chesebrough, 108–29.

48. Chesebrough, 125. Emphasis is Douglass's.

49. Chesebrough, 84.

50. Griffith, 162.

51. Theodore Stanton and Harriot Stanton Blatch, eds., *Elizabeth Cady Stanton as Revealed in her Letters, Diary, and Reminiscences*, Vol. 2 (1922; Arno Press, Inc., 1969), 64–75.

52. Banner, 68.

53. Griffith, 162.

54. Griffith, 118–43; Banner, 93–108.

55. Griffith, 162.

56. Griffith, 162.

57. Banner, 124.

58. Banner, 124–25.

59. Chesebrough, 69–71; 72.

60. Foner, 320. According to Foner and Chesebrough (71), the speech was given on April 14, 1876.

61. Chesbrough, 71.

62. Chesbrough, 71.

63. Foner, 324.

64. Foner, 324, emphasis added. The article appeared on June 1, 1877. Using these remarks and others, Foner convincingly argues that Douglass was neither co-opted nor gagged by his federal appointment. He openly criticized the Compromise of 1877 that led to the election in the House of Representatives of President Rutherford B. Hayes. A cornerstone of the deal was the removal of remaining federal troops in the South in the name of peace. This inevitably resulted in the region's descent into lawless intimidation of blacks who attempted to assert even a semblance of their equal citizenship (325).

65. In addition to his appointment by President Hayes as U.S. Marshall for the District of Columbia, he was appointed by President Harrison as Consul General to Haiti in 1889, and later that year, to the additional post of Chargé d'Affairs for Santo Domingo (Dominican Republic). Foner, 352.

Chapter Five

Morally Informed Action:
Two Examples from the Progressive Era

There are many who seek refuge in the popular side of a great question. As a Socialist, I have long since learned to stand alone.

—Eugene V. Debs[1]

[A]s all other forms of growth begin with a deviation from the mass, so moral change in human affairs may also begin with a differing group or an individual, who is at best designated as a crank and a freak, and in sterner moments imprisoned as an atheist or a traitor.

—Jane Addams[2]

By the 1880s, a new generation of core actors had emerged, influenced not only by mentors and exemplars like Stanton and Douglass, but by the context of accelerating change and newer forms of old injustice that were erupting across the American landscape. Eugene Victor Debs (1855–1926) and Jane Addams (1860–1935) began their activist careers just as Stanton's and Douglass's were ending. They came to maturity in an era characterized by the extremes that were generated by raw, unregulated human energy: wide-ranging optimism and utter despair; enhanced economic organization and concomitant social chaos; an explosion of specialized knowledge and the exploitation of massive, willful ignorance; the burgeoning of American nationhood and world power status. Each was justified by the cultural hubris and mythology of Anglo-Saxon superiority, reinforced by the appropriation of early evolutionary science to link power with fitness, fitness with survival, and survival with moral necessity. In the cultural and inner ether emanating from the energy and products thus generated, one could also detect a nagging sense that "communities were passing [and] men were becoming small units of a great system. . . . It was, in short, an age disquieting to all Americans."[3]

ORDINARY BEGINNINGS

Debs and Addams were each prototypes of the rapidly expanding Middle America. Their families could serve as economic bracket points and cultural exemplars for the broadly defined middle class in the latter half of the nineteenth century. Further, as with Stanton and Douglass, there was nothing sufficiently remarkable in the background or upbringing of either to suggest their subsequent adoption of nonconforming activism as their life work. Adjusted for time and circumstance, each of the four was merely bright, talented, and, except for Douglass, consistently loved and nurtured by one or both parents throughout childhood. In common with most of their contemporaries, again excepting Douglass, they were raised in large families, and imbued with values that were well within the mainstream for their time, place, and status. In sum, we cannot attribute their subsequent exceptionalism to some pattern in their early formation that was not shared by many of their contemporaries. Few of us are raised to be radicals, and neither Debs nor Addams was an exception in this regard. Historian Anne Fior Scott's observation regarding Addams applies equally to Debs: "This was a radicalism that began with experience, not with doctrine."[4]

Debs, at the low end of the middle-class spectrum, was born and raised in Terre Haute, Indiana, "the third of six surviving children" of parents who had immigrated to America from the Alsace region of France in 1849.[5] They moved to Terre Haute from New York City within a year, seeking, in a pattern familiar to many immigrants, to facilitate their future among at least some who might still share their native language.[6]

After failing in various efforts to support his family as a laborer, Debs's father achieved modest, small business success and community respect as a retail grocer. Young Debs attended private, then newly opened public schools through the ninth grade, leaving school at age fifteen (against his parents' wishes and concerns) to work for the Terre Haute and Indianapolis Railroad.[7] His entire railroading career spanned four years, ending after being laid off as a locomotive fireman during the depression economy of 1874. His father convinced him to take a job as an accounting clerk for a wholesale grocer in Terre Haute, a position he held for several years. In 1875, evincing his fondness for railroading—and for the hard-edged, masculine fraternity of railroad workers—he became a charter member and recording secretary of Vigo Lodge, No. 16, of the Brotherhood of Local Firemen.[8] He was bright, highly personable, and ambitious for conventional success and reputation.

Within five years he had moved from these modest beginnings to the appointed posts of Secretary-Treasurer of the national Grand Brotherhood and editor of its magazine.[9] In these and many other respects, Debs was imbued with the American enlightenment and cultural ethos.

"NATURAL" HARMONY

His initial view of unionism was one of general harmony with management. He saw his local lodge and the Brotherhood "less as a labor organization agitating for justice than as a sifter of personnel for the railroad corporation" and as a benevolent association for its members.[10] In the aftermath of the first nationwide railroad strike in 1877, in a speech to the 1878 Grand Brotherhood national convention, he "denounced, as 'sheerest folly,' accusations that his union would conspire against the railroad corporations, since its 'interests are so closely aligned with those of their employers.'" Although state militias and federal troops had been called out against the strikers from his own local and elsewhere, he sought to counter the growing radicalism of some Brotherhood members with the conservative, individualistic craft union "moral argument that placed the onus of maintaining harmony directly on the members," calling upon them to be "a class of men worthy of confidence and respect."[11]

GROWING DISHARMONY

Only gradually did Debs detect the shape and magnitude of what was then unfolding in the relationship of industrial labor to corporate industry in America. As political scientist Stephen Skowronek observed for a different purpose, "The years between the nationwide railroad strike and the Spanish American War define an era of labor violence unparalleled in any other industrial nation. . . ."[12]

Labor violence was only the second, largely reactive part of the change equation, however. Debs was slow to perceive the first—the pernicious effects of newly organizing capital and its powerful alliances with America's increasingly professional, largely sympathetic political, financial, and judicial elites. The emergence of class conflict in America ran contrary to the ethos of individual striving, success based on effort and merit within an overall harmony of equal, plentiful opportunity for free men of varied talents with which Debs—and most in his generation—had been imbued.[13]

He had vigorously opposed his local's participation in the 1877 strike and continued to oppose strikes and to work for labor-management harmony as

well as for skill-separated labor fraternity through much of the next decade.
He regarded William McKeen, the local developer-owner of the spur railroad
that ran through Terre Haute, as a personal exemplar, "'the model railroad
president' who believed in *'honest pay for an honest day's work.'*" Further,
he consistently argued that workers "must actively accept such men [implic-
itly including himself] as models, for left to themselves they tended to de-
generate."[14]

Jane Addams, born and raised in northern Illinois, was the eighth of nine
children, four of whom lived to adulthood. Her father and mother settled in
the then unincorporated region in the mid-1840s. By her birth in 1860 "he
was a successful miller, a large landowner, and a leader in public affairs in the
region."[15] He was also an abolitionist, elected to the state senate on the old
Whig ticket in 1854, shortly thereafter joining with Lincoln in the new Republican Party.[16] When he died unexpectedly in 1881, he left an estate estimated at $300,000, of which some $50,000, the 1998 equivalent of one mil-
lion dollars, went to his daughter.[17] In sum, Addams's father seems to have
been a man of strong republican and philanthropic virtue.

Much like Elizabeth Cady Stanton, Jane Addams enjoyed the early advan-
tages of an upper middle class upbringing in a supportive family. Her father
endorsed the evolving version of a traditional education for young women of
talent and means, serving as Trustee of nearby Rockford Seminary for
Women, founded by Congregational and Presbyterian clergymen in 1847.[18]
Rockford operated on the Protestant egalitarian and work ethic model of Mt.
Holyoke College in Massachusetts, and there Addams received a fairly rounded
liberal arts and science education at Rockford within its somewhat rigid religious regimen and its strong evangelical and missionary emphasis. Years
later, she would recall her "singular unresponsiveness to the emotional appeal
of religious evangelism" and her enduring resistance to all forms of religious
institutions and dogma.[19]

INFORMED UNEASE

Upon graduation in 1881, Addams entered young adulthood with a good
moral and intellectual education and a vague sense of unease. Reflecting on
the several years prior to her opening of Hull House in September 1889, she
described herself as being "absolutely at sea so far as any moral purpose was
concerned, clinging only to the desire to live in a really living world and refusing to be content with a shadowy intellectual or aesthetic reflection of it."[20]
She was aware that she had been both equipped and trained to do something
useful in the world, and imparted with a sense of both Christian and republi-

can duty to comply; however, Addams, like others of her class and gender, was left with few approved avenues for meaningful direct engagement with the great, pressing social and political issues of the day.

Hampered at first by the emotional and physical impact of her father's sudden, unexpected death as well as a prolonged convalescence following major surgery to correct a curvature of the spine, she spent the next six years traveling in Europe, first with her stepmother and later with friends, as well as visiting and corresponding with family and friends in this country. Then as now, travel, particularly in Europe, was seen as part of the cultural finishing process for a young woman ". . . who had money and education, but nothing to do."[21] Her journal notes reflected her angst over the incongruity between the material comfort of her life and that of her travel companions and the living and working conditions of rural and urban poor that she observed in Ireland, East London, and Germany.[22] She was especially moved by the Dickensian conditions she observed during a host-guided tour of the slums of East London—enough so that "for the following weeks [she] went about London furtively, afraid to look down narrow streets and alleys lest they disclose again this hideous human need . . . [and] bewildered that the world should be going on as usual." She was further troubled by "the assumption that she herself had nothing to do toward satisfying this human need," and felt "mocked not only by a sense of her own uselessness, but by the realization that *she was not expected to do anything.*"[23]

DEMOCRATIC IMMERSION

Entries in her personal journal and other accounts of Addams's second trip to Europe in 1888 permit two inferences: first, she was already aware that conditions for European immigrants and others mired in poverty in Chicago and other major American cities mirrored those in Europe; second, at some point prior to or during the trip she became determined to act on her concerns. While traveling in Spain she confided "her scheme" to her close friend and college classmate, Ellen Gates Starr, who immediately offered her "enthusiastic support." Returning to London, she arranged a "letter of introduction" to the head of Toynbee Hall, a new facility for helping the poor, located in Whitechapel, one of the most downtrodden neighborhoods in East London.[24]

According to Gertrude Himmelfarb, the

> chief purpose of Toynbee Hall, [founded in 1884] . . . was to humanize and civilize charity. The settlement 'implied no denial or even denigration of the distinctions of wealth, occupation, class, or talent. It was meant rather to be a civic

community, based upon a common denominator of citizenship . . . a citizenship that made tolerable all those other social distinctions which were natural or inevitable, but which should not be exacerbated and should not be permitted to obscure the common humanity of individuals. [It] was not an experiment in socialism; it was an experiment in democracy—which was no mean feat at that time and place.[25]

As first conceived, Toynbee Hall was as much "an aid and outlet to educated young men" as it was of intended benefit to the poor of East London.[26] Staffed initially by fifteen male "residents," all of them recent college graduates, its avowed aim was to avoid the class separation inherent in traditional institutional philanthropy. The task of the residents was to provide "people of Whitechapel with the kinds of services that would 'uplift them.'" This included "giving lectures and classes to workingmen and their families on hundreds of subjects," ranging from practical and health-oriented skills to all forms of cultural and educational enrichment, including courses in science, language, history, art, and literature.[27]

Toynbee Hall served as the model "by which, and against which," Addams and Ellen Starr founded Hull House in Chicago in September 1889. Located on Halsted Avenue, "a long north-south thoroughfare abutting the stockyards and shipbuilding operations and running through one of Chicago's worst slums," the old mansion was surrounded by ethnic enclaves of Italians, Germans, Polish and Russian Jews, and Bohemians.[28]

Unlike Toynbee Hall, the American settlement houses founded in its immediate wake were characterized by "less of *noblesse oblige*, less confidence that the upper classes were giving to the lower."[29] For her part, Addams moved into Hull House with the intention of learning from her new neighbors. She came to realize, however, that she and the other the Hull House founders initially shared the well-intentioned hubris of educated idealists of middle- and upper-class experience, varying only from the other American settlement models in Addams's and Starr's intent from the outset that their settlement would be run by college-educated women, not men.[30] She quickly learned, however, that this learning included not only the scientific gathering of facts, but also the garnering of knowledge in the form of practical, democratic wisdom that she, herself, did not yet possess.

Debs and Addams drew distinctly different lessons from their activist experiences during the 1890s. During that decade, Hull House grew exponentially—physically and in terms of residents, volunteers, and philanthropic supporters—as Addams and her colleagues launched a series of programs and reform initiatives, each undertaken in the spirit of what Gandhi would later refer to as "experiments with truth."[31] Truth, in other words, was not something static and objective to be simply sought, but rather a reality that was both actual and potential, something that could only be learned, reaffirmed, and expanded upon by each generation, by living life engaged with others and the world. Further, as Addams came to understand it, the process of learning from others was mutual *by nature and necessity*, and therefore inherently democratic.

By the early 1900s, there were few urban-related issues that Addams and the other residents had not learned about, acted upon, and achieved results: daycare, adult literacy and formal education, neighborhood playgrounds, garbage, sanitation and other aspects of public health, juvenile criminal justice, woman and child labor, industrial safety, and others.[32] In the process of doing so she had broadened and reinforced her nascent belief in the common humanity, dignity, and democratic capacity of her new neighbors, co-residents, and benefactors alike.

During the 1890s, Eugene Debs, like Addams, broadened his vision of social and political fraternity—but only to a clearly defined point. The change was marked by his two radical transitions during this period: first, from craft to federated and, ultimately, to industrial unionism; second, from union building to socialism and fulltime political action. Demonstrating the quickening pace of his activism, in the wake of an unsuccessful strike against the Chicago, Burlington, and Quincy Railroad in 1888, he was instrumental in organizing a federation of the rail craft and trade unions later that year, only to see it dissolve in internal conflict in 1892.[33] Confirming his growing awareness that the railroads and their financial and political supporters were both better organized and economically inclined to be more instrumental than fraternal in their dealings with labor, Debs joined the more radical ranks of industrial unionists. In February 1893, the American Railway Union was formally established, with Debs its key organizer and president.[34] Stimulated by a sharp depression as well as the tireless work of Debs and his colleagues, within just over a year the ARU comprised some 465 lodges and 150,000 members.[35]

Commenting indirectly on Debs's role during this period, sister labor and political activist Kate Richards O'Hare is said by one Debs biographer to have observed:

> For weeks, even months at a stretch, Gene would be dashing around from one city to another. . . . Sometimes at the end of grilling weeks of frantic labor he would come home utterly exhausted only to be called out again by urgent messages before he had enjoyed a single day of home and rest.[36]

The key event in the building of the new union was its successful strike in April 1894 against the powerful Great Northern Railroad. In the strike's immediate aftermath, membership burgeoned, as noted, and Debs "came to personify the American Railway Union and its efforts to develop an alternative to the corrupt policies of both the [union] brotherhoods and the [railroad] corporations."[37] In the process, Debs had become and would remain a national figure from 1894 onward.

The lives of Debs and Addams publicly intersected for the first time only a few weeks later during the Pullman Strike of 1894 when the confluence of corporate and political power at the national and state levels crushed the fledgling ARU. In the process, Debs was jailed for civil defiance of a court injunction, an event that directly contributed to his radical conversion to socialism.[38]

Neither Debs nor Addams was an admirer of George Pullman, the owner of the company struck by the ARU. According to Debs's biographer, Harold W. Currie, "even before the 1890's depression, the reputation of Pullman was odious in labor circles."[39] Prior to his complete transition from trade unionism, Debs already felt a growing animosity toward powerful owners, including Pullman. Writing for his union's magazine in 1887, he attacked the sleeping car manufacturer in an editorial, claiming that "The term 'Pullman' . . . has become . . . the synonym of almost anything odious that heartless, crushing, degrading monopoly suggests to the minds of honorable men." Assailing Pullman's wealth, autocratic management, and top-down paternalism, he confirmed his then continuing position in the mainstream of American *anti*-radical conservatism, as he observed: "It is such vindictive practices that breed unrest and vindictive spirit abroad in the lands that furnish anarchists and socialists with the raw material for their diatribes against law and order. . . ."[40]

AN IDEOLOGICAL CONVERSION

Within two years of serving his six-month jail sentence for contempt, Debs had become an enthusiastic convert to socialism. He accepted, without qualification, the Marxian analysis of the historical inevitability of class struggle, and, from that point forward, was a passionate foe of capitalism in general and capitalists in particular. His early, received belief in the American organic fraternity of man, superseding class, was abandoned for the narrower fraternity of labor. The socialist revolution that he now believed in must be constructed through the inculcation, by awakened leaders such as himself, of class-consciousness imparted with authentic moral persuasion. From this point forward, the focus of his activism reflected his customary salutation to his activist colleagues in labor and socialist politics, to potential working class converts, even much of his private correspondence with his father. His new greeting was "Comrade," not "Brother." He would, however, remain committed with equal authenticity to democratic values and nonviolence as he sought nothing less than an elite-led, working class controlled social, political, and economic democracy.

DEMOCRATIC ENGAGEMENT
VERSUS PLURALIST CONFRONTATION

In 1894, at the time of the Pullman Strike, Jane Addams was already well-known in Chicago. Before opening Hull House in 1889, she and Ellen Starr had spoken, met, and networked with many of Chicago's social, political, and philanthropic elite, soliciting and obtaining support for their new endeavor. In particular, she enlisted the financial and volunteer support of college-educated middle- and upper-class women, facilitated in this regard by the rapid growth of women's clubs and civic associations that coincided with her arrival.[41]

Addams's ties to Chicago's upper echelons through her background, her work with the poor, immigrant neighbors of the settlement house, and her brief efforts to intervene in the Pullman Strike afforded her the opportunity to view the controversy from several perspectives. Through her extensive engagement with her new neighbors in the early 1890s, she had strengthened her existing sympathy for the aims of the labor movement. Forming friendships with the muckraker journalist Henry Demarest Lloyd and several labor activists, "she was an early defender of the right, even the necessity, for labor organization." Supporting her belief with concrete action, "in late 1891 she helped to form two women's [textile worker] unions" in Chicago.[42] She further utilized the resources of Hull House to support efforts by labor organizers to unionize and to provide a variety of services to workers and their families affected by lock-outs, walk-outs, and strikes.[43]

Jane Addams, was certainly more radical concerning the needs of labor than the trade unionists, such as Samuel Gompers (founder of the American Federation of Labor—the AFL), and the politically liberal pluralists of her era. She took the opportunity, for example, in 1899 to publicly declare it deplorable that unions were "the [only] ones working for shorter hours, decent pay, healthy conditions, [and] the prevention of child labor . . . things that were the responsibility of all society."[44] As for corporate power and its anti-democratic influence, she was also in front of all but the socialists in the labor movement, in her calls for democracy in the industrial workplace.[45]

At the time of the Pullman Strike, Jane Addams was involved in an effort by progressive "good government" reformers among Chicago's civic elite to resolve labor disputes by arbitration. Prior to the initial walkout, she had been

appointed by the board of the Chicago Civic Federation, a progressive betterment group, to serve on its newly formed "Citizen's Arbitration Committee," specifically intended to help resolve labor-management conflicts. Her
group met with the Pullman workers and with ARU representatives in Pullman, the "model community" built by George Pullman to house some of his
factory workers. After securing their agreement to have the dispute arbitrated
by the committee, the "male members" of the committee met with Pullman,
who flatly refused to consider either arbitration or mediation [46]

A few months after the defeat of the strikers and the collapse of the ARU,
Jane Addams presented an essay to the Chicago Woman's Club and the Twentieth Century Club of Boston containing her reflections on the strike and, indirectly, on the lessons she had learned during her five years at Hull House.[47]
Her already prolific work with the poor in Chicago, her prodigious efforts to
raise funds *and* educate the social conscience of Chicago's elites, her investi-
gations into the conditions underlying the strike, her efforts to mediate its resolution, and media accounts of the extensive assistance given by the settlement house staff to striking workers and their families gave her words the ring
of authenticity. Unlike Debs, who is reported to have called her speech "just
another attempt to put out fire with rosewater,"[48] Henry Demarest Lloyd, a reformer respected by both Addams and Debs, found her critique of George
Pullman so strong and implicitly broad that he advised her not to attempt to
have it published in its current form.[49]

With devastating effect, Addams compared Pullman to Shakespeare's King
Lear, relating his reputation as a generous, progressive employer and bene-
factor to the paternal beneficence Lear had afforded his daughter, Cordelia. In
fact, she continued, Pullman had been criticized by Wall Street several years
earlier when he had used extensive corporate funds to construct a model community, on his solely conceived, minutely detailed physical and social design,
for Pullman Company employees on the outskirts of Chicago.

Of the strike, she observed that Pullman, "like King Lear, could not imagine that his child [his workers] 'should be moved by a principle obtained outside himself,'" or have acted so ungratefully.[50] She carefully crafted the analogy to show how industrialists, including those such as Pullman who claimed
the mantle of enlightened philanthropic virtue, were really engaged in individual, primarily ego-gratifying pursuits, creating a dependent social order
"not only in the factory, but the form in which in which [their] workmen were
living."[51] Referring to Pullman's stubborn refusal to either arbitrate or nego-
tiate in the face of the strike's massive national and local human impact, she
inferred his self-righteous sincerity, concluding that "he must have been sustained by the consciousness of being in the right. Only that could have held
him against the great desire for fair play which swept over the country."[52]

Addams's essay was far more than a critique of the excesses of what she and most other progressive reformers acknowledged as the new industrial order in America. For her the Pullman Strike was evidence not simply of structural growing pains, but of a growing "social disorder," which needed to be understood "not alone in its legal aspect nor in its sociological bearings, *but from those deep human motives*, which, after all, determine events."[53] The strike affirmed for her the evidence of class warfare that now informed Debs's action; however, unlike Debs, she refused to treat it as either a normal or inevitable part of the American system. Further, although she weighed in strongly on the side of labor in her appraisal of the resulting injustice, she strongly felt that class warfare itself was only the latest version of man's primitive, gendered state.

In Addams's view, class struggle was part of the recurring cycle of arbitrary assertion of self-interest by some elites and the reactive violence of those oppressed by a newly configured coercion—one that high-handed benevolence, however well intentioned, could not adequately soften. The culprits were wrongly informed human agents, both organized and individual, not social structures or some diaphanous force of history.

For Addams, the counter-mobilization of organized self-interest by labor, while understandable, even justified and noble given the magnitude of the injustice, was equally primitive, likely to descend into violence, and inadequate in its social motive. Both parties, each convinced of their legitimacy, were isolating themselves from the other, each regarding the other with increasing contempt.

In her first book, *Democracy and Social Ethics*, a collection of speeches and articles published in 1907, Jane Addams addressed more fully what she saw as the need of her generation, particularly its powerful elites, for a new social ethic. She attempted to share with an educated and privileged audience what she and her activist colleagues had learned as they worked at and from the Hull House venue during the preceding decade that had included the Pullman Strike.[54] She aimed her argument at those of her strata who, as she had been, were "unhappy in regard to their attitude toward the [new] social order; toward the dreary round of uninteresting work, the pleasures narrowed down to those of appetite . . . who are denied the relief that sturdy action brings. . . ."[55]

Her solution was simple and direct: the individual, perhaps once enlightened, motive of rational self-interest that governed the existing order needed to be abandoned, or at least subordinated to a broader, more inclusive social motive. We must "cast our experiences in a larger mould if our lives are to be animated by . . . larger social aims."[56] What was needed was a conscious seeking by those genuinely disaffected of broad, democratic experience, "a wider acquaintance with and participation in the life about them."[57] By bringing one's self into contact "with the moral experiences of the many," she argued, one is more readily, and *naturally*, able to "procure an adequate social motive."

> Such] experience gives the easy and trustworthy impulse toward right action in the broad as well as in the narrow relations. . . . Our social ideals are developed through our ability to . . . reflect on experience and our strength to attain them is secured from interest in life itself.[58]

ACTING FOR PEACE

Jane Addams's activism, informed by early, ongoing learning from her Hull House neighbors and the often hotly discussed proposals of her sister and fellow residents and colleagues, such as John Dewey and many others, was constant, local as well as far-ranging, and frequently controversial during her first twenty years. No single aspect of her career, however, generated more conflict and, by necessary inference, greater evidence of her authenticity as a core social and political actor than her unqualified opposition to World War I.

As Addams understood it, pacifism and nonviolence were merely logical extensions of the democratic social ethic, the emotional and rational product of the "cosmopolitan" experience of one's active engagement with life—most especially with those on the margins of society, such as in Chicago's immigrant neighborhoods where she lived and worked. They were also qualities that women, she believed with Stanton, learned more predictably than men, through their nurturing and affectionate relationships their parents and with their own children. Accordingly, it is not surprising that she voiced her opposition to war at the first opportunity, during America's intervention in Cuba and the Philippines at the turn of the century.[59]

In 1907 she set forth her arguments for peace, grounding them in neither the empirical nor romantic principals of human equality and universal rights that had characterized eighteenth-century political thought, nor in the pragmatism that justified peace secured by international law as a rational, less costly alternative to international violence. While she saw both as signs of moral progress and as important rationales, she understood that neither contained the necessary motive force to enable us to withstand the primitive and selfish urges that led to conflict. She also found the parallel arguments of many pacifists—appeals to human pity or sensibility based on the horrors of war and arguments of prudence or good sense that sought to avoid war by setting forth its cost "with pitiless accuracy"—truthful, but inadequate.[60]

In her analysis, she came down on the side of human emotion informed not by abstract principal but by democratic, social experience, which, as she had encountered it, deepened pity into compassion and abstract equality into equality based on mutual relationship, interpersonal affection, and respect. She fully understood the lure that war held for many, perhaps most, men in America. The spirit of war animated them to heroic action, furnished them with a moral raison d'être by stirring "the nobler blood and the higher imagination of the nation, and thus free[ing] it from moral stagnation and the bonds of commercialism."[61]

Addams's solution, as she had proposed for ameliorating the clash of labor and capital, was the substitution of a new motive force, a "virile good will" as she artfully called it, at least equal to the spirit of warfare and its corresponding moral claim on the hearts and minds of men, yet as "compatible with their spiritual natures, as war has proved itself to be incompatible."[62] She deeply believed that man was an evolutionary creature, uniquely equipped to learn from such experience, supplemented with formal knowledge, such as she had gleaned from—and brought to—the Hull House neighborhood. She detected in her own social learning, and the similar education she had observed among her colleagues and immigrant neighbors, evidence that this "substitute motive" was already taking hold in America at large:

> We care less each day for the heroism connected with warfare and destruction, and constantly admire more that which pertains to labor and the nourishing of human life. The new heroism manifests itself at the present moment in [the] ... determination to abolish poverty and disease, a manifestation so widespread that it may justly be called international.[63]

As Addams's, biographer Daniel Levine observes, her growing "respectability" in the mainstream-entering current of Progressive Era reform was essentially unaffected until the entry of America into World War I in April 1917.[64] As with Elizabeth Cady Stanton, she had become an activist at what we can now easily discern was a propitious moment in our history, enabling her to tap into the moral discontent and search for meaning that she had experienced and detected in many others of her generation. Accordingly, her qualified, pragmatic support for Roosevelt's Progressive Party candidacy in 1912 was solicited and welcomed.[65] Even her pacifism was shared as an ideal, or at least tolerated, by many reformers and conventional actors. They included Woodrow Wilson, who saw the outbreak of war in Europe as anachronistic—a spasm of first generation, unenlightened nationalism, enhanced by modern means.

During 1914 and 1915, Addams's participation in efforts organized by men and women alike to end the war in Europe was prodigious. In September, 1914, only weeks after the outbreak of hostilities, she met with members of various American and international peace societies in New York, searching for ways to keep America out of the conflict and, if possible, to end the war itself. The group decided upon the strategy of organizing a purely women's peace group, based upon the belief, strongly shared by Addams, that "there are things concerning which women are more sensitive than men, and one of these is the treasuring of life."[66]

Upon her return to Chicago, Jane Addams worked with noted suffragist Carrie Chapman Catt to organize a national peace congress in Washington in January 1915. The convocation was attended by some three thousand women, primarily delegates from existing national women's organizations. The Woman's Peace Party (later the nucleus of the American branch of the Women's International League for Peace and Freedom) was formed at the congress, with Addams elected as its chair.[67]

Later that spring, Addams traveled to Europe, heading a delegation of the WPP, to attend an international congress of women at The Hague, together with 1,136 women from 12 countries. The organizers, members of the international suffrage movement, had invited Addams to chair the meeting, intentionally comprised of delegates from both neutral and warring nations.[68] Following the congress, she and other delegates spent the next several weeks traveling with great difficulty through Europe, meeting with belligerents and neutrals alike in an attempt to convince them to participate in a neutral nation mediation of the war. Addams took on the toughest challenge, traveling to the capital of each of the principal warring countries, attempting (and sometimes succeeding) to meet with key state leaders.

Addams continued her efforts for peaceful resolution and to keep America neutral in the war for the next several months. In the 1916 election, she supported Wilson, given his overall progressive record and his pledge to maintain American neutrality. However, in early 1917, as Germany resumed unrestricted submarine warfare and President Wilson shifted rapidly with growing public sentiment to enter the war, Addams quickly found herself "on the radical fringe of society, a troubled outcast."[69] Nonetheless, she persevered, testifying before Congress against both the Espionage and Conscription Acts, as America formally entered the war and war fever quickly became an epidemic.[70]

The low point arrived in June 1917, two months after America entered the war, when she delivered one of several speeches she had given that spring, of "Patriots and Pacifists in Wartime," this one to an audience at the First Congregational Church in Evanston, Illinois.[71] Her speech, which was greeted with awkward silence, confirmed both her unalterable opposition to the war and her awareness of the personal cost of standing largely alone. According to her nephew and biographer, James Linn, she observed with personal and gendered irony:

The pacifist is making a venture into a new international ethics. He is afforded an opportunity to cultivate a fine valor . . . for new ethics are unpopular ethics. . . . [Yet] the pacifist must serve his country by forcing definitions if possible. . . . He should insist that the United States declare its refusal to regard the deliberate starvation of the woman and children of any nation [a reference to the then widespread effects of the total naval blockade imposed by the allies at the beginning of the war] as a proper war measure.[72]

PRAGMATIC ADJUSTMENT

Addams was one "of only a handful of urban progressive reformers who opposed American participation in the war," throughout the war. She stood in opposition not only to overwhelming American public sentiment and reactive war hysteria, but also to a majority of her Hull House colleagues and supporters, including her friend and former Hull House resident, John Dewey.[73] Realizing that speaking from a principled stance alone was ineffective as a vehicle for promoting peace in the midst of the patriotic, sacrificial fervor of war, she sought a new means of concrete action to define and express her wider moral view. As she had written several years earlier, she understood that

action is indeed the sole medium for the expression of ethics . . . that speculation in regard to morality is but observation . . . that a situation does not really become moral until we are confronted with a question of what shall be done in a concrete case, and are obliged to act upon our theory.[74]

By the last months of the conflict she had turned to food aid for starving children and women in Europe as both an urgent need and the most effective means to promote the social ethic of cooperation and mutual aid and to highlight the heinous consequences of war. She found a new national voice while traveling the country, speaking to women's groups in particular, in support of an expanded vision of the federal government's wartime food program.

Addams joined in the official call for public food conservation and increased production, and especially in the plea for international institution-building to aid the starving in Europe and to stave off what many saw as a looming world food crisis.[75] Her further reflection on experience had triggered a new insight, based in part on women's primal, life-preserving roles as child nurturers, agriculturalists, providers of basic sustenance, and their corresponding empathy for suffering children:

As I had felt the young immigrant conscripts caught up into a great world movement which sent them out to fight, so it seemed to me [that] the millions of

American women might be caught up into a great world purpose, that of conservation of life; there might someday be found an antidote to war in women's
all-embracing pity for helpless children.[76]

After the war and the subsidence of the reactionary events of 1919–1921,
Addams spent the next decade in relative obscurity, until, like Stanton, her
age and occasional reminders of her association with the institutions—juvenile courts and the University of Chicago School of Social Work among
them—that had been built upon her once controversial initiatives, restored
her name to one that socially minded organizations "wanted on their letter-
heads."[77] Throughout the decade, she continued to write prolifically and to
speak out for a new, more inclusive social morality, urging American ratification of the League of Nations treaty and humanitarian relief for war-rav-
aged Europe, and endorsing various battles being fought by others seeking social justice. As with Stanton and Douglass, she was fortunate to live long
enough to again be seen as safe and saintly by the media and the state. In
1931, three years before her death, she was awarded the Nobel Peace Prize,
donating most of the honorarium, much as she had done with her inheritance
in the founding and early operation of Hull House, to the Women's International League for Peace and Freedom.[78]

ANOTHER FORM OF NONVIOLENT ACTION

Following his conversion to socialism in 1895, Eugene Debs devoted the rest
of his life to raising the "public conscience" of "[t]he heart of the country,"
which he equated with the proletariat or working class and their families.[79]
Having discovered the general course of historical development, his goal was
to lead the vanguard of the Marxist-conceived class struggle in America and
to establish a "working-class republic" via a democratic revolutionary victory
over the capitalist plutocrats to be achieved at the ballot box.[80]

To his credit, the working class that Debs identified with and sought to persuade included both women and African Americans as political equals.[81] As
with Stanton, Douglass, and Addams, he saw women as playing a vital moral
role in any politics of reform. He also believed that their emancipation and
enlistment in the socialist cause as voters and party workers were each essential to the movement's democratic success in America.

His support for African American political equality, as well as greatly improved economic freedom, also appeared to be supported by sincere belief,
although clearly subordinated to his efforts to build the Socialist Party in a
strongly racist labor environment. In a 1903 article, for example, he unequiv-

ocally condemned the injustice of slavery and its racial aftermath, in a simple declaration: "The history of the Negro in the United States is a history of crime without parallel." He focused his sharpest critique, however, on the South, where it was evident that neither unions nor socialism were likely to take root. At the end of the piece he accepted both the reality of social discrimination, although decrying the injustice of its causes, and acknowledged that his party "had nothing special to offer the Negro.[82]

Socialism, as Debs saw it, was inevitable throughout the industrial world; its peaceful democratic evolution—as a process and an outcome—was not. For Debs, democracy was inseparable from socialism, not simply the most practical way, given the conservative individualism with which he had earlier been imbued and which he knew was endemic in American labor. In fact, he counted on the American revolutionary spirit and the radical individualism that informed it, for socialism's ultimate success in this country. Awakened by experience and the educative persuasion of actors like himself to a proper understanding of the cause of the lack of freedom that they had come to live with, reminded and prodded to assert their revolutionary "manhood," American workers would organize economically, politically, and nonviolently—unless required in self-defense, as at the American founding.

Like Addams, Debs's efforts to achieve his above goals were immense and overwhelmingly authentic. He headed the Socialist Party and ran as its presidential candidate from 1900 to 1912, helping to build its active member base from less than 10,000 in 1904 to its peak of 118,000 in 1912. In that year the Debs ticket garnered 900,000 votes, some six percent of national presidential total.[83] In each campaign, he traveled, spoke, wrote, organized, and often struggled with internecine conflicts over doctrine, strategy, and egos to the point of physical exhaustion.

The second aspect of his strategy, seen by him as indispensable to the "socialist movement," was the organization of industrial unions. Writing in 1911 concerning strategy for the upcoming election, he stated with typical clarity:

> Of far greater importance than increasing the vote of the Socialist party is the economic organization of the working class. To the extent, and only to the extent, that the workers are disciplined and organized in their respective industries can the Socialist movement advance and the Socialists party hold what [it gains] by the ballot. . . . Each industry must be organized in its entirety, embracing all the workers, and all working together in the interests of all, in the true spirit of solidarity, thus laying the foundation and developing the superstructure of the new system within the old, from which it is evolving, and systematically fitting the workers, step by step, to assume entire control of the productive forces when the hour strikes for the impending organic change.[84]

It was at a point of maximum exhaustion, in the waning months of World War I, that Debs demonstrated the full depth of his sincerity for all to see. In the late summer of 1917, following America's entry into the war and the first major wave of arrests of his leftist radical colleagues under the new national Espionage Act, he had "suffered the third major physical collapse in his activist career and entered a sanitarium."[85] As one would expect, he had openly, strenuously opposed both the war and Wilson's policy of preparedness alongside neutrality.

Unlike Jane Addams, his opposition was not based on opposition to all forms of organized hostility, but "to ruling class war," national conflicts commenced by the ruling class, whether characterized as offensive or defensive, "or what other lying excuse may be invented for it."[86] Much as Douglass had accepted the necessity of the Civil War, Debs saw the necessity of violence in the class struggle for nations, such as Russia, where democratic persuasion and confrontation were not possible.

That summer was also the nadir for American socialism, much as it was for efforts to promote the democratic, nonviolent resolution of international disputes. Late that fall, he was buoyed by the success of the Bolshevik-led Russian Revolution, praising those who "by their incomparable valor and sacrifice added fresh luster to the fame of the international movement." His enthusiasm was tempered, however, by his awareness that "the movement in America would face further persecution, for capitalists as well as Socialists understood that 'the truth alone will make people free.'"[87]

In early June 1918, determined to demonstrate his solidarity with his comrades and to lend personal testimony to the importance of his cause, Debs left his sick bed, "expecting, even anticipating his arrest," under the Sedition Act adopted by Congress the previous month. Within two weeks he was successful, following his delivery of an impassioned speech to a crowd of one thousand state party members in Cantonsville, Ohio. It was an address carefully calculated to inflame both his supporters *and* his enemies, without stepping over the line of national disloyalty.[88] He was tried that September and presented no defense other than an eloquent, passionate closing argument to the jury. The following day, he was found guilty. At sentencing, he addressed the court, informing the judge that he "sought no mercy and . . . [pled] for no immunity." He continued to predict that the course of history, the foreseeable interaction of economic structure and human nature theorized by Marx, would ultimately prevail, as he gave his perception of the present and prophecy of the future:

> Your honor . . . I realize finally that the right must prevail. I never so clearly comprehended as now the great struggle between the powers of greed and ex-

ploitation on the one hand and upon the other the rising hosts of industrial freedom and social justice. I can see the dawn of a better day for humanity. The people are awakening. In due time they will and must come to their own.[89]

The judge "acknowledged Debs's sincerity and courage" as he sentenced him to ten years in prison, implicitly condemning him along with "those 'within our borders who would strike the sword from the hand of this nation while she is engaged in defending herself against a foreign and brutal power.'"[90]

Eugene Debs served over three years of his sentence at hard labor in federal penitentiaries in West Virginia and Atlanta before his sentence was commuted by President Harding in 1923. In his late sixties when incarcerated, with his health already largely spent for his cause, Debs died in 1926. Notwithstanding his decades of effort, his skilled rhetoric, and his dogged persistence, the American working class was not ready to heed the call to revolution by Debs and his numerous socialist core actor contemporaries.

That many millions listened to his call and that a great many of those chose to act in repsonse, is, in the context of early twentieth century America, powerful evidence of two things: first, that authenticity is a prerequisite to moral suasion; second, that authentic action, even when accompanied by extraordinary will and rhetorical skill, lacks the full human content necessary to overcome power, whether supported by individualism or some variant of communal conformity—or both, as in America.

NOTES

1. Nick Salvatore, *Eugene V. Debs: Citizen and Socialist* (Urbana: University of Illinois Press, 1982), 292. Taken from his spring, 1918 speech in Canton, Ohio, which led to his arrest on federal charges of sedition soon thereafter.

2. Jane Addams, *Peace and Bread in Time of War* (New York: MacMillan Co., 1922), 141.

3. McWilliams, 380.

4. Anne Fior Scott, introduction, Jane Addams, *Democracy and Social Ethics*, ed. Anne Fior Scott (Cambridge, MA: Belknap-Harvard University Press, 1964), xxxiv.

5. Salvatore, 9–10.

6. McAlister Coleman, *Eugene V. Debs: A Man Unafraid* (New York: Greenberg, 1930; Ann Arbor, MI: University Microfilms, Inc., 1966), 4. The French had traded and settled along the river networks of Ohio and Indiana well prior to the Revolution and the American push westward.

7. Salvatore, 17–18; Coleman, 13–17.

8. Salvatore, 19–20.

9. H. Wayne Morgan, *Eugene V. Debs: Socialist for President* (Syracuse: Syracuse University Press, 1962,) 3–4; Salvatore, 26.

10. Salvatore, 27.

11. Salvatore, 28; 31.

12. Stephen Skowronek, *Building a New American State: The Expansion of National Administrative Capacities, 1877–1920* (Cambridge, UK: Cambridge University Press, 1982), 87. Skowronek attributes the widespread state enactment of legislation creating the National Guard and the passage of federal funding to states for this purpose to the poor training and questionable loyalty of state militia troops called to "restore order" and defend against during the 1877 strike. He also blames the establishment-stoked fear of immigrant radicals and anarchists that emerged during this era (98–105).

13. Salvatore, 19; 36.

14. Salvatore, 48. Italics in original.

15. John C. Farrell, *Beloved Lady: A History of Jane Addams Ideas on Reform and Peace* (Baltimore: Johns Hopkins Press, 1967), 27.

16. James Weber Linn, *Jane Addams: A Biography* (New York: D. Appleton-Century Co., 1935), 13–17. Linn, a nephew of Addams, wrote an admittedly partisan account of her life; however, he also had extensive access to her papers and wrote most of his account while Addams was alive. He claims that she reviewed and commented on the first eight chapters. Linn, vii–viii; Farrell, 20.

17. Gioia Diliberto, *A Useful Woman: The Early Life of Jane Addams* (New York: Lisa Drew/Scribner, 1999), 82.

18. Farrell, 29.

19. Farrell, 34–35.

20. Linn, 65. Quote attributed to Addams but not referenced.

21. Diliberto, 98.

22. Diliberto, 105–6; Linn, 71–74; Scott, intro., xvi.

23. Linn, 73. Italics in original.

24. Diliberto, 126–27.

25. Diliberto, 130–31. Attributed to Gertrude Himmelfarb, *Poverty and Compassion: The Moral Imagination of the Victorians* (New York: Knopf, 1991), 243.

26. Farrell, 46.

27. Diliberto, 130.

28. Diliberto, 151. According to Linn, in 1889, seventy percent of Chicago's inhabitants were foreign born (100).

29. Levine, 40. Italics in original. Hull House was the third settlement house in America. The first two were established in New York City in 1886 and early 1889.

30. Diliberto, 131.

31. Gandhi, *An Autobiography.*

32. Both Levine and Diliberto's biographies contain thorough accounts of the early accomplishments, many of which were models for later nationwide reform, of Addams and the other Hull House activists.

33. Harold W. Currie, *Eugene V. Debs* (Boston: Twayne Publishers, 1976), 23–24.

34. Currie, 25; Salvatore, 115.

35. Salvatore, 125. He notes that this compared with a total membership of 90,000 in all of the brotherhood craft and trade unions.

36. Coleman, 111–12. Attributed but no source given.

37. Salvatore, 123.

38. By 1894, Debs was regarded as a highly effective, therefore dangerous, labor leader in Washington, Chicago, and New York. Debs and the ARU were reluctantly caught up in the strike against Pullman, a Chicago-based manufacturer of sleeping car and other rail coaches. The strike began as a spontaneous walk-out to by Pullman workers to protest the firing of three from a larger employee-appointed committee who had presented a grievance petition to Pullman's management. At the time the ARU, under Debs's leadership, was assisting local, nonmember efforts to organize the Pullman plant. Nick Salvatore, in his extensive account of the events leading to the nationwide boycott by the ARU of all trains pulling Pullman sleeping cars and the subsequent crushing of the union, concludes that Pullman, and the major railroad corporations more generally, welcomed the strike, seeing it as an opportunity to eliminate the threat posed by an industry-wide labor union. As Salvatore observes, "The federal government, in the persons of Grover Cleveland, [Attorney General] Richard Olney, and the ubiquitous Walter Q. Gresham, . . . Secretary of State, was hardly neutral." Salvatore, 131. With palpable irony, Olney, a thirty-five year veteran of corporate legal service to railroads, secured an indictment of Debs and the entire ARU executive Board for conspiracy to violate the Sherman Anti-Trust Act of 1890. In a concurrent civil action, the ARU leaders were also enjoined from essentially all union activity. It was for violating the injunction that Debs was found in contempt and sentenced to six months. Cleveland also dispatched federal troops to Chicago on July 4th, against the wishes of the Mayor and Governor, authorizing their deployment to insure the uninterrupted flow of the mail and interstate commerce (127–35).

39. Currie, 25.

40. Currie, 25–26. Debs's quotes are from editorial entitled "Pullman" cited by Currie as follows: *The Locomotive Fireman*, 11 (1887): 8–9.

41. Skocpol, 328–40. She confirms that Addams was right in her assessment that there were many young, educated women like herself who were seeking outlets to do something useful for their society and polity. In 1880, she notes, "some 40,000 women constituted a third of enrollees . . . in all institutions of higher learning" (341).

42. Farrell, 73; Levine, 161.

43. Diliberto, 197–99.

44. Linn, 165, summarizing Addams's argument in Addams, "Trade Unions and Public Duty," *American Journal of Sociology*, IV (1899): 448–62.

45. Addams, *Democracy and Social Ethics*, Chap. 5, "Industrial Amelioration."

46. Diliberto, 207–8; Linn, 165–66.

47. Jane Addams, "A Modern Lear," *The Social Thought of Jane Addams*, ed. Christopher Lasch (Indianapolis: Bobbs-Merrill Co., Inc., 1965).

48. Linn, 167.

49. Christopher Lasch, ed., 106. Debs corresponded with Lloyd from at least 1893 on. In a letter to Lloyd written from jail in Chicago in July 1894, Debs, speaking for himself and his jailed colleagues, praised Lloyd, stating "We are not unmindful that

your great heart throbs in unison with every movement that has for its purpose the rejuvenation of men." *Letters of Eugene V. Debs*, ed. J. Robert Constantine, vol. 1 (Urbana: University of Illinois Press, 1990), 73–74. Addams's essay, although publicly presented to at least three audiences, was not published until 1912. According to Christopher Lasch (Addams, Lasch, ed., 106), she followed Lloyd's advice in 1895 not even to attempt to have it published; however, both Linn (167) and Diliberto (212) claim that she made several unsuccessful efforts to do so, including the *Atlantic Monthly*.

50. Diliberto, 211.

51. Addams, "A Modern Lear," in Lasch, ed., 111.

52. Addams, "A Modern Lear," in Lasch, ed., 117.

53. Addams, "A Modern Lear," in Lasch, ed., 107. Emphasis added.

54. Many of the women who lived and worked with Jane Addams at Hull House were, like Addams, powerful social and political actors in their own right. The following are only the first "generation": Julia Lathrop—child and women's labor advocate, and first Director of the U.S. Children's Bureau in the Department of Labor; Florence Kelley—pioneer child labor investigator, Chief Factory Inspector in Illinois, and long time head of the National Consumer's Union; Alice Hamilton—industrial illness researcher and industrial medicine pioneer; Grace and Edith Abbott—distinguished pioneers in social work and social worker education. Levine, 47–53. The above is only suggestive of the range and extent of their activism. In her biography of two further Hull House residents, sisters Grace and Edith Abbott, biographer Lela B. Costin illustrates this well: "Before their careers had ended, the Abbott sisters had turned their energies . . . to a wide range of social and political issues—woman suffrage, the rights of women in industry, . . . child labor, . . . international traffic in women for . . . prostitution, the immigrant 'problem,' tenement housing, delinquency, prison reform, the peace movement, [and] the right of women to safety in child-bearing." Lela B. Costin, *Two Sisters for Social Justice: A Biography of Grace and Edith Abbott* (Urbana: University of Illinois Press, 1983), vii.

55. Addams, *Democracy and Social Ethics*, 4–5.

56. Addams, *Democracy and Social Ethics*, 5.

57. Addams, *Democracy and Social Ethics*, 5.

58. Addams, *Democracy and Social Ethics*, 5–6. Emphasis added.

59. Farrell, 17.

60. Jane Addams, *Newer Ideals of Peace*, ed. Richard T. Ely (New York: MacMillan Co., 1907), 3–7.

61. Addams, *Newer Ideals of Peace*, 26–27.

62. Addams, *Newer Ideals of Peace*, 24. In part she is quoting from philosopher William James.

63. Addams, *Newer Ideals of Peace*, 24–25. As she wrote these words, she had in mind an international effort, then underway, involving the United States, France, Germany, Italy, and England to rid the world of tuberculosis, as well as several other efforts where new institutions of cross-national cooperation were being developed to study, research, share knowledge and develop projects to improve living conditions and public health (25–26).

64. Levine, 194.

65. Addams was, in fact uncomfortable with Roosevelt, particularly his foreign policy, his opposition to the seating of Southern Negro Delegates, and his paternalistic dismissal in 1908 of her pacifist views in *Newer Ideals of Peace*. Her seconding speech at the Progressive Party convention was carefully crafted to show as much support "on the platform and as little on the candidate as common courtesy would permit." Levine, 188–91.

66. Farrell, 151. The words are attributed to Addams as part of her keynote address to the first convening of the Woman's Peace Party in Washington, D.C., in January 1915.

67. Farrell, 151–52; Levine, 203–204.

68. Farrell, 153–54. The English government refused to allow its 180 delegates to attend and held up the ship carrying the American delegation to Holland, for several days. There were also no delegates permitted to attend from either France or Russia. Linn, 302.

69. Levine, 220.

70. Levine, 220–21.

71. Levine, 221.

72. Linn, 331.

73. Farrell, 19; 171–73.

74. Addams, *Democracy and Social Ethics*, 273–74.

75. Linn, 335–36.

76. Addams, *Peace and Bread in Time of War*, 82–83.

77. Levine, 238.

78. Levine, 240–41.

79. Eugene V. Debs, letter to father, 14 January 1895; and letter to parents, 8 January 1895, *Letters of Eugene V. Debs*, Constantine, ed., I: 81–82.

80. Salvatore, 220. Chapter title.

81. Currie, 103–10; Ronald Radosh, ed., *Great Lives Observed: Debs* (Englewood Cliffs, NJ: Prentice-Hall, 1971), 60–65.

82. "The Negro in the Class Struggle," *International Socialist Review*, November, 1903, in Radosh, ed., 61.

83. Salvatore, 190; 221; 264.

84. Eugene V. Debs, "Danger Ahead," *International Socialist Review* (Jan. 1911), in Radosh, ed., 53.

85. Salvatore, 287–88.

86. Currie, 86. Attributed by Currie (note 9) to a speech by Debs dated or delivered on September 11, 1915, entitled "When I Fight."

87. Salvatore, 292. Quoting Debs, in part, from his famous speech at Cantonsville, Ohio, on June 16, 1918. See Radosh, ed., 71.

88. Salvatore, 291–94. There was little, if anything, seditious in the speech from a legal perspective. A review by the Attorney General and his senior staff supported this conclusion; however, the final decision as to whether to seek an indictment was left to the U.S. Attorney in Cleveland, who immediately convened a grand jury and obtained what he sought. 294.

89. Debs, Radosh, ed., 83–84.

90. Salvatore, 296.

Chapter Six

Some Contemporary Actors

If we are to understand the nature, capacity, and effect of core actors in our midst, it is helpful, as earlier argued, to first look back at earlier periods of social and political reform, to achievements that conform to our fundamental moral outlook and priorities in the present, and to the actors associated with such accomplishments. Having endeavored to do so, we are now more prepared to identify such actors in the present, to consider the nature and potential impact of their action, and to determine what, if anything, this reveals concerning our own moral nature.

The relative ease of understanding our actual and potential individual, social, and political nature by recourse to history should not, however, be assumed. To do so requires that we imaginatively enter the lives, past circumstances, and understandings of others who are no longer available to witness or interview. Our task is to convert them from abstractions—words and visual images—into breathing actors or agents who, like us, were influenced by the results of past action, who in turn acted in ways that influenced their time and ours.[1]

This is a difficult task for many since we are commonly taught to regard imagination as a false conscious or prerational path to ignorance—a reverie that leads only to unicorns—and our capacity to imagine is therefore often woefully undeveloped. Moreover, our effort to understand ourselves with the assistance of the past inevitably requires that we contend with narrative myth-making and scholarly bias that either artificially enhances or diminishes human accomplishment, often omitting entire sets of actors and frequently mis-replicating the stage on which they performed.

Finally there is the problem of our own ontological perspective. If, for example, we are of the view that human nature is somehow fixed, predetermined, and essentially static, or that it is determined *and* dependent upon

131

structures and forces that reflect our nature but that are beyond our control, then our history is only useful as a tactical manual or as a developmental chronology of a species subgroup. If history is to offer us inspiration, it must offer evidence of individual and socialized moral learning and growth at the original instance of identifiable human actors. Fortunately, to the extent that we can shed our liberal republican and communitarian blinders and discern the full range of our own moral nature, the other distortions can be overcome and we can discover a past that offers hope through our genuine enlightenment in the present.

The task of discovering inspiration and hope in the present—of identifying core actors and understanding their actual and potential role in our lives—is much more difficult. In addition to the personal moral discomfort that their words and deeds so often impart, there are the following factors to contend with:

1. Our still-growing attraction to rational methodology, which limits our comprehension and discussion of nonelite individual and group action to aggregated, quantifiable, highly qualified facts and equally qualified mid-level structural-behavioral models and theories that are mildly predictive, at best[2];
2. Our concept-of-the-year social and political, moral, and ethical discourse by privatized observers that so largely comprises the commercial "marketplace of ideas" for intellectual consumers, and offers only a short-lived tonic of clever surface analysis for their malaise[3];
3. The ongoing political and rabidly corporate, market-driven closure of democratic informational space, exemplified by the imposition of scant, often misleading, media coverage of authentic moral activism unless accompanied by violence or expressive anarchistic disruption, together with an almost virtual guarantee of public anonymity ensured by the group characterization of core actors; and
4. Our pervasive Enlightenment-informed, postmodern-enhanced, systemically structured social, political, and ontological isolation from authentic engagement with one another, even as we rationally acknowledge, with singular cultural reluctance and resigned irony, our increasing instrumental interdependence and mass conformity.

Accordingly, it has never been easier to overlook, mischaracterize, or dismiss core actors, or to perceive them as ineffectively scattered here and there. They continue to work among us, however, and retain the capacity to potentially persuade and include us, living and acting as they do, authentically at all levels of our social and political landscape. They are lacking only in ready opportunities meet with us intimately, authentically, face-to-face, where we are neither inclined nor required to make the first effort to do so.

IN THE TRADITION OF STANTON AND ADDAMS

At age eighty when interviewed, Frances Crowe is one of the oldest and likely the best known peace and social justice activists in the Pioneer Valley or five-college region of Western Massachusetts. The range and duration of her activism—of most of her adult life—is suggested by her most recent, ongoing effort "to get her life in a manageable shape."[4] Although much earlier like efforts had led her to avoid doing "much international work," she has traveled and acted extensively in this country, in the course of which she has "met people, and you network, and [attended] national meetings." She neglects to mention that she made dozens of these trips to engage in nonviolent protests. Frequently, these have included intentional acts of civil disobedience, many of which led to her arrest. In an article published several months earlier, covering her trial with five others for her most recent civilly disobedient act at the Raytheon defense plant in Andover, Massachusetts, the journalist overheard her hosts at a pot luck supper on the night before her hearing asking Crowe if she was "afraid of going to prison." "Well," she replied, "I have been in jail a number of times; to be honest, I've stopped counting."[5]

At this point in her life, the engagingly direct, unfailingly polite, physically diminutive Crowe described something of her philosophy as she reviewed her efforts to cut back. "I just [have always] felt, I'm trying to live simply so that others may simply live." Referring to her decades-long work with the American Friends Service Committee (AFSC), a Quaker-founded organization established in 1917 "as a practical expression of the philosophy of William James, . . . [and] a prototype of the later Civilian Conservation Corps and Peace Corps," she mentions the changes she has made since "retiring" as director of that group in 1994[6]:

> [N]ow that I'm retired from the AFSC, I've picked up some pieces from the AFSC office . . . focusing on economic justice and youth empowerment. But I also feel strongly about this situation in Iraq—lifting the sanctions—and started a weekly vigil and [helped form] a local committee to look at the sanctions and stop the bombing. . . . And then, when we were bombing Yugoslavia, we included [that] in our campaign. And I'm active in another group I started, the Nuclear Weapons Abolition Task Force. . . . I'm a member of the Atlantic Life Community, which is the east coast people who are working . . . resisting nuclear weapons. So, those are the things that I really focus on now.

Judging from the phone calls during her interview, the far from museum-like appearance of her basement office (the former location of the AFSC regional office in Western Massachusetts), and the number of times that her name was mentioned in other interviews, though Frances Crowe may, like Stanton and Addams before her, have slowed down in her later years, morally informed action continues for her to be fully a part of life itself.

Her activism began at least as early as high school in Carthage, Missouri, when she became upset that girls couldn't take physical education, and started a petition drive that succeeded in getting the matter considered by the school board.[7] She recalled being born and raised in that town as part of a large, middle class family (four children), in which she experienced love, relationship, mutual support, and interdependence. She credits her parents for furnishing her with a good "moral education," and for imparting to her and her sisters a sense of their competence to act, "always saying [to them] you can do something with your life. . . . Life is what you make of it."

Asked to further explain the origins of her activism, she displayed only a trace of impatience as she observed: "You don't just sit down and decide what you are going to be. We get sort of propelled along." Evidencing her understanding of expanding moral awareness, she continued: "and if we live good, lengthy, thoughtful, conscious lives, that's what happens." In her case, the more generic early propulsion in that direction was a combination of full-blown adventuresome youthfulness and her strong desire to leave Carthage, which she saw then (and now) as a conservative community, "with a lot of racism and classism. I think that really bothered me a lot . . . you know, really wanting to get out . . . and get to know some very interesting people . . . who aren't living on who their Grandparents were." The latter reason further suggests the influence of an already expanding, inclusive world-view.

After graduating from Syracuse University where she majored in psychology, she moved to Columbia, Missouri, to do student personnel work at Stephens College. At about this time, the attack on Pearl Harbor spurred her to action. She left Stephens, feeling that "I just had to get out of there and get involved in the war effort in some way. After considering the military and other service options, "I chose [the] war industry." She took a special summer course offered by Mount Holyoke College "in engineering science war management training," and "ended up at Bell Laboratories."

Now living in New York City, she was also exposed to "new ideas" from reading a local progressive newspaper, and from living at International House, a well known group residence, and doing part-time graduate work at Columbia.

And then I switched from Columbia to [evening classes] at the Hunter School for Social Research, and was getting lots of ideas, so that, by the end of the war,

I was developing a lot of anti-war feeling, feeling that war was not the answer and that we had to figure out something else.

Married and living in New Orleans toward the end of the war, while her husband served as an Army Medical Corps surgeon aboard a ship whose home port was in that city, she recalls with utter clarity the moment when she learned that America had dropped a nuclear bomb on Hiroshima, an event that strengthened her predilection toward nonviolence into a strong conviction:

Tom [her recently deceased husband] was . . . on a ship that went between Panama and New Orleans. He heard a lot about the bomb from his contacts, so we sort of knew what it was, and he was planning to go into radiology, so he was very interested in that whole field. So we knew a little bit, but my immediate feeling was . . . I remember I was ironing a placemat when I heard on the news that we had dropped this bomb, and early reports said that maybe a hundred thousand people had died. I just thought . . . [long pause].

She recalled with gentle, self-deprecating humor her naïveté in reaction to that news, and her determination that she must immediately do something about it:

[A]nd I went out looking for the peace center [laughing] . . . in New Orleans! . . . I did find a used bookstore. . . . I asked the man if he had any books on the peace movement, and he wisely sent me to Tolstoy's writings. So I started reading about nonviolence.[8]

While living in Rochester, New York, after the war, Crowe and her husband were exposed to Quakerism through friends. Shortly thereafter, around 1951, they moved to the Pioneer Valley so that their son, second of their three children, could attend the Clark School for the Deaf in Northampton. They decided to seek out a Friends' meeting in the area and became active members.[9] It was this decision, motivated by a combination of spiritual need, an evolving, quickening concern over issues of peace and social justice, and the simple human desire for local friendship that facilitated her transition into what would later become a support network for her fulltime activism.

During the 1950s, the living and learning process continued for Crowe and her husband, as they gradually became more morally informed and active. By the early 1960s, judging by the actions each took, they had incorporated activism into their respective life routines. The primary social and political issue for Crowe, now in her early forties, and her husband continued to be the bomb, in particular the recently discovered concern over nuclear atmospheric testing and its effects on human health. Her husband became an early member of

Physicians for Social Responsibility (PSR), a group founded by several nationally prominent physicians in 1961 to act on this and related nuclear concerns, and organized a local chapter in the valley.[10]

Searching for a means to work on the same issue, Crowe learned through
another mother and Quaker friend about the still-active Women's International League for Peace and Freedom (WILPF), which, as previously noted,
Jane Addams had been instrumental in founding and leading two generations
earlier. In the tradition of Addams and Stanton before her, Crowe and her
friend decided to start a local chapter of WILPF by inviting seventy-five
women to come to her house for tea. Looking back at that moment, she recalled: "Anyway, we started—and [all] seventy-five people came. . . . It was
really incredible! So we started a very active chapter here. It was the fastest
growing chapter . . . in the country. We did all kinds of wonderful things."

Shortly thereafter, she helped organize a local chapter of the Committee for
a SANE Nuclear Policy, a national organization established by long-time *Sat-
urday Review* editor and noted social philosopher, Norman Cousins, and others to address the wider issues of nuclear weapons and to call for disarmament. However, when SANE's steering committee decided to adopt the
government-fostered policy of requiring its members to sign statements declaring that they were not communists, "we decided, you know, we weren't
going to work with them anymore."

As was somewhat the case with each of the four historical actors, Crowe has
remained most persistently active in her first cause, the effort to ban the use of
nuclear weapons and to eliminate the weapons themselves. Never content with
the mere communication of her moral stance to others, she has acted repeatedly, speaking out, organizing, writing, demonstrating, and getting arrested to
call attention to this fundamental moral issue, to inform and persuade others to
see for themselves the truths that underlie her view.

Reminiscent of Jane Addams, new learning from events, extensive contacts
and relationships with others, and further experiences have led Crowe to oppose war much more broadly. In common with many of us, Vietnam was another watershed event in her life. William Norris, a local long-time lawyer-
activist, was a fledgling attorney when he first met her in 1967. Crowe had
decided on draft counseling as a local strategy, part of a national effort just
then getting underway. Hoping to obtain legal expertise for the cause, she publicized "an open invitation to all lawyers in Hampshire and Franklin Counties
to meet First Church in Amherst to discuss draft counseling for young people
opposed to the Vietnam War. I was the only attorney to show up."[11]

Crowe enlisted Norris to help with draft counseling and set up an office and
meeting place in the basement of her home, conveniently located, as mentioned, in the "five colleges" region. Prior to doing so, she attended a week-

long training course in draft counseling at the Philadelphia headquarters of the Central Committee for Conscientious Objectors, a Quaker-affiliated organization like the AFSC, having its roots in the immediate post-World War II era.[12] Its policy called for potential draftees to be counseled individually and confidentially, in the rights tradition of American liberalism. Again reminiscent of Addams, Crowe recalled,

> I had always thought that this one-on-one thing was wrong . . . that you can best find yourself in the group process. . . . I could tell them about the draft law, but the personal decision he had to make—and it was "he's"—about who he was, and where he was going, and why . . . had to be done in a group setting.

For the next few years the Crowe's house, even by their usual standards, was a busy place. She and her volunteer staff worked hard and creatively, going repeatedly to the University of Massachusetts, Hampshire and Amherst College campuses, and elsewhere, throughout the valley and Western Massachusetts to both recruit students and run workshops. They reached out to inform young men about the war, to encourage them to reflect and consider their options, and to offer, in a sea of apparent overwhelming conformity, the refuge and support of a small group community that she had created at her home. Crowe herself recalls traveling the main road between Amherst and Northampton, picking up young male hitchhikers. "They all had the draft on their minds." In one year, she proudly recounts "we had 1,776 visits in this office."

In all, approximately one hundred and fifty young men applied for conscientious objector status. "As far as I know, no one was denied." In the process, in response to a petition from her neighbors, the city council ordered "no parking" signs posted along her upper middle class cul-de-sac street. "That's right," she wryly remembers, "They had too many kids with motorcycles and long hair coming in here."

LEARNING AND ADAPTING

Frances Crowe and her home office remained at the center of peace and social justice activism in the region for the next two decades. Following the pattern of many couples of their generation and circumstance, her husband, although continuing his work with PSR, performed a largely supportive role, providing the family's economic means that allowed Crowe to devote herself to the position she had grown into, that of a core social and political actor.

As she became aware, informed, and active on an increasing number of issues of national and global concern, matters where she concluded that her society and state were ignorant, in the wrong, or at least could do much better, she drew in part from her experience with anti-draft activism to develop a strategy to reach and involve more people. Now running the regional AFSC office from her home, she sought out and encouraged existing and new activist colleagues to form and join specialized, long-term and ad hoc "working groups" utilizing the administrative, informational, and other support she could offer through AFSC and otherwise. Starting with nuclear energy and disarmament, she helped to form similar groups and, whenever possible, to connect them with others to form coalitions and task forces. Among the efforts mounted in this manner were those to end apartheid, to change American policy in Central America, the Balkans, Iraq, and the Middle East, address the devastating effects of economic globalization, and act on other issues of national and world-wide import. Commenting on the change, she observed:

> [T]hey met separately and sometimes, you know, I was more or less involved. . . . When I got busy, I didn't go to all their meetings, but I knew what was going on, and I could give them information that came from Philadelphia and other avenues. So [now] we always work this way, as a collective within the group.

Although a great deal of what kept her busy led to her frequent arrests, most of it came from other forms of her prodigious activism. In the 1970s and 1980s, for example she worked extensively with her AFSC-affiliated local Disarmament Working Group and others in the Western Massachusetts First Congressional District, then represented by a nationally powerful long-term Republican, Silvio O. Conte.[13] She helped organize and coordinate drives to place four different nonbinding questions on local ballots in the district, the best known of which was the "nuclear freeze" initiative undertaken in 1979. In another such effort, a resolution calling on the Massachusetts congressional delegation to vote against funding for the Reagan administration's Star Wars program, they prevailed in a majority of towns in Berkshire County, including Pittsfield, Conte's hometown.

Crowe had developed somewhat of a relationship of mutual respect with Conte. Her persistence and overall authenticity in her dealings with him—including a well-publicized sit-in at his Holyoke office several years earlier after his repeated unwillingness to meet with her group to discuss American policy in El Salvador—likely helped to foster this relationship. According to her clearly relished story involving the Star Wars campaign, she had arranged a small group meeting with him at his Holyoke office, bringing along a map of Berkshire County that she had garnished with "gold stars" to graphically depict the number and location of cities and towns whose voters had supported the question. Conte, surprised (and quite possibly pleased) by the compiled evidence that so many constituents were opposed to the Reagan policy, voted against the appropriation and helped to kill funding for the program from his influential position as a ranking minority member on the House Appropriations Committee. About a year later, when Crowe met with him on other concerns, "he really leveled with me":

> "You'll never know what that vote on Star Wars cost me," he said. "I'm glad I did it, but these things are not free. Just last month I was invited by President Reagan down to [New York City] . . . and they were honoring [the Centennial] of the Statue of Liberty, and they [the administration] had a destroyer in New York harbor." Reagan was on [the battleship] and he [Conte] had been invited on board with his family on Fourth of July evening to see the fireworks. So he got his children, his grand children, his mother . . . and they all got down there on the gangplank to go out, and they were told that their tickets were no longer honored.

Conte concluded, as Crowe undoubtedly has many times over her forty plus years of activism—much of it highly unpopular—"'That's what happens when you do the right thing.'" One can imagine her core actor forebears both informing and echoing the same sentiment, often from positions much more difficult to endure.

Core actors, like the rest of us, are imperfect models of what they would like to be. In response to a question of whether she had ever experienced the kind of moral political dilemma posed by Michael Walzer in his essay "Political Action: The Problem of Dirty Hands,"[14] Crowe recalled two instances where she and others who shared her beliefs "seized the moment," using tactics that gave her what has become, in our time, a frustratingly rare opportunity to express her views to a larger public audience. In one, a well publicized speech at Smith College, in 1979, to be given by a "high government official . . . involved in the military aid program in El Salvador . . ." she recalled: "I was working with the Central American working group and they wanted very much to stop that speaker." Concerned over a shift in U.S. policy away from democratic reform to leftist suppression in the wake of Somoza's overthrow by the Sandinistas in neighboring Nicaragua,[15] the group worked hard for several days in an unsuccessful effort to get the college to rescind the invitation, seeing it as yet another attempt at official disinformation:

> They worked out this plan. They had all of these slides that they wanted to show about what was really happening in El Salvador, and [wanted] someone who would stand up and speak. So the plan was, they went in [into the hall] and I was there helping them leaflet. . . . Just before he was to speak, they . . . turned out the lights . . . turned on the projector—it was my slide projector—[and] projected the slides. They got up on the stage [and] they took over. And I started talking about what was really going on in the slides. Well, it really broke up the [planned] meeting of course. I mean, people really listened to what [we] had to say. So the speaker didn't get to speak at all.

Crowe's democratic discomfort—still implicit in her above selection of personal nouns—and her concern over the likely harmful effect that such tactics would have on her ability to reach and authentically persuade an even broader audience were outweighed in this instance by her moral outrage and pragmatism. She acted in order to enlarge the public space available to actors with unpopular views, to surmount the overwhelming absence of authentic debate, and to overcome both the official intentional withholding of vital democratic information and the powerful dissemination of misinformation and outright lies when official silence is pierced or deemed inadequate.

VARIED BACKGROUNDS, TALENTS, AND FORMS OF PERSUASION

As suggested in the first chapter, morally informed core actors come from the same variety of life circumstances as the rest of us. Some, like Frances Crowe, are blessed with a relative abundance of favorable circumstances of birth, comfort, and moral nurture through to adulthood. Others are more rudely introduced to life. As a result of this diversity of circumstance, early received experience, and predisposition they may enter adulthood more immediately aware of what life should not be, which itself implies that they have somehow acquired a foundation of affirmative knowledge as well.

Those core actors who have been abruptly, directly awakened to social and political injustice at a point in their lives where strong passions are easy to arouse and more difficult to constrain can be powerful nonconformists. Further, even when they are informed by a moral tradition that is ideally inclusive and eschews violence, their early activism, at least, is also likely to be more impatient, less tolerant, more agonistic, and more intense.

Living the Social Gospel

Donna S. is a forceful example. For the first eleven years of her life, she was nurtured and sheltered by her parents, a "very extended family, lots of security, safety, no money, but we [she and her two siblings] didn't even know it." In addition to family, much of their life routine was centered in the German-American community of Kingston, New York, a small city located an hour's drive north of Manhattan, and its fundamentalist Lutheran church, part of the Missouri Synod.

The abrupt transition in her life was caused by a combination of economically structured self-interest and the desire of her father to better provide for his family. Repeating a story that she was obviously aware had strongly influenced her subsequent life course, she continued:

> My father swept the floor in one of the garment factories there. My mother worked in a sausage factory. We were happy until he decided to move up. That was when unions were starting to come in, the whole story about why [clothing manufacturers] left the Northeast and went south. . . .

Her father was offered a job training low-wage, mostly African American female workers to perform machine sewing piecework at a newly opened location in the South. He was likely unaware that his employers did not intend to keep him in one location for long. Conscious of the Faustian bargain that her father made, and remade, with his employers, she continued:

> There's just no question that I am the educated and well-off person that I am today because he went into management. But we moved every year . . . from the time I was eleven until . . . I went to college. He trained black women to run sewing machines throughout the South. He was fired four times . . . and he would go crawling back . . . so that's why we kept on moving. They basically just used him to do this training and then would move him on. . . . Then, when he was sixty, they just fired him so they wouldn't have to pay his pension. So, I'm [from] a family that sort of went kicking and screaming into the middle class, but at tremendous cost—costs of joy, cost in security.

Confrontation as Persuasion

Experiencing the deterioration of her father and family triggered her initial foray into activism. Now married to a Jew, she recalls with irony her adolescent, visceral hatred, focused on the Jewish owners of the company for which her father worked and suffered his "utter humiliation":

> I went when I was seventeen to their corporate headquarters in Philadelphia and walked in and threw things at the guy, and said "you know what you're doing to me and my family and why!" . . . [At the time] I was not tutored. I was just angry because I was a fundamentalist kid who really didn't think you should do this to people.

It is impossible to determine if this, Donna's first direct, confrontational action, was at all persuasive. Perhaps it was, on an individual level, over time. It was, in any event, undeniably authentic.

According to Donna, her father died "a destroyed, angry, 'Archie Bunker' Republican. He could never understand his complicity. . . . I didn't get it for a long time either." Her experience during adolescence also provided much of the knowledge and motive strength of her activism. "I know what economic evil is from a very first-hand experience, and I know it's very wide-spread and pernicious. So there is a lot of payback in what I do." This strikes one as a surprisingly candid self-assessment from someone who has engaged in much of her activism since her ordainment as a clergywoman.

Her decision to become—and remain—a minister suggests that there is much more to her radicalism than experience-informed anger. For one thing, she also credits "great mentors, good timing, [and] my faith in God." Among her mentors she includes her chaplain at Gettysburg College, the small Lutheran-founded school she attended, who "very slowly, took me through [the process of] understanding." The timing she refers to was a combination of what she sees as her good fortune to have gone to college in the mid- and late 1960s, yet having gone to a school that was relatively detached from the social and political upheavals that moved like storm surges across most ur-ban campuses. "If I had gone to a big school, I would have flipped out. I would have been a casualty because I was so angry and unformed, but in-stead I had this extraordinary experience." She would later accept his invi-tation to work with him as an associate chaplain at Yale, and they remain close friends today.

Learning from Core Actors

In 1970 she entered theological school at the University of Chicago, thanks in part to a full scholarship from her childhood Lutheran Synod. In short or-der, she was exposed to the burgeoning ideas and movements from which she had been somewhat isolated while at Gettysburg. Soon after arriving, she met her second major mentor, noted urban social and political activist Saul Alinsky.[16] Indirectly acknowledging his influence on her, she ob-served:

> If I had met him while I was still being a fundamentalist Lutheran about the war in Vietnam and about civil rights—you know, "as soon as we tell them it's wrong, they'll stop it" . . . I had no conception of power, and when I met Alin-sky and learned [from him] about power, that, I think, made me capable of the long haul.

In the process of gaining new insights that included not only a broader so-cial analysis of capitalism, but also a perspective informed by rapidly emerg-ing feminist thought, Donna also developed her unusual capacity to inform and lead others in social and political action and, in the process, to instigate change. The Chicago Divinity School was her first target for reform. During her first year of classes, she recalls:

I became so impressed with what Alinsky was saying and so unimpressed with what the professors were saying. . . . So I basically organized the students [she was the only woman in her class] not to go to the divinity school [but instead] to go down to the Woodlawn Organization [an African American grassroots political organization organized by Alinsky several years earlier and located in a dense, poor area near her campus]. . . . So basically we did an action on the University and took our whole divinity schoolwork at Woodlawn, and made the professors come to Woodlawn to teach us.

Confronted with their moral dilemma—the same one that Protestant social gospel clergy had confronted their institutions with at the outset of the Progressive Era—the faculty responded positively:

[T]he professors came and taught us there, and Alinsky taught us, and we just became his band. I mean, it was incredible. We lived there, took our classes there, we took the professors around, even to places that we didn't know ourselves, and I just had my mind blown. Just blown. . . . So, for the whole time I was there, I just really saw what was happening . . . *I could never really look at the world the same again.*

Without elaboration, Donna further explained that the University also "came around," awarding her and her fellow activist classmates their degrees on schedule. In the interim, she and several student colleagues became involved with the Urban Institute, another Chicago-based offshoot of Alinsky's work.[17] In the course of performing her requisite internships at suburban white churches, she "insisted" on taking teenagers on "urban plunges," a technique that she learned at the Institute. "Basically [we would] take twenty or thirty white kids" into a poor neighborhood and guide them through informational meetings and a brief period of living in the setting and economics of poverty."[18] While she readily agreed to a suggestion that the plunge strategy runs the risk of denigrating those who are unable to leave when the plunge experience is over, she countered with the unavoidable dilemma of moral activists who attempt to forge reform in any context of systemic injustice:

I think we always had a lot of students who basically thought it was just so phony to go on a plunge, that it was manipulative of the poor, that it was denigrating, that it was morally suspect on so many grounds. And, if anything, it leaves you with more of a sense of the rift between rich and poor, as opposed to less. I would acknowledge every one of those really bad things . . . and say that unless you have first-hand experience of the poor, you'll never care long enough to last as an activist. You won't think it's real because it is just too easy to live in this world and never see them. . . . They are really invisible and their plight is invisible or we say it's their fault. . . .

Reflecting on her argument, one is reminded of its resonance with the experience of others. Jane Addams, for example, might never have chosen to live and work *with* the poor if she had not first been moved by the close-up sight of visceral poverty in her first, *guided* tour of East London. Further, she might not have taken and sustained broader actions on their behalf if she had not first lived in their neighborhood, or if she had not frequently returned to them after her activism had extended its reach.

Finally, as for the current isolation of the urban poor, one of the more poignant visual metaphors of that reality is captured in Jonathan Kozol's description of the government-funded painting of beautiful urban landscape murals on the side of vacant apartment buildings facing Interstate Route 95 as it passes through the South Bronx. The effect is to disguise the physical, absentee-owned ugliness of poverty that lies behind their thin veneer for the aesthetic benefit of those of us who are able to drive by.[19]

The Role of Gender

Donna's path to the ministry was further complicated by another rude awakening—this time to the institutionalized social reality of gender. After graduating she contacted her synod to inquire about ordination, only to be informed that the church that had financed her formal religious training did not ordain women. When she asked what they proposed to do with her, they suggested that she could teach. One can imagine her reaction. Her ordination committee seemed blissfully ignorant that she had grown her strength in an all-male environment at divinity school, at one point requiring her to take a career aptitude test designed for men and learning that she would make an excellent Army general.

In response, she decided to bring her denomination into the world as she was then discovering it. "So I had to organize the Lutheran Church to ordain women." Using her newly acquired organizational talent, she spent the next year doing so. She quickly learned that "there were a lot of other women around [the Missouri Synod] who were like me . . . maybe twenty or thirty [of them]." Minimizing her own efforts, she continued: "We found each other and the day they voted [at the Synod's annual meeting] that they would ordain women—by a two thirds vote—three of us were on the front page of the *Minneapolis Tribune* . . . saying 'yea us.' And the next day I said 'forget it.'" Although Donna did not say so in so many words, one suspects that she had learned something else in the process of acting to reform her church, an institution that had nurtured her in the exclusive community of her childhood. She had grown to realize—gender issues aside—that she no longer belonged.

At about the same time, as she was rapidly gaining new insights from feminism and personal experience, she briefly became nationally prominent in the movement to legalize abortion. Newly ordained in the United Church of Christ (often referred to as the Congregational Church) and active in a clergy-established network that provided information and access to abortion services, she "ended up on all the talk shows. . . . I debated all the fastidious women on the Oprah Winfrey Show and did all that stuff."

In the mid-1970s, she left Chicago, as earlier mentioned, to join her college chaplain mentor, the newly installed chaplain at Yale, where he had succeeded one of America's best known and most controversial civil rights and antiwar activists of the sixties, William Sloane Coffin.[20]

As Donna summarized it, she spent her time at Yale "taking students into the community [and] doing plunges of one kind or another. Bought a taxi company, did some economic development, had a ball. Got fired from Yale." In fuller garb, what she had done was to become involved with the Downtown Cooperative Ministries in New Haven, adding her energy and organizational skills. A conventional institutional view of undivided loyalty landed her in trouble with Bart Giamatti, then acting President of Yale.[21] She had conceived the idea of purchasing a local cab company and converting it to an employee-owned cooperative. To that end, she approached a new friend, a multi-millionaire retired businessman who had been invited to teach and live at Yale, asking him to donate the lion's share of the quarter-million dollar down payment. They agreed that if she could get some of the "well-heeled" downtown churches to invest the first fifty thousand dollars, he would "put up the rest." It worked:

> We bought the cab company, we did worker ownership, we were having a ball. Everyone looked good, even Yale . . . which is what I tried to tell Giamatti. But he didn't get it, and he said "You have violated one of the policies of Yale [private fund-raising], when you're an officer of the University. . . . You are fired" . . . . Well [the donor friend] wrote them out of his will . . . and they lost lots of money.

According to Donna, when Giamatti learned of this, he appointed her to a second three-year term as Associate Chaplain, an offer that, upon detecting the implicit quid pro quo, she characteristically refused.

If she had accepted the reappointment, with its status and potential for fame, Donna wouldn't have been invited to become the pastor of the Congregational Church in Amherst in the 1970s. She also would not have met Frances Crowe and found herself, "nine and one half months pregnant," doing the sit-in, earlier mentioned, with Frances and an area nun in Congressman Conte's Holyoke office.

Well, Frances is probably the pre-eminent activist in the valley, has been for all
these years. And you know, I've been here twice, in two different incarnations.
The first time I was here Frances and I were together every day. She did AFSC
and I was involved with the El Salvador group [Central American Working
Group], and . . . we got to know Silvio Conte on a first name basis.[22]

She recalls that at the time of their action she was married and expecting
her first son:

You know, I didn't know how to be pregnant. I was thirty-six. . . . It never occurred to me to stop doing whatever I was doing and Frances was very concerned that I figure out how to go off and have this baby, but she also needed me
for things we were doing with Conte.

Commenting on the frequent frustration from being a core actor, she continued:

[What we were trying to do] was tremendously important—you know, if regions
have anything to do with national policy, that's a good story. I always feel like I
haven't really [accomplished] anything, and I think that Frances and many of us
feel the same way. It took us two years of daily harassment of Silvio Conte and
getting literally dozens of others to do the same thing—to break through.

Action as Existential Hope

After a few vigorously active years in the Amherst-Northampton area, she
moved back to Chicago as director of the Urban Institute, the Alinsky-
founded training school for activist organizers and urban ministers. She then
moved to a church assignment in New York, ultimately returning to Western
Massachusetts in 1992 to work as regional administrator for her denomination. In the process her family grew from one to three and the nature and pace
of her action changed. She moved away from direct action, explaining "I
think I gave up being an out front leader when I had kids."

Pressed to explain further, she offered other reasons that confirmed her ongoing effort for rigorous self-honesty, an important component of reflection
and the inner counterpart of her authentic, confrontational, social, political,
and spiritual nature:

And then, there is the theological answer that I do think that I went a little crazy
trying to change the world. I became quite the idolater and much too full of myself. [I] stopped trusting God's work and trusted only my work, and I really had
to back off of that active and controlling space and [get] into an acting space. So
I've lost some of the ferocity . . . and [right now] I do what I can.

For the past few years, Donna has tried to apply the Alinsky model in her professional work in order to encourage individual pastors and church members to become more aware, better organized, and more involved in peace and social justice issues at the grassroots level. In a related vein, she helped to organize the Pioneer Valley Project, an ecumenical consortium of large and small religious organizations and nonprofit action agencies to identify and take coordinated action on issues of poverty and race in the Springfield-Holyoke area.

Near the end of the interview, Donna mentioned that her children were now getting older and, in November, she planned to travel to the School of the Americas at Ft. Benning, Georgia, to join the years-long protest vigil there and, possibly, to get arrested.[23] At the same time, however, she expressed little confidence that what she and "all the good people . . . I've partnered with" had done had made any real difference. At that moment, however, the personal grit that drives core actors when inspiration fails emerged.

As the interview ended she stated that she had no plans to give up, even in the face of her assessment of the even greater challenges of our current situation. "And now, the globalization stuff that is going on, it's unbelievable. What happened to my family, instead of happening less, is simply being enlarged. It's just enormous." Without morally informed initiators—people such as herself acting at all levels of society—however, she sees no hope at all. Commenting further, she spoke implicitly of her struggle to gain a long-term perspective, while searching for new forms of authentic action to deal with what she perceives as a massive, mounting crisis: "[I]f anything, we need to be doing more radical things. I would not leave you with the lovely credentials that I have. I mean, I have wonderful credentials and I'm not ashamed of what I've done, but it hasn't changed very much." It is clear, however, from examining the past that she may well be wrong.

Earlier that day, in the middle of our outdoor interview conducted on a breezy, beautiful morning in an urban downtown park, we had observed a flock of pigeons flying in an exquisite, seemingly synchronic display as they abruptly changed direction in apparent retort to the shifting wind currents sweeping through the park. In response to my observation, "There's organicity to their action," she replied, "Yes, there's a leader in there." Donna was offering a hopeful human analogy in which individuals who are associated in a group, each of them aware of their freedom to fly in his or her own direction, could readily discern the most capable, authentic leader among them—the best embodiment of profound idea and dedicated action—and be inspired to move in the same direction. It was further apparent that for reasons much more profound than personal payback, she had no intention of stopping her own attempts to demonstrate and lead, regardless of her uncertain future success.

MORE LOCAL FORMS OF ACTION

A Quiet Actor

Some of those interviewed, although no less radical in their action from the perspective of conventional wisdom, are less dramatic or visible in their apparent reach. James M. is a good example. Jim lives and works in Berkshire County, the westernmost county in Massachusetts. It is a region known much more for its cultural and historical attractions and year round natural scenery than for its social or political activism. Jim is a college-educated carpenter. He is reserved, enduringly modest, and does not think of himself as a core actor, even when encouraged to do so. Yet, his history of morally informed action confirms that he is.

He grew up in a conservative rural community in neighboring New York, one of six children. His father worked in a mid-level position for the New York State Department of Highways and his mother was a homemaker. He recalls nothing out of the ordinary in his middle class upbringing, simply that he and his siblings were raised in the Roman Catholic tradition, were taught to cooperate and expected to help out at home, and were at least adequately loved and nurtured. His father, who served as a member of the local school board and as a volunteer fireman, also demonstrated that republican duty to one's community was important.

After high school, he went to the University of Rochester, according to Jim also a fairly conservative place during the 1960s, where most of the students were career focused and "somewhat self-centered." Like most of his classmates, Jim was only somewhat politically active in protests involving student rights, and not at all on broader issues such as Vietnam, although he read and kept himself informed. In fact, he had decided that the war was immoral but did not see how he could do anything to bring about change.

After graduating in the late 1960s, he took a teaching job in Southern Berkshire County. It was the unlikely event of attending a summer teacher workshop at Central Michigan that provided him with the opportunity to gain fresh insight and precipitated his first foray into activism. As he described it,

> I met some people [seminar leaders] who were talking about taking personal responsibility for [one's] actions, that it's not easy to change the world, but it's a heck of a lot easier to change yourself. How you interrelate, how you relate to people, how you relate to the environment—your participation in things that may be too large to change—is something you can do today. And maybe [what you do] will have an impact and maybe it won't, but that's not the ultimate value, that's not the ultimate test. . . .

At the end of that summer, in "August 1969" he precisely remembered, he wrote a letter to his local draft board, enclosing his draft card and saying, in effect, "I'm not interested anymore." He explained his action as "a personal decision—certainly moved by others' examples. I didn't come upon this decision through meditation or self-examination. It was through conversations, discussion. . . . It was also a time of growth [and] reflection."

Although Jim's above action was privately implemented, he did disclose his decision to a few friends and family, as well as his further refusal to accept CO status, which led to his indictment and trial as a draft resister in the U.S. District Court at Albany. Around this time, he recalls, "I [also] became involved in demonstrations. Whenever there was a demonstration going on at the Pentagon, we would go down for that." He also participated in local and regional protests organized by the War Resistors League and the AFSC.[24] He further attempted to use his trial, "at a minimum, to confront the twelve jurors with this [moral] question and, maybe, shake [their convictions] a little bit."

Notwithstanding his attempt, he was fairly quickly found guilty and sentenced to two years probation, upon terms that amounted to the rough equivalent of the CO alternative service he had refused. He finally recollected with his typically modest candor that he

> could have refused that [sentence] but my mother, who could never understand why I was making such a fuss, was saying very strongly that she didn't want me to go to jail. So, the question was how much more was I going to upset her. I decided that I had done a lot of what I had wanted to do . . .

After Vietnam ended, Jim's activism waned for over a decade, "until Reagan came in which, in a lot of ways, was like Vietnam all over again." The issue that drew him back into the fray was American policy in Central America and, in particular toward Nicaragua. After a few years of mounting concern and frustration over a change "in the political atmosphere in the United States and conversations in Washington concerning Soviet [or Cuban] influence in Central America [and that] we were going to have to invade Nicaragua to deal with the problem. . . . That sounded rather extreme." At about that time he came upon a notice in the local paper inviting the public to a meeting to "talk about the situation and . . . to decide what might be done to avert the kind of destruction [that] we have seen in the Balkans more recently."

Jim was one of about twenty-four who attended that meeting at the Unitarian Church in Pittsfield in 1984. Over the next several years he and other members of an existing group known as the Berkshire Committee on Central America—a likely offshoot of the working group organized in 1979 by Frances Crowe and others forty miles away in Northampton—organized rallies, vigils,

leafleting, and protests. In 1986 he took part in a sit-in at the Marine Corps re-
cruiting office at the modest federal office building in Pittsfield, resulting in
his arrest, with sixteen others, for trespass.

Since the mid-1980s, Jim has made social and political activism part of his
life. As with most core actors, his concerns are much broader than a single
people, cause, or region. This is supported by his occasional participation in
rallies and civilly disobedient antinuclear and antimilitarism protests, such as
those at the Pentagon and at the General Dynamics Electric Boat Works facility in Groton, Connecticut, both of which resulted in his arrest. He is also
active in a local affiliate of Habitat for Humanity where he is able to demonstrate and perform with his carpentry skills his commitment to human betterment.

Although public attention has long since shifted away from Central America, that region, particularly Nicaragua, has remained as the primary focus of
Jim's activism. In a rare departure from his customary brevity, he describes
his approach to action in practical, existential terms:

> You see so many things that really aren't as good as they can be. Some people
> say, "Well, I don't listen to the news anymore . . . it's too frustrating. There's
> nothing I can do about it." And that's one approach; [however], for some other
> people, myself included, [we] say, "well, let's see what piece of this we can deal
> with, and focus on one . . . part of that." Then, being aware of other [issues] that
> are frustrating or aggravating or angering, occasionally finding some energy to
> deal with some . . . of those things as well.

Like Jane Addams, Jim's work for justice in Nicaragua is informed and
strengthened by concrete experience as well as by formal learning and the experiences of others. In 1985 two of his friends, a retired bluecollar union local leader and the managing editor of the regional paper, decided to travel to
that country and learn about the social, economic, and political situation first
hand. Already informed and active on the issue of U.S. involvement in the region, Jim was further educated by the information his friends returned with.

Several months later, upon learning that two professors from the local community college were organizing a trip to that country, he and his partner decided to go and see for themselves. The group spent much of its time in Marapasilo, a small city some distance from the capital. Although he was further
powerfully informed by the conditions he observed, it was the mood of many
of the people he met that most profoundly moved him:

> To see people living in a very difficult situation, without access to health care
> and their kids are sick, without access to education . . . they're—you could find
> many people who were not bitter, who were not angry all the time as I think that

I would be if I were in their situation. . . . To meet people who laughed and had a good time and wanted to celebrate life despite all they had to live through . . . I think is an inspiration.

At about the same time, Jim began to realize, as did Frances Crowe, Donna S., and others, that direct confrontational action to change official policy, while highly important, was not solely adequate for the task of morally informed change. He noticed, for example, how the nuclear freeze initiative had quickly grown into a movement and had just as rapidly lost traction in the quicksand of congressional inaction and the Reagan Star Wars initiative. For these reasons and the simple desire to offer concrete help to the people of Marapasilo, he and his colleagues formed Berkshire Amistad. "We [had] to find a way of sustaining ourselves despite whatever Washington might say. And the suggestion was made that we start a sister city program."

Berkshire Amistad was a way to reach a broader local audience and, in the process of gathering financial and other support for concrete "self-help" projects, to educate and raise awareness indirectly but authentically. As Jim put it,

Rotary [clubs], schools, woman's groups are interested in sister city work [and] living conditions, and [people] begin to ask [as he did] the same questions of themselves, after getting engaged in that way. . . . Why is there this poverty? Why is there such poor healthcare? Why can't kids go to school? [Then] maybe they become active, maybe they don't, but they are at least willing to listen to us.

The approach has had some success in the Berkshires and has spread elsewhere. The City of Pittsfield officially established a sister city relationship with Malpaisillo, more than once receiving visiting officials from that city. Together with Amistad members, they have spoken frequently throughout the county, mirroring parallel efforts by a network of such groups throughout New England. Local Rotary clubs and other service organizations have responded, donating funds to help the city obtain potable water and enable local residents to acquire a degree of self-sufficiency with a micro-enterprise loan program funded by the Amistad group.[25]

Of at least equal importance to the prospects for eventual morally informed change, more than thirty county residents have traveled to the community over the last decade, not including Jim and his partner, who have been back on several occasions. Each time they go there they are renewed in purpose and each time they speak they inform the minds of many, change the minds of a few, and perhaps inspire one or two to become core actors, initiators of moral progress in the social and political arena.

Teaching Peace and Social Justice in the Classroom

For two of those interviewed, the classroom has been their primary vehicle
for action. Karen P. is a public school teacher and school adjustment counselor who, until recently, taught social skills in an elementary school in Berkshire County. Father Leo is the Catholic chaplain and a professor at a small,
private Catholic college in Springfield, Massachusetts. Both were in their
classrooms during a portion of their interviews and it was quickly apparent
that each was clearly "in their element." One quickly notices that they impart
a sense of self-comfort, warm affection, and enthusiasm to their students that
is authentic beyond question. Father Leo was observed teaching one of his favorite subjects, liberation theology, a more recent Catholic equivalent to the
late-nineteenth-century social gospel theology of Protestantism.[26]

It is at once apparent that Father Leo does not accept the various value neutral models of pedagogy, so prevalent on the American campus today and yes-
terday. He offers his students his fluent, passionate analysis of how Max Weber and Hannah Arendt were right in their depiction of the way that modern
organization and mass society make evil seemingly routine and necessary.
They do so, he suggests, by diminishing our capacity to think deeply about
life and publicly act on what we learn:

> We don't question our institutions. We don't question . . . what is right or what
> is wrong about institutions. We got sucked into believing—and there are more
> and more people in prosperous times that get sucked into believing—in institu-
> tions because they just know that they live in a house of cards. If you remove
> one card everything collapses, and because they have such prosperity today, fi-
> nancial prosperity, folks are not going to [seriously] question the institution,
> whatever the institution is.

To further illustrate his case against modern institutions—and his implicit
willingness to challenge the official dogma of his own institutional leaders,
he berates our political elites, using them to illustrate how much easier it is to
distance oneself from injustice and morality by talking in terms such as "policy" and "options." Continuing in the rising and receding tidal rhythm somewhat akin to an evangelist preacher, he describes how even our religious institutions encourage us to depend on them, fostering our moral passivity:

> We don't have to experience pain, so we don't have to experience growth. They
> teach us to believe in "original sin," not "original blessing" and this lets us off
> the hook. We're fallen creatures, so what's the point. With "original blessing"
> we have to acknowledge that we're co-creators with God, [therefore both] rad-
> ically free and accountable.[27]

Father Leo clearly believes in both as he applies liberal doses of blunt candor to his students, affectionately chiding them at the same time for their woeful, lazy ignorance. Using his favorite metaphor for our time, he tells them that they are

> living in tunnels . . . of darkness and [your] parents have brought [you] to those tunnels of darkness by not challenging life, not challenging themselves. They're not challenging their offspring, not challenging their children that are now young adults.

It is not a Greek philosophical cave he is describing, but rather a cavern of lazy ignorance—his definition of original sin for our era—self-delusion, and fear.

Pressed to explain his metaphor in more detail, he uses the example of how we fail to identify obvious issues of human injustice, to connect them to our own hubris, ignorance, and misdeeds, and to support core actors who seek to ameliorate them. He illustrates his concern by using his colleague and friend, Father Roy Bourgeois, and the general public failure to understand and support his protest outside Ft. Benning against the "School of Assassins" (his term for the recently-renamed School of the Americas):

> I think that people have given up believing that there's an alternative and even that there it is a hope factor, believing that people can gather together and celebrate together and trust in celebration that there's an alternative view. But I really do believe most people have just dismissed that by saying, "Oh, how naïve! We've been through that in the 60s, 70s, 80s." It's like saying my father did that, my grandfather did it, my great-grandfather did it.

His frustration becomes more evident as he continues:

> I'm not saying everyone needs to "walk the walk," but they have to be palpable in their support of those who are . . . not only palpable about supporting them but understanding why the others are walking the walk, without fear.

Focusing again on his students and their parents, his tone abruptly changes, softening in apparent distress as he imaginatively, empathetically re-enters their caves. He explains:

> I mean, they're so frightened, filled with such darkness and fear running through the cave that they look upon those people [core actors] as lunatics, and we have many more people being looked down upon today as lunatics who are struggling to walk the walk.

Based on his analysis of the current conditions in our society—our institutions and state of mind—he has turned, as have James M. and several other interviewees, to action that is primarily local and interpersonal in order to inform students by his own example, the words and action of others, and, to the extent possible, by guided direct experience. Further explaining, he continued: "We don't have to be in the city streets trying to get others to join us," he explains. "That kind of classroom . . . that's over, because [it] didn't work. We thought it worked [but] it failed." Pointing to one of many cases from the last thirty years that make his point, he continued, "There would not be an East Timor today if that classroom was [still] effective. People are not listening [to] the city streets [to public protest]. We're not listening today."

Commenting on the current ineffectiveness of mass public protest, Father Leo is angry and despondent at his nation and society, and deeply worried about a world that he dearly loves. He seems to have arrived at a point in his life not unlike the one that Frederick Douglass reached as he experienced the collapse of reconstruction. As with Douglass, however, he has neither given up hope, nor has he abandoned action, only a form of action that he believes has largely lost its effect. For one thing, he remains actively involved in area social justice work, mostly through small groups who work with the poor and on human rights concerns in several locations in the Pioneer Valley. He chooses the organizations that he works with carefully, given his premise that many have become overly institutionalized, vested more in their own existence than in serious reform, engaged in "endless meetings" rather than action.

As suggested above, he recognizes that his mere words in a classroom or in his campus ministry are inadequate to inspire more than perhaps one or two of his students to shed their ignorance and discover their capacity as moral agents through action. To further stimulate the imaginations of his youthful flock, he brings core actors from his extensive network of colleagues and friends to campus each semester. In face-to-face encounters in his class and elsewhere, students become acquainted with flesh and blood actors, Father Bourgeois among them, enabling them to discover, as he did, that they do not match their "lunatic" cultural image.

Father Leo knows that the direct encounter approach is effective because it was for him. He attributes his moral awareness and his turn to activism both to his mother while growing up and to the "crazy lunatics"—the activists he met while at St. Anselm's, a small catholic college in Manchester, New Hampshire, run by the Benedictine monastic order. He credits his mother— and mothers in general—for teaching both an awareness of injustice and compassion for the poor and weak. Looking back at the customary pattern of upbringing in his middle working class Irish Catholic neighborhood in Holyoke, he observes: "When I look at moral development, most often women teach

[it]. Men teach fear, or legislation, or doctrine, or dogma. . . . Mom[s] raise questions. Dad[s] give us periods."

While at St. Anselm's he met and got to know several powerful core actors, including Catholic Worker co-founder Dorothy Day and fellow Worker Ammon Hennacy.[28] Their effect on him was quick and long-lasting:

> By the time I was a sophomore, I saw Dorothy Day as a solid citizen. So my [childhood] activism from passing out leaflets for Irish Catholic liberal Democrats [part of his mother's activism] now became—it's no longer the Irish Catholic liberal Democrat; it's a question of morality . . . a question of spirituality . . . a question of justice.

While direct encounters with core actors are highly persuasive, Father Leo is keenly aware that Jane Addams was right: one learns most effectively about the content and status of justice in our society, state, and world by living and working with those most affected by its absence—the very poor. About fifteen years earlier, he set out to create such an opportunity for his students. From a simple initiative—"Just a couple students and myself and some other campus ministries in the beginning"—it has grown into a yearly program involving some sixty students traveling to work in Haiti from his campus alone. In recent years, he has had to turn students away, something that obviously disturbs him; however, from the beginning the program has been carefully built to foster mutual learning and assistance, not to offer guided tours through slums on a climate-controlled bus, nor to expose students recklessly to the violence that reflects the anomie of chronic despair. Describing how the initiative developed, he elaborated:

> So we went to Haiti and we had some guidelines. We were going to do whatever the Haitians wanted us to do. They said they needed to dig a ditch here and over there and to help us dig the ditch here and over there. We were not going to say "well that's wrong by the way. It should be done like this because we learned about this [at] the university in America." So we dug the ditches the way they wanted them dug. But eventually, then, they'd ask us some questions about some medical intervention or health or something like that and we'd bring in that medical intervention and the next time we'd have some training done. We would have some trainers train trainers and then have the Haitians train their own people.

Reflecting what Addams had learned almost a century earlier, he described the common-sense, worldly knowledge that the Haitian peasants, lacking in material resources and technical expertise, possessed in abundance. They respond to questions that students, witnessing extreme poverty for the first time, are stimulated to ask and motivated to learn:

> They know more why they're oppressed than we know [about our own oppression] in America. They know about [then Secretary of State] Madeline Albright,

they know about the International Monetary Fund, they know about the World Bank. They're called illiterate people [but] they know who their oppressor is. They know it's capitalism, they know it's Wall Street. They know it's . . . Alan Greenspan. . . .

Father Leo is not suggesting that the Haitian people he has encountered are ignorant concerning their local thugs and corrupt leadership, or that they exclusively blame the above American officials or America for their plight. He is claiming that they understand the facilitative connection between U.S. policies and their local political and economic conditions, that the past and current architects and administrators of these policies have names, and that they are morally accountable for their action and inaction.

A Most Unconventional School Teacher

Karen P. is likely the most unselfconsciously authentic, unconventionally radical actor that one might encounter. The locus of her activism, a public elementary school, is, accordingly, all the more surprising. The interview was conducted in her classroom where, once every two weeks, every class—all the students at her school—spends about an hour with her. Originally hired to do educational-behavioral assessments, she was approached by two other teachers who suggested that most of the students sent to her for special needs evaluation had behavioral problems that were caused or aggravated by poor social skills.

The teachers who had approached her were likely aware that she was then teaching a graduate education seminar at the nearby state college, entitled "The Peaceful Classroom." As she described it,

> What happened in the course, which I absolutely loved, is it wasn't a course where we really learned a lot of written material and documented fact. What we basically did was create the peaceful classroom that we need to experience so that we can create it for our students.

Asked to explain the concept further, she continued:

> To me, it needs to be a setting where there's safety and you're able to share who you are without the risk of being, you know, ridiculed, misunderstood . . . authentically who you are. I would basically start my course with an activity that would really touch us in the heart and after that first night together we were already like a family and it happened every single semester. . . . I probably taught it [for] five semesters. . . . I was amazed because the first year, when it started to flow so smoothly and it was so deep, you know, the experiences we were having, I almost didn't trust it because I thought can this happen again? Will it hap-

pen again if you have that intention? And you know what? It kept happening and happening.

In the three years that she has worked in her unique classroom, she has replicated her approach with adults in her work with children, creating a comfortable, secure place that they are invited to help define and create. Her credentials for doing so are impressive, extending far beyond her dual teacher certifications and her Masters in educating the emotionally disturbed that she earned at Columbia. For one thing, she was adopted into a strong nurturing family, a household full of foster children that was "open to the neighborhood" as well. For another, there was her early passionate identification with the needs of others less fortunate than herself, a quality that led her into frequent trouble in high school, including trips to the principal's office for unauthorized fundraising from fellow students to contribute to humanitarian relief in Biafra during the 1960s.

Finally, she has combined her concern for others with a tenacity to do whatever it takes to reach students and to broadly educate them. This trait is evident from her account of the six years that she spent teaching and living in the Park Avenue area of Hartford, Connecticut, one of the poorest minority areas in a city that has been extraordinarily fled from by whites.[29] She describes that experience graphically:

> I mean, I had thirteen-year-old drug runners in my classroom who came in and couldn't read "Go Sally Go." But you had to validate them for being somewhere so we basically started. When I first started teaching, I started in an empty classroom. I asked for the class to be empty [of books and furniture]. People thought I was nuts [but] I didn't know what we could have in there that made sense. So the first few weeks of school with all these Hispanic boys that were bigger than me and spoke mostly Spanish, we kind of sat around in an empty room and I said "what do you want to do? How are we going to make this work and help you to learn?" [After a while] it was incredible the kinds of [educational] things that were happening. [And] I started to learn about their lives and spent a lot of time in their homes, walking up urine-smelling tenement buildings and taking the kids bowling on weekends and showing them that there's another way.

Returning to her present classroom, filled almost beyond capacity with tables, chairs, an inviting "peace lounge" area with bean bag chairs and Indian cotton print décor, and student creations depicting various peace themes throughout, Karen concludes, "and I think that's what I try to do with these guys."

During her first year, something dramatic began to happen in her class and in the school. It started within the conventional curriculum, with the students raising issues about the various forms of violence that they encountered in school and elsewhere in their daily lives. She led them in discussion, helping them to identify and try out nonviolent solutions. She imparted her belief that they could and should take responsibility for the conflicts that inevitably arise in daily life—that they were capable of choosing how to act and react and of learning new means of establishing and maintaining peace.

Inevitably, this led to questions about peaceful relations in the larger world, a natural extension of logical childhood wonder that asks not only "why not?" but "what can we do?" Not one to discourage what she was endeavoring to teach, Karen assumed the power of human agency that she was then striving to impart to her students, asking them what they would like to do. By late winter or early spring, they began to implement answers in amazing, highly unconventional ways.

Karen P.'s students are mostly the descendants of French Canadian and Polish immigrants who came to the North Berkshire County community to work in the mills, a familiar New England pattern. Although those jobs have disappeared and the economy has indefinitely slowed, their families have stayed longer than most, content in the community and scenery that surround them. One suspects that many were surprised when their children came home that spring to tell them that they were going to be in a peace parade, with their whole school, marching down the main street.

The parade was an idea that came from the students. It started with a suggestion by one that they could do a peace march around the school corridors; however, when another asked why it couldn't be outside, down the sidewalk, sort of like a real parade, she knew that she should not dismiss the idea unless she first checked it out. To understand what followed, one must imagine an innocent-appearing, enthusiastic, diminutive, and utterly sincere teacher presenting her students' idea:

> So I asked my principal. He goes "well, you know, go for it." He's very supportive of what I do because, actually, it helps take care of a lot of discipline things and stuff. So he's very supportive, not actively advertising it but he'll let me do just about anything I want to do and then he says "but beware of, you know, somebody else." Like maybe some of the teachers and such. Okay, that's fine. I'll do my thing and just stand up with the kids. I feel stronger because I've got the kids—right. [Next] I called up the police department and asked them if there were any way at all that I could get some sort of permit . . . to maybe walk down the sidewalks or something, but the kids really would like to walk in the street. The cop said "that'll be no problem." And I said "you're kidding me?" And he said "No. We can stop the traffic. What would you like to do? How big would you like to make it?" And so we were already starting a conversation. So again, here's that social change and that activism because you step outside of our school building and now the cops are behind us. I went to the Board of Selectmen and asked them if they would be supporting it because actually the cops

sent me to them. The cops said you have to talk with the Board of Selectmen. So I talked to those guys [and] they were so supportive it was unbelievable.

The Select board issued a proclamation declaring the day of the parade, June 11, 1998, "Piece of Peace Day" in the town. That morning, some seven hundred children marched down the main street carrying hand made banners, signs, and posters with a variety of peace messages and slogans relating to family, community, country, and world. At the end of the parade the children formed a giant peace symbol in front of a fire department aerial ladder truck, with a photographer perched at the top.[30]

In a press release Karen explained how the event was the outgrowth of the students' response to her suggestion that the best way to deal with their varied responses to the violence of contemporary life—fear, confusion, anger, apathy, and powerlessness—was to take action. She presented them "with the notion that change begins on the inside of people (with thoughts, feelings, and ideas), and that kids have the power to create [such] change." The parade was the result of that process, an action generated by the children "that would demonstrate that [they] can help teach others about tolerance and building a safe community."

The parade was a growing annual event for the students and the town for four consecutive years. Karen built her social skills curriculum around the concepts of peace and nonviolence, using the parade project as the capstone activity for the year. In the spring of 2002, however, there was no parade. A combination of changes in school administration and, one suspects, some furtive expressions of discomfort with Karen's nonconformity resulted in the elimination of the social skills position, the closing of the "peace classroom," and Karen's reassignment as a special education teacher.

Although saddened by the change, her idea remains alive as she remains active, working with other teacher activists in Berkshire County and elsewhere who are now engaged in similar projects in their schools. In 2001, for example, an organization called Peace Crew was formed as "a community initiative dedicated to peace education and safety in Southern Berkshire schools."[31] One can also readily imagine that her ideas and practices remain vital in the lives of some of the several hundred students who spent time in her classroom, discovering their competence and finding there a refreshing oasis from our public culture of violence in the cause of justice, and for the sake of self.

OTHER ACTORS

The selection of Frances, Donna, James, Father Leo, Karen, and several others from the twenty-six persons interviewed results in a necessarily incomplete portrait of morally informed actors and action in our society. There are, for example, Andrea, a Protestant college chaplain and wide-ranging social justice activist, including protest against U.S. military policy and advocacy of gay and lesbian rights; Steve, a grassroots community builder, pacifist, and environmentalist in an economically distressed former mill town; and Betsy, with her husband a long-term peace and social justice activist whose focus when interviewed was on clean elections and other democratic reforms, as well as running a rehabilitative horticultural program she developed for inmates at a local jail. Each of them, along with an estimated four hundred others in the same region, join together each spring in public ceremonies to declare their ongoing refusal to pay federal taxes to support war.

Also omitted are Don and Marion, a rural husband and wife partnership who for years have taken part in national, regional, and local protests, peace walks, vigils, and other forms of public action. They have also organized a wide variety of community college symposia, international exchanges, and other informative gatherings to better understand and communicate the principles of nonviolence at all levels of social and political life. Further not mentioned are Dora, Tenagra, and Michael Ann, each of whom has worked full-time in a variety of creative and confrontational ways to alleviate racial and ethnic injustice and poverty in the distressed Hispanic and African American enclaves of Springfield and Holyoke, Massachusetts.

In addition there are several others not yet mentioned and those thus far referred to only briefly in the introduction. Each has learned that they possess the capacity to act, and to act authentically, in a wide variety of settings and around a number of moral issues. What remains to be learned from them, and from the four core actors from our past, is what informs and sustains them, matters that have thus far only been abstractly introduced or mentioned as part of the narrative of their action. If, as has been suggested, they have acted with some discernable success in our past and if we accept that success as moral progress—as achievements that we are willing to at least verbally defend—we should now be prepared to accept the possibility that they can further succeed in our present.

To understand how this can happen we need to examine more than the ability of core actors in our midst to act authentically, and illustrate the current forms of such action. We need to know what other capacities they possess that undergird and inform their capacity to act, and which enhance their power of moral persuasion. In the process, we can also discover what our history, properly understood, informs us is true: that each of us must have at least some of the same knowledge and abilities if even a portion of what they are now seeking is to be achieved, whether in our time or ever.

NOTES

1. Arendt, *Human Condition,* 164–65.

2. The professional realm of Social Movement Theory affords a particularly cogent example. Originating as a self-conscious sociological subdiscipline in the immediate aftermath of the Southern civil rights era of the 1950s and 1960s, its adherents constructed successive structural-functional metatheories ranging from Marxist to pluralist and cultural to rational choice, each motivated by an apparent earnest desire to understand the external causes and effects of the most recent "movement." In turn each theory lost favor as the most recent explanation failed to account for, let alone predict, the next wave of activism. Finally, beginning in the 1980s, many sociological theorists, along with their counterparts in political science, largely abandoned attempts at offering empirically verifiable comprehensive explanations, and began to focus their attention on mid-range theorizing, some under the rubric of New Social Movement Theory. For an excellent, compressive summary of this history, see James M. Jasper, *The Art of Moral Protest: Biography and Creativity in Social Movements* (Chicago: University of Chicago Press, 1997), 19–41. See also Thomas R. Rochon and David S. Meyer, eds., *Coalitions and Social Movements: The Lessons of the Nuclear Freeze* (Boulder, CO: Lynne Rienner Publishers, 1997); Russell J. Dalton and Manfred Kuechler, eds., *Challenging the Political Order: New Social Movements in Western Democracies* (New York. Oxford University Press, 1990).

3. David Brooks's book, *Bobos in Paradise: The New Upper Class and How They Got There* (New York: Simon & Schuster, 2000) offers an interesting, humorous analysis—and cogent example of this phenomenon.

4. A note on quotations attributed to contemporary actors who were interviewed for this project. As noted in Chapter 1, each was interviewed by this writer. All interviews were taped and transcribed, and the originals of each have been preserved. Further, each interviewee was given the opportunity to review their quoted material, not to censor their remarks, but to ensure the contextual accuracy of their use. Finally, some of their names have been altered—at my urging, *not* theirs. Their friends and colleagues can still recognize them by their deeds; however, other readers have to assess their authenticity—and mine—for themselves.

5. Claudia Lefko, "Conscientious Objector," *Hampshire Life Magazine*, supplement to the *Daily Hampshire Gazette*, 18 Dec. 1998, 10.

6. Lynd and Lynd, intro., xxiv. James expressed his views with exceptional clarity in his famous essay "The Moral Equivalent of War," first published in 1910. Evidencing the cross-fertilization of ideas between James and Jane Addams, he first describes the primal motive force of warfare, and of the "dignity" and "pride" that it fosters in men as a noble, sacrificial service to their "collectivity," and encourages pacifists to "enter more deeply" into "the point of view of their opponents." He argues that by doing so, one can detect that the ameliorating benefits (for some) of liberalism, capitalism, and rational international co-existence afford an inadequate alternative to the emotions stirred by war. People need to be enlisted—in James's assessment, "conscripted"—in a heroic, disciplined, self-sacrificial struggle for human betterment, particularly those born into

privilege and leisure. Only through such endeavors, akin to Addams's democratic ex-
perience, can an alternative "social motive" be instilled. The essay can be found in John
J. McDermott, ed., *The Writings of William James: A Comprehensive Edition* (1967;
Chicago: University of Chicago Press, 1977), 660–71.

7. Lefko, *Hampshire Life Magazine*, 9.

8. Jane Addams was also influenced by Tolstoy, as were most opponents of war
at the turn of the twentieth century. She traveled to Russia to meet him in 1896. Diliberto, 226–28.

9. "Friends," short for Society of Friends, is another, more formal name by which
Quakers are known.

10. Congress ratified the Limited Nuclear Test Ban Treaty, which banned atmospheric testing, in 1963.

11. Edward K. Shanahan, "Tracking is Attorney's Latest Cause," *Daily Hampshire
Gazette,* 24 May 1997.

12. According to Cooney and Michalowski, eds., the CCCO was founded in 1948 in
response to the jailing of numerous conscientious objectors during World War II (117).

13. Conte was well known as a partisan maverick. For example, less than a month
before his death in February 1991, he was one of three GOP house members to vote
against the congressional action that sanctioned the use by the Bush administration of
military force against Iraq, preceding the Gulf War. Mary McGrory, "Their Passion
Was Politics," *Washington Post*, 12 Feb. 1991, A2.

14. Michael Walzer, "Political Action: The Problem of Dirty Hands," *Philosophy
and Public Affairs*, II (Winter 1973): 160–80. The moral dilemma that Walzer posed,
whether an official charged with protecting the inhabitants of a city should authorize
the torture of a suspect reasonably believed to know the whereabouts of bombs timed
to explode and claim many lives, is not as far-fetched as it once seemed in America.

15. Martin Diskin, "El Salvador: Reform Prevents Change," in William C. Thiesenhusen ed., *Searching for Agrarian Reform in Latin America* (Winchester, MA: Unwin
Hyman, Inc., 1989), 432–33.

16. Saul Alinsky (1909–1972) had a long activist career, well-summarized in a
web-published account by the Independent Television News Service, "The Democratic Promise: Saul Alinsky and his Legacy" (http://www.itvs.org/democrat-
icpromise/alinsky1.html) from which the following is condensed:

He established his reputation as a highly effective grassroots political organizer in
Chicago's massive slum area, adjacent to the Union Stockyards, the same region where
Jane Addams's Hull House had been established and where Upton Sinclair had set his
novel, *The Jungle*. In 1939 he succeeded in forging a working coalition, the Back-of the-
Yards Council, comprised of several Eastern European ethnic group leaders, the CIO, a
major industrial union, and the Catholic Bishop. His book, *Reveille for Radicals*, published in 1946, he called upon America's poor to reclaim democracy. In the 1950s he
turned his attention to civil rights, organizing the Woodlawn Organization in 1959 to
achieve effective political power for blacks on Chicago's South Side. In 1969 he turned to
a conscious effort to train organizers for the next generation, setting up the Urban Training Center [where Donna S. met him a year or two prior to his death]. In 1970, *Time Magazine* hailed Alinsky as "a prophet of power to the people."

17. Shortly before his death in 1972, he had arrived at the same conclusion that Jane Addams had come to via a different route, namely that "America's poor would have to ally themselves with the middle class, whom he was afraid would move to the right." ITVS, http://www.itvs.org/democraticpromise/alinsky2.html.

18. The "urban plunge" experience was apparently widely copied in other parts of the country by trainees from the Urban Institute. In the late 1960s or early 1970s, two other Western Massachusetts interviewees, Don and Marion L., had taken part in one in the Los Angeles area. They recalled the experience as "intense" and, judging from the details recounted years later, deeply informative.

19. Jonathan Kozol, *Amazing Grace: The Lives of Children and the Conscience of a Nation* (New York: Crown Publishers, 1995), 30–31.

20. Coffin and Donna S. had known each other through their activism and later became friends. When interviewed, she informed me that her husband was in the middle of writing his biography.

21. Giamatti was President of Yale from 1978 to 1986. He left to become president of the National League in that year and later became the commissioner of Major League Baseball. http://www.BaseballLibrary.com.

22. The Conte archives (Special Collections, William E. DuBois Library, University of Massachusetts Amherst) contain a section devoted to such correspondence, dating from the Vietnam era through the 1980s.

23. This facility, renamed in 2001 the Western Hemisphere Center for Security Cooperation, has been operated by the Department of Defense since the late 1940s as a training center for military and civilian security forces from Latin America and elsewhere. Initially located in the Canal Zone, it was moved to Ft. Benning, Georgia, in the late 1970s. Its sixty thousand trainees to date include former Panamanian dictator Manuel Noriega and several members of the military junta that overthrew the Allende government in Chile in 1973. Since 1990, Father Roy Bourgeois has headed a protest campaign from a location just outside Ft. Benning in an attempt to close the school. His group's website is http://www.soaw.org. Cf. Howard Zinn, *A People's History of the United States: 1492–Present* (New York: HarperPerennial, 1995), 557.

24. The War Resistor's League was founded in 1923 in response to the harsh treatment of conscientious objectors during World War I. Two of its four founders, Tracy Mygatt and Frances Witherspoon, were life-long "co-workers for peace and human rights, working with each other until their deaths . . . in 1974." Indicative of the often wide range and intensity of the work of core actors, they authored a volume of public correspondence "as well as articles, petitions, plays and short stories. [In addition] Mygatt was the founder of the Campaign for World Government, and both . . . were socialists, feminists, and active members of FOR [Fellowship of Reconciliation], ACLU, SANE, WILPF, World Federalists, and the U.N. Association." Cooney and Michalowski, eds., 45–46.

25. This writer, then a practicing attorney in Pittsfield, Massachusetts, had the pleasure of hearing the group speak more than once at the Pittsfield Rotary Club.

26. Liberation Theology, according to Lynd and Lynd, is a "synthesis of Christianity and the need for social revolution." It developed largely out of the experiences of some Catholic missionary clergy working with the poor in Latin America in the late

1960s and 1970s and their efforts to practice a "preferential option for the poor" in settings of systemic institutional oppression and violence. One of its most prominent exponents was El Salvadoran Archbishop Oscar Romero, apparent victim of a government ordered assassination as he conducted Sunday Mass at the cathedral in San Salvador in 1979. Lynd and Lynd, intro., xlii–xlv. Practioners of both Liberation and Social Gospel theology seek to return Christianity to the simple teachings of its "founding," namely as a servant ministry to the poor and dispossessed. Practioners of this form of ministry typically emphasize the achievement of basic social and economic justice at least as much as the imparting of their doctrinal or formal faith. Accordingly, as with the Catholic Workers (Kathy Kelly, Chapter 1), neither has been welcomed by the institutional leaders of either tradition.

27. The concept of "original blessing," borrowed from Matthew Fox's book, *Original Blessing* (Ch. 1, note 15), is strongly contrary to the official Roman Catholic doctrine of original sin.

28. Hennacy was a Socialist sentenced to federal prison in 1917 for advocating resistance to the draft. He became a Christian pacifist and anarchist while in prison and later became active in the Catholic Worker movement during the 1930s. At the time that Father Leo met him, he was actively opposing the war in Vietnam. Lynd and Lynd, 103–4.

29. According to 2000 U.S. Census Bureau data, whites comprise 17.8% of Hartford's population, Hispanics or Latinos 40.5%, and African Americans 36%. For Hartford County, the comparative figure for Hispanics or Latinos is 12% and for African Americans, 10.7%. Source: Census 2000 Redistricting Data (P. L. 94–171), Summary File, Connecticut Matrices.

30. *Berkshire Eagle*, 12 June 1998, A1.

31. Taken from the first newsletter published by the group, based in Great Barrington, Massachusetts, dated summer 2001.

Chapter Seven

The Capacity to Care

All feeling is for the sake of action, all feeling results in action. . . .

—William James[1]

Feelings accompany the metaphysical and metapsychical fact of love, but they do not constitute it, and the feelings that accompany it can be very different. . . . Feelings one "has"; love occurs. Feelings dwell in man, but man dwells in his love.

—Martin Buber[2]

The domain of morality is not just what people do but how they think about what they do . . . how behaviors come to be called moral and immoral [and] what that means to us. . . .

—Helen E. Longino[3]

We need to develop a moral system that will combine the virtues of what the historical discourse has relegated to men on the one hand and to women on the other.

—E. Ann Kaplan[4]

The willingness to die is the ultimate guarantee of moral standards, of purposes, and of the self.

—Wilson Carey McWilliams[5]

INTRODUCTION

When an intended action affects us, its authenticity is only part of what we attempt to discern. We are concerned to know not only the identity of the actor or agent, and whether he or she is sincere and committed in their effort, but also the nature and quality of care that their action signifies. It concerns us, for example, to learn that someone is hostile or indifferent to our well-being, regardless of the sincerity and candor with which they act.

There is little question concerning our capacity to exercise care for ourselves in our reaction to action by others, and in our own action. Further, few will argue that our self-focused concerns, particularly when justified by some form of rational or traditional moral sanctity, do not inform action that has, in its cumulative effect, considerable—often dominant—social and political import. We take legitimating refuge in such rubrics as national interest, economic necessity, "way of life," law, and individual right, particularly when there is public debate over the morality of our action, or when we find ourselves privately uneasy. Slavery, once again, is a powerful example of an institution created from the impetus of powerful, individual, and purposively aggregated self-regard, legitimated by each of the foregoing moral claims along with supporting "facts" of racial superiority and paternal benevolence.

Given our undeniably ample appetite for self-service, enlightened and otherwise, the questions to be considered in this chapter concern what many of us believe is our *lesser* capacity to care broadly and deeply for others and for things that lie physically outside the coterie of the self. To accomplish this, two tasks are or critical importance. *First*, we must examine the particular problems we have in our culture with our comprehension of caring for self and other. Having examined the historical development of our two most common beliefs concerning the nature of the self and its relationship to others, namely, those offered by liberalism and communitarianism, it is time to focus our attention inward, in order to assess how we become morally informed and stirred to action in ways that belie our culturally dominant beliefs. In doing so we discover something that core actors have simply learned more profoundly—that our capacity to care lies at the heart of all morally informed action.

Second, we need to explore the actual and potential relationships of caring to moral knowledge and the role of caring in social and political action. Any such effort within a larger undertaking must be partial, illustrative in scope, although hopefully sufficient to suggest the content of the rest. Perhaps the most noteworthy omission stems from the fact that the core actors selected herein to furnish testimony and inferences for the nature and role of caring in morally informed action happen to act more on the strength of concerns for others than for other life forms or the environment. This is not to suggest that they, or other core actors, have a fundamentally divided or inflexibly prioritized foundational world-view, or that their concerns are informed only by human interaction.

As with the examination of action itself, evidence from their self-understanding and deeds is substantially relied upon to inform and support the argument. Fortunately, each of them is accustomed to carrying heavy loads uphill, which makes their use for this purpose entirely appropriate. As always, we must furnish the balance of necessary input from our respective reservoirs of learning, caring, and action.

THE NATURE OF CARE

Caring, regardless of its form or object, is a state of mind that is present in all intended action. It is associated with a wide range and depth of emotions that are important to both the actor and those who are affected by the action, either with or without the actor's specific intention. We typically overlook its presence in action where, as discussed in the previous chapter, most of our daily acts and those of others that reach us are habitual, instrumental, or both. Depending on the agent source, if that can even be reliably determined, our occasional reflection on the routine of simple and densely complex daily interactions reveals little if any care specifically targeted at us. Much of it is organizationally scripted, coordinated action aimed at our demographics, our assumed existence, our gathered preferences, or not at us at all.

At those moments when our cognition and reflection inform us that we are the intended recipients of an act that has some of the qualities of genuine affection, concern, and respect, our state of mind is favorably affected, our sense of self enhanced, our spirits lifted—the list continues. It matters greatly to us that we are valued in some affirmative regard by others for *who we are*, whether the person knows us well—or not at all—and cares for us nonetheless.

It is also highly important to us that we are able to regard ourselves favorably for the "who we are" that we are able to authentically disclose to the world, for our particular capacity to act authentically. This "is" quality is often especially evident in those who initiate morally informed change in unfamiliar, uncertain settings that contain the risk that they will find selves standing alone in unpleasant circumstances, or worse. At such times, the affectionate, caring acts of lovers, family, friends—and similar regard from those who stand with us in broader fraternal and sororal kinship—provide much-needed nourishment for the self.

CARE, KNOWLEDGE, AND ACTION

When we examine our personal repertoire of care and its particular associations, we are quickly reminded that the relationship between care, knowledge, and action is neither casual nor significant only for the security and comfort that it affords to one's self or, when rendered, to others. Caring, regardless of its form or object, is the motive energy that propels us from contemplation to intention and into action, influencing our premeditation, the nature of our action, and the intensity or "single-mindedness" with which it is undertaken. It is also part of the information that we consult prior to deciding how or whether to act—a vital component of our ability to prioritize moral knowledge. Moreover, it is the only part that *finally* motivates us to act, and the ultimate arbiter in our deciding to reformulate our plans, alter our means—even our goals, when necessary, and to act again.

All other forms of knowledge, regardless of their content, lack the motive power to determine our course of intentional action until we consider their implications and attach some form and level of care to each, or are more immediately informed by the form and intensity of care that attends them. In other words, when we consider whether and how to act in some context where our decision may have serious, nonroutine implications, we go through an interactive process of thinking, feeling, and caring.

Caring, as just suggested, is also the substance that morally informs our intended action. The fact that, for some, caring may happen in a moment and be recognized as awareness more than conscious thought does not render it any less important. It may mean that we have acquired an all too rare ability—that of forming profound moral habits.[6]

The varied contents of our conscious thought, concrete and abstract, individual and grouped, personal and impersonal, emotive, cognitive, and intellectual—everything that informs and urges our attention—can be overridden by the form and intensity of care associated with a particular knowledge composite that moves us to choose its form of action. In this process, we relegate our other knowledge, feelings, and concerns to either supporting roles or to some lower priority along with its associated forms of action. Even our seemingly unadorned will is unable to move us unless we first care enough about someone or something to employ it. That someone, in the first instance at least, is often the self, our inner voice urging action for the sake of our fundamental integrity, our congruent self, vital in the world and within.

EXTREME CARING

Examples of how care operates within us are abundant among the more extreme conditions of intended action. In accounts of famine, for example, there are invariably stories of parents and others who, having exhausted all avenues of possible relief, and considering what to do with the last scant ration, have chosen to go hungry, accepting the stark consequences of physical sacrifice for the sake of a loved one. Alternatively, there are those, who out of mutual love and the respect for the other's decision that mature love entails, have shared—or jointly, defiantly refused to consume—the single insufficient ration. Finally, there are those who have eaten while the "loved one" knowingly went without, although their stories are less often told. In all cases, it is the form and intensity of care, not hunger or reason, that has had the final word in their action.

In the above example, or in others involving nonfamilial forms of deep human caring, since most of us likely believe that one of the self-abnegating actions is the right, moral, or noble course, the form of caring that attends it seems patent, therefore somehow secondary, of less importance than the act. However, the caring demonstrated in the intentional but *nonconforming* action of morally informed actors in equivalent extreme conditions and in other less dramatic contexts is substantially more difficult for many to fathom. This is mostly due, as shall be considered more fully, to the fact that our caring—our capacity to care and the form and intensity of our caring—is informed at any given moment by a combination of inheritance, culture, experience, including the experience of caring itself, other acquired knowledge, and our resulting capacity to imagine and reflect. Since all of these are variables in our respective lives, so our personal repertoire of care and our ability to comprehend the caring of others vary also. Fortunately, our capacity to learn from others, and from life more broadly, is formidable and ongoing.

GENDERED CARING

It is no accident that men, in particular, are apt to dismiss or deprecate our capacity to care broadly and intrinsically for others as part of the human apparatus that informs moral action in civil society and in government. As most of us are aware, this is a much more universal problem than can be laid at the collective feet of men in America or the Western world to which this discussion is confined. Having been almost ubiquitously informed since at least the dawn of the virtually all major civilizations that they are the natural superior to women in strength and the intellectual skills of government, men have acted within a moral framework that fosters male caring in the service of self, the protection of those cared for within the private coterie of self, and sacrifice either for social honor or for the sake of those to whom one becomes bound in the pursuit of noble purpose.[7] It is not that men do not care deeply for others, whether intimately or fraternally. They are, however, powerfully encouraged to express profound interpersonal and other concrete care only in private or other limited domains, and to subordinate such care for the sake of abstract goods, attachment to which is seen as distinct from and superior to concrete caring, whatever its form or objects.

In contrast, women have long been associated with concrete, particular care and nurture of others linked by bonds of birth, love, affection, and intimate friendship, as well as empathy for the weak and vulnerable. For them, such "virtues" are portrayed as natural, and at least somewhat unique to their sex and gender. As one result of the structural enforcement of this male-female dichotomy, the objects of caring by women and most forms of expression have not been as bifurcated into private and public, exclusive and general, concrete and abstract. To appreciate the role of social reinforcement in this gender divide, we have only to look at such phenomena as the Madonna-whore duality of Western culture, most visible in our history of criminal justice administration, to appreciate the extent to which men have and continue to strive to "preserve" the "higher" nature of women.[8]

With the powerful installation of the rationally enlightened understanding of human nature and the resulting decline of common public goods, the elite male tradition of sacrificial public service as a duty inherent in one's station or class has been gradually devalued. Freed from the limits of tradition by the logic of equality and economic power, newly liberated middle class men shifted the focus of their profound concerns to ideals and ideologies that were informed by reason, rather than more tangible, acknowledged caring for the extended family of ethnic group, country, or their religious and other cultural icons.

We are now somewhat more aware that our history and its selection of heroes and other exemplars has been driven by the persistent myths of masculine physical and intellectual superiority, the reality of male dominance by sheer strength, and the almost primordial social and political instantiation of both into customs, mores, law, and constitutions. The gradual amelioration of male dominance in America over the last one hundred and sixty or so years is a powerful story of gradual moral awakening, informed in each generation by women such as Elizabeth Cady Stanton who refused to conform, and by men and women who were persuaded by their efforts. It is not a tale of men awakening either on their own or around some fraternal campfire. Myths must be confronted if they are to lose their luster of truth.

The still ongoing, thirty-year debate between feminists and traditionalists in the field of developmental psychology illustrates that the debate over the relationship between caring, gender, and the nature of morally informed action in all areas of life is far from over. Psychologist Carol Gilligan cogently argues that the stages of individual moral development model relied upon by Lawrence Kohlberg and other cognitive psychological theorists explicitly assumes the immature inferiority of morality derived from caring for others and the valuing of concrete relationships, both of which he associated with women in particular. In his version of the enlightened moral hierarchy, the highest stage of moral development for men and women is reached when we acquire the capacity to formulate, from an empirical and Kantian perspective, "Universalizable, Reversible, and Prescriptive Ethical Principles."[9] Gilligan notes the historical paradox, observing that "the very traits that have traditionally defined the 'goodness' of women, their care for and sensitivity to the needs of others, are those that mark them deficient in their moral development."[10]

The foregoing is not offered to suggest that many men are not good caregivers, or that their capacity for local, familial love, deep friendship, and related care is not showing signs of significant individual growth, as well as slight social and political impact. The observation is made to point out a key reason for our widespread assumption that in the political and associated social realms, such affectionate caring is still considered to strongly inform only the pluralistic, instrumental pursuit of private self-interests that can only be aggregated, never durably joined. In contrast, core actors, such as those discussed thus far, reveal that in some fashion, our capacity to intrinsically experience and express love, and act with caring affection toward family and friends, can, with modest further input, inform and motivate equally powerful caring that spurs us to act socially and politically for the benefit of others whom we do not concretely know.

BROADLY AFFECTIONATE CARING

It has been suggested in the foregoing that concrete, particular, and affectionate caring, particularly that associated with women, somehow informs our capacity to move beyond the limits of kinship and desire to more broadly encompass others and the world. The vehicle suggested by enlightened modernity is our capacity to abstract and conceptualize from the perspective of self and our framework of experience and knowledge, or, failing in that effort, to at least learn tolerance. Such means, as McWilliams powerfully argues, are partial, temporary at best, and ultimately doomed to failure, as are all projects conceived with an exclusively rational, self-oriented, prudent mindset.[11]

The means of broadly affectionate caring—of moving from the particular to the general—are inherent in our existing, developable nature, a nature that must be seen as combining the gendered capacities of women and men and blending the somewhat artificial categories of intellect and reason with profound feeling in order to obtain caring, the state of mind that is the subject at hand.

Gail K., one of the contemporary activists not yet introduced, told a story during her interview that further illustrates the content, formation, and expansion of our capacity to care. For at least the reasons suggested, some readers will relate easily to the form and intensity of care expressed or evident from her action, while others will not. Before recounting her story, therefore, it is especially important to learn something about her as a person in order to understand her moral formation and to relate her life to our own.

Married and the parent of three grown daughters, Gail has lived in a Western Massachusetts hill-town overlooking the Pioneer Valley for the past twenty years. For almost all of that time, she has engaged in an extensive range of social and political activism that has long since become a customary part of her life. Gail is a morally informed, highly competent, deeply passionate core actor.

The range of the concerns that she has acted on is impressive. They include nuclear disarmament, United States military and political interventions in Central America and elsewhere, and a whole range of issues having to do with violence, historical gender beliefs, and structured subordination that uniquely disempower women. Like her friends and activist colleagues, Frances Crowe and Jean Grossholtz, introduced in earlier chapters, she has taken part in many direct action protests on a variety of peace and social justice concerns that have led to her arrest on perhaps one hundred occasions. The first occurred when she and her youngest daughter were detained at a Pentagon sit-in in the early 1980s, shortly before she moved to Massachusetts.

By the time she moved to Massachusetts, she had been a core actor for well over twenty years. For as long as she can remember, Gail has "always had this kind of underlying drive toward social justice." She was born and raised in New York City as part of an average-sized middle-class Jewish family. Both of her parents were public school teachers, socially and politically engaged and informed but not unusually active. When asked if they gave her and her siblings a religious upbringing, Gail replied with affectionate humor: "Well, I grew up in a kosher home [kept for the sake of a Grandmother who lived with them], my parents were Conservative [and we] went to temple, but they were atheists." She indicated that she views herself today as a "spiritual person," informed by her sense of being "connected to nature and, in some very deep way, to my roots as a Jew."[12] She is also strongly connected to others.

Gail recalls that social and political issues were part of the regular family conversation that occurred around her and that spirited discussions on these topics were a vital part of her family experience, including the evenings she spent eavesdropping on her parents' passionate conversations with friends while she was supposed to be sleeping. The only activist she knows of in her family tree was her maternal grandfather, a socialist who died when she was five. She learned about his "soap box" speeches and other activism from family stories and adopted him as a role model early on.

Gail has a tremendous capacity for caring of all types, most of all, affection and altruistic concern for the welfare of others.[13] She evidenced the conventional ability to form strong attachments with her family while growing up, and within her own family where the intimate ongoing bonds between Gail, her husband, and her daughters are apparent not only in her conversation, but in the photographs and family memorabilia that adorn her home. Her early broad ability to form friendships and communicate warmth and concern for others is further suggested by her selection in high school as the captain of the cheerleading team and her election as "most popular" in her graduating class. Such adolescent peer judgments are by no means the consistent rewards for broad, genuine caring; however, in Gail's case, until science has enabled us to reliably reorder entire personalities, one must suspect that her peers had this quality much in mind.

It was Gail's concern for others, informed by her growing awareness of what she now sees as many forms of institutionalized, systemic oppression and injustice, that motivated her to become an activist. After graduating from Cornell around 1959, she taught in New York City schools for several years, while marrying, having children, and earning her masters degree in social work. Her experiences as a teacher in inner-city schools, particularly in the South Bronx, exposed her to the underbelly of American class prejudice and racism. In one junior high school to which she was assigned, she recalled "kids went into the schools with shotguns . . . [it] was literally a war zone." Although she quickly discovered that "teaching didn't happen" in that environment, she was able to do more that "stick it out." She subsequently volunteered to teach over the next several years in some of the toughest classrooms in New York City.

Gail's words and actions confirm that the primary objects of her compassion were the children she had been assigned to teach. It motivated her to learn more in order understand the causes of their precarious, chaotic, deprived lives and to strive to do whatever she could to educate them. When interviewed, her informed passion for learning was physically confirmed by the hundreds of books that fill her home library, covering subjects relating to social understanding and to social and political change.

LIVING IN CONTRADICTION

The existential and moral dissonance of undertaking this task—of attempting to live and work coherently in two vastly different worlds—was considerable. As she described it, "There were difficult teaching conditions, *and they were very difficult learning conditions* [hers]. So I would leave [after school], and in about fifteen minutes I would go to my nice house . . . over the line in Yonkers, and it was like . . . [lengthy silence]."

It was during this period, as her awareness grew that her students were the innocent victims of organized mistreatment and neglect beyond their control, that she took her first direct action, crossing a picket line of her fellow and sister teachers who were on strike, refusing to teach until their own needs were addressed. Forced to choose between the legitimate concerns of her colleagues that would also benefit her in many ways, she learned that she cared more for the students and their much greater, more immediate needs.

For the next several years, as her young family grew and her husband's career as an accountant took hold, she continued in this pattern of known contradiction, moving "upward" and slightly more outward in the process to the south side of New Rochelle, next to Yonkers. As a progressive, engaged, suburban couple, they were involved in various groups that met, discussed, and sought to address community and the broader social and political issues of the time, including the Vietnam War. She recalls that her social circle, at one point, included liberal intellectuals, E. L. Doctorow, and others: "We would go to parties with these . . . friends of ours . . . people who were very progressive, and [who] were storytellers. But when I would tell stories, it wasn't a story that they wanted to hear. . . . [W]hat I had to say was too intense, and I . . . was considered abrasive."[14] Deep caring was something to be either avoided or left elsewhere, outside the realm of informed banter, networking, and intellectual relaxation.

Their move to rural Massachusetts was not to escape her social and political concerns for others, but engage them more fully while better tending to the need to maintain a healthier self. Her move enabled her to obtain a quieter, less hectic home life in more natural, less material and overtly status-conscious conditions, while facilitating her ability to develop and nurture a few deep friendships, while avoiding many casual ones. In addition to tending to self-care, she was able to expand the scope and reach of her activism through involvement in groups, primarily with other women, where she experienced "the sharing of ideas in a way that challenges me and also nourishes me . . . [where there was] feeling for each other as people . . . a real feeling of connection and caring." What Gail describes is the sororal counterpart of McWilliams description of fraternity, referred to in the first chapter.[15]

Like each of the historical actors and most of those interviewed, she is aware that she still lives in the midst of moral contradiction, given her concerns and world-view. However, she concurs with her activist colleague and close friend, Jean Grossholtz, who sees any form of middle- or upper-class life in America, including their own, as a life that almost daily contradicts the values that each of them ardently supports. Each, however, actively attempts to reduce the scope and quantity of such incongruities to an extent much greater than most of us who share their world-view and concerns are able to manage. As with ourselves, Gail and Jean reflect the need for self-regard that comes from acting up to ones beliefs, and the virtual impossibility of doing so when you can only act effectively from, as Gail described it, "within the very world you're trying to change."

While living in New York during the late 1960s and 1970s, she became aware of the problem of battering, the use of violence by men to establish and maintain control over women in families and other intimate relationships, long before it was identified as a widespread social problem in the 1980s. After moving to Western Massachusetts, in addition to getting involved with political and social justice activism via the area office of the American Friends Service Committee and directly with Frances Crowe (see Chapter 6), she also joined with women in the Northampton area who had organized to work together on a range of women's concerns. Using her social work credentials and experience (she had worked as a school counselor after getting her master's), Gail began to work as an advocate for battering victims and with them as a personal counselor. After eighteen or so years she has come to see her individual work with battered women as a vital, grassroots component of her activism.

Her work with these women is the basis for her story. Occasionally Gail has been asked to help battered women referred to her by other colleagues. She has done so by various means, including assisting them in "going underground" in order to escape from especially dangerous abusers. This has occasionally meant giving higher priority to her informed concerns for the safety of women and children that to the sanctity of court orders and general respect for the rule of law. She does so in reliance on her experience, that of her colleagues and those whom she has helped, that many in the legal system have been slow to grasp the dynamics of domestic violence and their personal and social severity.[16]

One of the many consequences of this failure has been the charging of women with murder who have killed their male batterers in the belief that they were acting in self-defense, but under circumstances that men, as originators and enforcers of the law, have been slow to grasp.[17] Several years ago, Gail became familiar with one such case through a local colleague who had worked with an accused murderer during the lengthy time that she had been held in state prison awaiting trial. The friend believed the woman's story of horrendous abuse leading to justifiable homicide and persuaded Gail to accompany her to a further pre-trial bail hearing that had been obtained on her behalf. Gail trusted the friend and was prepared to help the accused with bail if possible. After meeting her at court for the first time that day, Gail offered to secure the woman's release with a second mortgage on her home as surety for the multi-thousand-dollar bail. After a surprised first reaction, the court accepted her offer.

Confirming her husband's long, ongoing role as her closest "supporting actor," she recounts her call to him that day to discuss her unusual plan. His simple response was "'Fine.' And we knew that she could have fled. If she had . . . we would have supported that . . . because I knew that the system was not going to be a just system for her." Gail's decision to act to help a factual stranger was prompted by care for the woman in circumstances furnished to Gail by the woman, by a trusted colleague and friend, and further informed by her extensive direct experience and other knowledge concerning the dynamics of domestic violence. "I knew her story" is the way Gail described it.

RELATIONS WITHIN ACTION, KNOWLEDGE, AND CARING

If we are to fully accept the presence and power of some form of care in all of our intentional actions, and to acknowledge caring as an essential part of that which morally informs us, we need to further explore the nature of both. In doing so we discover that intentional action, profound moral knowledge, and caring are relational. All premeditated action has a subject—the actor—and an object—someone or something else whom or which the act is intended to affect. That someone or something lies outside the self, in the world of other selves, other forms of life, inanimate things, and in our shared ideas and organized arrangements. That is the locus of action, the place where it will have its external effects.

Caring, because it is expressed in and conveyed with our intended action, also has a subject actor and an intended target, the object or objects of our affection and concern. Unlike action, our caring may be only incidentally evident in the world outside the self. We go there only because we have to. Its exclusive object is the subject, the actor, the self. Thus, while our action relates us to the world, the form and quality of caring that we impart to our action informs those who experience or witness it of the manner and extent to which we see ourselves related to them and the world *as they know it*. Inferentially, they also learn something about how we define *our* world, and the degree of confluence of the two.

MULTIPLE MOTIVES

We often experience the motives that accompany our acting, the several forms and relative strengths of our caring, as complex and mixed. This awareness stems from the reality that one important situation or event can trigger several concerns involving others, the world, and one's self as we contemplate our response. We either sense or more consciously determine that our motives—our cares and concerns that finally motivate us to act—contain a blended mix of caring for our self and for others.

It appears to follow from the above that all human caring, including that which attends social and political action, exists along a continuum—a line strung between two opposing objects of care. The action of morally informed core actors would presumably attach near the pole of deep, altruistic concern for some "broad constituency" of others, while the action of those who are informed by more extreme versions of self-interest or exclusive views of community would gravitate to the pole of self-regard.[18]

The foregoing is neither the exclusive nor likely the dominant view. Many evolutionary biologists, for example, join with liberal rationalists in accepting the neater hypothesis that holds that most, if not all, of our caring, along with our associated action, is undertaken for the benefit of the self. Our moral capacities evolve in the same manner as our physical characteristics via natural selection "because they help the individuals who possess them to survive and reproduce."[19] Others argue with equal fervor (and apparently with Darwin) that we act mostly for the larger sake of some socio-biological group, upon the basis of information, including the forms and methods of care that the group maintains for its own benefit.[20] A further few assume the possibility that the truth lies less neatly in between and elsewhere, in the realm of cooperation, as is argued by evolutionary adaptationists, rather than in the dangerous realms of individual or group competition.[21]

Hopefully, on the strength of what we know with reasonable certainty about our own caring, and what we further are able to learn from the morally informed core actors such as those presented herein, we can discern that *neither* the continuum nor the evolutionary either-or alternatives explain us completely, either as individuals or as groups. Our common experience of mixed or multiple motives, of concerns for self and other, is likely correct and, although often painful or messy, not of any inalterable necessity, either fixed or inherently contradictory.

CONGRUENT CARING

Self-care and caring for others are not, or need not be seen as either mutually exclusive or as involving a zero-sum competition within the self. We have the demonstrated, varied, and developable capacity to care for our selves, the world, and others in ways that are neither mutually exclusive, nor inherently preferential, nor determined as to the objects of affection and concern. This is not to suggest that "win-win" scenarios of the utilitarian, New Democratic variety abound. Everything we do for the sake of another may not yield psychic rewards of equal weight to the self. The conditions of life impinge on our range of options for action and require us to make difficult, imperfect choices. At our best, we act in response to that composite of what we have come to know that informs us most deeply. Where that knowledge establishes some close connection between the self and others, or the self and the world, the continuum collapses, the dichotomy dissolves. The mixture of concerns relating to self and other becomes more complementary, less competitive, more amenable to peaceful resolution both within and outside of the self. That does not mean that our decision and resulting action will be easy or volitionally pain-free. We often have little control over the context of choice, and we must frequently decide on the strength of factual uncertainty. Almost invariably, however, we retain the radical freedom to choose and to act.

Our capacity for accommodating self and other in a single action becomes apparent when we return to the example of the person who, acting from deep love for another, gives over the food that will only keep one of them alive. From the perspective of the recipient or someone who later learns of the story, the act may be seen as selfless only; however, from the vantage point of the donor, to have acted otherwise would have been contrary to the most his or her fundamental understandings—say that of a parent's automatic, loving duty to her or his child. For that person, such an act is simply the most competent that one can take both for the sake of another and for one's self.

As caring for another does not invariably crowd out self-regard, care or regard for one's self that is expressed in action does not, of any pre-fixed necessity, crowd out our capacity to experience and express care for others or the world, whether in separate acts or in the same action. In a self that sees itself as radically free (in the sense of having the capacity to choose), as competent to act, and connected to all or some part of its known, believed-in world by a form of knowledge and corresponding level of care that exceeds that then afforded to the continuance of its physical life, then the self may be well served by its own apparent destruction. We are capable of deeply caring for others, the self, and the world—indeed, we must endeavor to do so if we are to live our lives to their full existential capacity. The inevitable imperfection and unforeseeable consequences of actions informed by such caring cannot and must not be accepted as an excuse or justification for the intentional encouragement of profound ignorance, exclusively self-serving instrumental action, or rote obedience to an individual, organization, tradition, or cause.

Extreme forms of intended action demonstrate the maximum thrust of human agency, its potentially devastating as well as uplifting effects, and reveal the form and intensity of caring that such action demonstrates. As suggested, extreme action intended for the benefit of others and motivated by concern for their welfare is sometimes further motivated by concern experienced for the sake of self—that we live up to our highest capacity and deepest insights, overcoming our insecurities, fears and other self-concerns. What we experience as will in the realm of morally informed action is really our striving to overcome the inevitable gaps that appear between our imperfect ability to know with constant clarity and to care with consistent strength.

Our inherent, developable capacity to care, much like our capacity to act authentically, is subject to inner variation over time and circumstance and is also strongly affected in its form and intensity by the quality of knowledge that informs it. The diverse patterns of care among individuals, societies, cultures, and states are simply a larger, much less exact expression of the varied quality of knowledge that affects caring in the self. This is apparent in the relationship between caring, ideals, and beliefs.

CARING AND IDEALS

Our social and political ideals and beliefs need to be understood as much more than rationally sensible arrangements for life in close proximity to others. For many, they serve as authentic symbols for past action and caring, as shorthand reminders of some better imagined way of life, and as concise expressions of hope for their greater instantiation in the future. Ideals, in other words, serve as terse, summary expressions that open our personal and common repositories of knowledge, care, and forms of action that we associate with the name. Like institutions, they exist most powerfully in the self where they are stored and can acquire an extended shelf life. They become thus known and vital in the world only through action and, to a lesser extent only, in written and oral accounts of their formation, preservation, and enhancement.

Democracy and freedom are cogent examples. The fact that the knowledge and forms of care associated with each varies widely among individuals and groups is evident in the practices that comprise American pluralism. Our dominant knowledge and belief concerning human nature, liberalism, informs us that representative democracy and freedom are fundamental requirements of the self, created and abstracted for the sake of the self and those instrumentally or affectionately important to our needy nature and particular circumstances. We may want these symbols to have substance for others, but not approaching the extent where their exercise might restrict *our* freedom by reducing the power, property, and other resources that define and secure it. Their demonstrated and symbolic reference point is the self.

Accordingly, our motive energy for deepening or extending freedom and democracy is a combination of instrumental self-care and weak sympathy for others. The latter is confirmed by our preference for charity or philanthropy rather than the sharing of power that comprehensive democracy and positive freedom entail. This dominant content of each symbol is evident in the acts of many who are excluded from their ambit, both at home and abroad. To the extent that they share the Enlightenment view of self in relation to others and the world that we disseminate so powerfully through institutional and systemic action, they offer themselves for easy enlistment in organizations and regimes that offer them a measure of enlightened access—symbolic inclusion—or in coups and revolutions against those that do not.

Others who are excluded, or who have refused the narrow terms of inclusion, forming instead fraternal and sororal communities for mutual support and democratic reform, evidence broader, more inclusive knowledge and forms of caring in association with these symbols. They resist the temptation to accept some form of co-optation while working to inform, confront, and persuade those who practice democracy only within exclusive bounds. Finally, there are a few who also strive to accomplish change by working within the traditions and practices of the system where the most influential of those whom they seek to persuade preside. John B., one of those interviewed, is an excellent example of this latter group, and of the attempt to inform deeply valued ideals with altruistic and concretely informed concerns.

CARING FOR DEMOCRACY
VERSUS DEMOCRATIC CARING

John B. and his democratic reform colleagues associate democracy and freedom with broad forms of knowledge and caring.[22] When interviewed, he was the director of the National Voting Rights Institute, a Boston based group that he founded in 1994 for the immediate purpose of "challenging the constitutionality of the current campaign finance system at the federal and state levels."[23] Since then, he has been active fulltime, employing his legal talent (Harvard Law School) and persuasive skills both to challenge "our campaign finance system in voting rights trials, and to defend [public financing] campaign reform laws that pass at the state and local level and then get subjected to constitutional challenge."

John is clearly determined to increase the level and quality of citizen democracy in our society. He has been instrumental and has lent support, for example, in the defense against court challenges to public campaign finance laws in Maine, Arizona, Massachusetts, and elsewhere. Moreover, he has learned that he must attend to these laws after they are upheld, and even where they have been the result of strong majority enactment via direct voter initiative, as was the case in Massachusetts.

After extensive efforts by other citizen democracy advocates in getting the proposed law on the ballot, the voters enacted it by a two to one margin in 1998.[24] The law, which is similar to one adopted and implemented in Maine, provided for funding in stages, with the law to go into full effect with the state-wide election of 2002.

As the first election under the new law approached, the notoriously non-democratic, Democrat-dominated Massachusetts legislature balked. Next, emboldened by the success of their initial action, the leaders in each chamber, with apparent majorities of their colleagues standing tacitly behind them, refused to authorize the release of the monies already appropriated to at least partially fund qualified candidates. At this juncture, John B. and his colleagues assisted supporters of the initiative by filing suit in the state high court. To the surprise of many, the court decided by a slim majority to order the executive branch to comply with the law.[25] When that did not occur, and the legislature remained unresponsive, John's group obtained a further court order allowing the seizure and sale of state-owned non-cash assets, the only further remedy that the court would allow under its view of the Massachusetts constitution. This course of action contained a mine-field of potential harms to the legitimate needs of other citizens whose programs would be affected. Accordingly, it was gingerly pursued by the NVRI.

The hope of the reform coalition, reflected in its seizure strategy, was that the publicity generated by a few targeted seizures, such as new SUVs purchased by the Lottery Commission or the desks of lawmakers, would embarrass them into honoring what the reformers fairly regarded as a democratic mandate.[26] Although their strategy did work for the Fall 2002 election, the legislature voted in early 2003 to repeal the law in direct defiance of the 1998 voter mandate.

When one becomes familiar with John B.'s background, it becomes apparent that his concepts of democracy and freedom are more strongly informed by his care for others than by a rationally informed idea of democracy leading to the logic of obligation. His idea of democracy and of freedom is part of his ideal vision, a future dream "that we have to fight for"; it is equally a morally informed way of life that is inspired by his experience of the world and of his caring for others in the present.

Of all the actors interviewed or studied for this project, John B. is perhaps the most positively nurtured and consistently mentored in the direction of core activism. This is largely due to his parents who were activists and went to great lengths to expose him to the world as they had come to know it. He readily acknowledges their role in his first answer to a general, open-ended question: "Well, my parents provided me with an enormous amount of influence growing up."

His mother, who founded and directed a nonprofit co-operative to support low-income artists from around the country, introduced him

to a number of amazing people from the Deep South and Appalachia who taught me a lot about different realities, [their] faith in their lives, the day-to-day struggle to survive that many of them didn't live through. And some of these people were involved in the equal rights movement and told me stories, taught me songs, that sort of thing.

His father, an Ecuadorian native, was a chemical engineer with E.I. du Pont de Nemours and Company when John was a child, attending law school at night. "He was also very engaged in working with farm workers in Tenant Square, Pennsylvania, which is the mushroom capital of the world. I went to some of the camps with him and was exposed to some of the conditions people were forced to live in." His father also took the family to Ecuador every other summer to visit his family, where the conditions of extreme poverty were further laid open.

His parents, although non-Quakers, further tended to his moral learning by sending him to the Wilmington Friend's School, located near where they lived in Delaware. It is part of a small number of Quaker-run schools across the country. During his twelve years at the school he was further furnished with both a grassroots and a global perspective of humanity and the planet and taught about each in a peace and social justice framework that related ideas to caring and acting. By the time he was in high school, he was already an activist, something that conventional schools discourage. Commenting on the school's teaching philosophy, he indicated his awareness that caring cannot be directly taught, only informed and stimulated: "So they certainly take a position. They're not as neutral as some other schools might be. They teach—they *encourage* a [sense of] responsibility to do something that would improve the world for everyone."

When he left home to further his education, his early influences persisted. At Brown University, he recalls, "I spent my junior year in India, and that had an enormous influence on me." He further easily withstood the enlightenment forge heat of a top-tier law school, spending one summer on a Navajo reservation in New Mexico, and another working as an advocate for farm workers in Florida.

Following law school, John spent some time in Washington, D.C., doing research on the influence of money in elections for the Center for Responsive

Politics. While there, he "helped develop a legal strategy that led to the founding of the [National Voting Rights] Institute."

For John, democracy "is a fundamental question," a matter of how one sees one's self in relation to others and the world at a basic ontological level. It is clear that his experienced and learned, felt and conceived connections to others, although expressed in ideals such as democracy, are what inform him, motivate him, and sustain him. He readily acknowledges his strong base of support, beginning with his family, extending to his fraternal and sororal colleagues. There is also his sense of present and historical connection—informing his heart and mind—to other activists, especially those who "have very little resources, but have the spirit to fight on. . . ." He summarizes the emotional component of his motive energy, stating: "I think that there's no question that you have to be passionate and committed to this work." We need to remind ourselves that "passion" and "commitment" are terms that signify the intensity of one's care.

The concretely informed human focus of his care becomes even more apparent when he discusses his less democratic and anti-democratic opponents. When offered the opportunity to label them as "the enemy," he declines, expressing his belief that "there is always the opportunity to move people in the right direction." While he sees, as did Eugene Debs, that there are some elites whose actions suggest that "they would be more satisfied in a dictatorship," he feels that many politicians are basically well-intended but misinformed about the actual conditions of life.

Showing the same insight and faith as Jane Addams and John Dewey, he believes that his opponents "have this supreme fear of [democratic] process" due to their fundamental distrust of the capacity of average citizens. They would not trust the poor to govern, because they believe the poor "are not capable of that." Echoing Frederick Douglass, he continued, gently critiquing elites *and* average citizens as part of a common human puzzle:

> People need to be confronted. . . . I don't think there's any chance . . . that people will just change [automatically]. . . . But I think people can change and I definitely believe that we can really persuade people to; [however], you can't just let them off the hook. Sometimes it requires a fair amount of pressure.

Any residual doubt concerning the role of care in informing John's passionate core activism and his sense of individual duty was erased toward the end of his interview. As he discussed his problems with moral relativism, he further revealed his understanding of human nature, and his own motivation:

> We have a lot of wavering. We have a lot of looking at the center and then compromising. We need some steady, demanding voices our there. . . . There is no

compromise when it comes to poverty in America. It needs to be abolished.
There is no compromise to big money controlling our democracy. It needs to be
abolished.

When asked whether his basis for knowing or believing that these proposi-
tions were morally right was rational, he related rational thought to moral
knowledge and caring in a manner that we need to consider for ourselves:

Question: How do you know what's right and what's wrong?

John: I would say it's world experience. People come from different places, you
know, but my world experience gives me a set of guideposts to understand . . .
how I think of what's right and wrong. I'm not suggesting that on every single
question I automatically know what is right and . . . wrong, but on certain core
questions, I don't find there's a whole lot of difficulty in determining. . . .

Question: Describe to me how that is grounded in you. . . . Is it rational, logical?

John: Yeah. And, you know, it's connected to human needs and that we ought to
be able to stand up for other human beings.

Asked to further explain the ground for his concerns, and whether it might
stem from religion or some broader spirituality, he replied: "Well, it's not that
I don't respect that others have religious faith and so forth . . . but you know,
I personally find that power *in individual humans—in relationships* [empha-
sis added]."

ICONIC AND INSTITUTIONAL CARING

Just as caring in some form is present in all intended action, the attitude of
certainty is characteristic of all action that has been informed by some combination of profound knowledge and intense caring. Certainty originates in
our knowledge and feeling, in the fundamental nexus of heart and mind. It is
a quality associated with our most profound insights, awareness, and reflection but not, for reasons previously discussed, necessarily with any *particular plan* or course of action. Depending on the content of our certain knowledge, the forms of action and the means to be employed are constrained—as,
for example, with the eschewing of violence. Certainty is present—our certain knowledge is reflected—in the strength of our perceived *need* or *desire*
to act, and is discernable to others in the nature and manner of our acting. Because, however, there is often still a wide range of specific choices within
moral constraints, as well as a lot of facts and contingencies that are unknown
or uncertain, there is a great deal of room left for humility, or as Gandhi ex-

pressed it, for regarding even our most deeply informed projects as "experiments with Truth."[27]

Morally informed certainty is often expressed in elemental terms of knowing right and wrong, as with John B. It is also stated in personal terms of overriding duty or unconditional obligation, such as is indicated in the common refrain of the rescuers of Jews during World War II. When asked why they had put themselves and their immediate loved ones in palpable mortal peril, they replied, in effect: "What else could I do?"[28]

It has been argued thus far that our deeply informed caring, regardless of its object, has at least two primary effects: it prompts us into action, and it strongly affects the form and method of action that we choose. Since caring as a conscious state of mind results from of our varied ability to learn, feel, and reflect, the form of knowledge or object that we direct our attention toward and to which we attach the highest moral significance indirectly affects the nature of our action. More succinctly put, we act with our greatest strength, our fewest doubts, to install, defend, and enhance that which we come to know most profoundly—with the greatest certainty—and therefore care about most deeply.

The qualities of certain knowing and caring that result are often expressed in abstract formulations of fundamental truth, universally applicable as categorical absolutes. Principles, canons, doctrines, creeds, and articles of faith are only a few of the generic titles we have assigned to them. They are not the same as ideals, except to the extent that ideals such as democracy are construed as part of an overarching ideology—some set of beliefs and practices that are binding on everyone, regardless of circumstance or preference.

As John B.'s actions to achieve greater democracy in America reveal, such abstractions can be powerful reservoirs of knowledge and inspiration. His life experiences and his activism suggest that his ideas and precepts of democracy were formed—and remain—in the world of exposure to and interaction with a wide array of persons, present and past, to whom he became deeply attached. His dedication to the concept and practices of democracy, and his lesser, related respect for liberal republican institutions and the rule of law, are informed by, therefore subordinate to, his learning that stems from relationship to others and the care for them which that experience helps to instill. John's *primary* attachments are to others, his fundamental faith is in others, and his political vision is the expression of the social, economic, and political relationship that he wants for their sake *and* for his. His idea of democracy is therefore informed by concrete, interpersonal, affectionate warmth, not the sterility of a process that is derived from life-detached ideation.

When we become more attached in our caring to social and political moral precepts than to what and who has informed them, we locate ourselves in some at least partially ethereal realm, a world informed first and foremost by ideas. That is the risk that is inherent in the false notion of the pure rational idea, the timeless conception around which the past is reconstructed, the present is framed, and the future preordained.

When Eugene Debs experienced his "jailhouse conversion" to Marxist determinism and socialism, his initial world-view of general basic human decency and his youthful, cultural exposure to Horatio Algerism, the centaur-like offspring of the American enlightenment, were each recast into a dichotomy of labor and capital—good and evil— on a single, inevitable grand stage of history. From that point onward, he never sought to persuade, only to defeat, those who were not at least closely allied with the proletariat. Fealty to a set of beliefs became as important, if not more so, than his deep, affectionate fraternal association with workers who, by and large, did not share his iconic ideology, but revered him for his efforts on their behalf nonetheless.

His caring, however, continued to inform his idea of democracy and his clear preference for nonviolence. This suggests a close relationship between the idea of democracy and certain knowledge of a world that was still broad and vital enough to inform him. It also explains why labor was moved by his caring even after his rigid adoption of a world-view that explained more of the past, present, and future that we are capable of knowing with certainty.

CARING NEAR THE EDGE OF ABSTRACTION

Our ideas concerning life have had tremendous social and political ramifications in America. Enlightenment-informed knowledge has led to political relativism, given its pragmatic assumption that individual life in the active, contested world of politics is all that we can address safely with a majority voice. The question of when life begins before it can vote or revolt is a matter of private secular, spiritual, and religious concern that involves government only indirectly through its generally accepted role as our pluralist referee. The demonstrable fact that governing elites have never succeeded in maintaining their own neutrality on this issue only confirms its basic importance and the degree of caring that each of us attaches to it.

Mary McD., another interviewee for this project, is part of a significant minority who ardently believes that human life begins at least as early as conception. Given their relative pluralist political weight at the national level, they have formed an often uneasy alliance with the Republican Party where their rewards have come in the form of federal court appointees and policies that seek to thwart public funding of abortions either at home or abroad. Regionally and locally, they have been somewhat successful in indirect political strategies to weaken *Roe vs. Wade* (1973) by efforts to restrict access to abortion services, such as waiting periods, parental consent for minors, and grassroots support for candidates to city councils and school boards who support the pro-life agenda. Finally, in cities, communities, and states where political strategies are unlikely to be successful, they struggle as core actors and supporters in organized, persuasive efforts to inform others of their views and to broaden their acceptance as profound truth.

Mary has become a persistent, humble, yet visible activist on this issue. She demonstrates a strong preference for authentic action, and is by no means a supporter of violent action as a morally justified response to abortion, although she believes it to be a form of homicide. For her and for millions of Americans, the moral right to life for all human purposes begins at conception, not at viability or at birth. It is a principle of the highest moral certainty, a fundamental belief involving the nature and origins of life itself.

The "right-to-life" or "pro-life" precept lies near the border of belief that is abstracted or derived from life in the concrete world, and the abstract idea that both symbolizes and constitutes certain belief. In the former, life in the flesh for some is sacrosanct, for others it is entirely relative to self, and for most of us it is in the sometimes agonizing "in between" of situational encounter and moral conflict. Albert Schweitzer is one notable example of those for whom "reverence for life" in virtually all detectable forms is expressed and confirmed in lives of caring, congruent action.[29]

For others, it is the content of the abstraction, understood as a fixed, inviolable principle or doctrine whose subject matter is life *as therein defined*. This does not imply that those of us who adhere to such certain beliefs are devoid of any sense of value or caring for life outside their scope; however, it does mean that in a concrete conflict between one form of life and another—a mother-to-be and the unborn within her, for example—the form that is protected by the principle should prevail. The form and intensity of caring that connects us to each life is acknowledged and experienced by many adherents but does not factor into the decision. Something more important than interpersonal caring is involved.

Abstract principles of the latter form are grounded on certain belief in the *a priori authority* that formulates the abstraction. In is the authorship of the principle that gives it its certainty. Certainty based on the false notion of pure reason has little durable social and political weight because, by its nature, such authority is individual in its origins, inherently subjective, and cares first and finally only for its author, the self.

When the ultimate authorship is seen as divine and furnished to us in a long, widely shared, and valued institutional tradition, the principle becomes powerful and persuasive not only individually, but socially and politically as well. The fact that the principle also relates to a matter of basic importance to each of us—and offers a clear rule for resolving our fundamental concern—only enhances its influence on our action.

Mary McD.'s personal belief reflects the close association between principle and institutional transmission, in her case, via Roman Catholicism. She was raised as an only child in a loving, working-class family that devoutly observed the beliefs and ritual practices of the Catholic Church as they existed in the Springfield, Massachusetts, area during the 1940s and 1950s. Neither of her parents was active on either social or political issues, devoting themselves, as most of us do, to work, family, and the raising of their daughter in a nurturing environment. "My parents gave me every benefit" is how she summarizes her upbringing that, from a child's perspective, seamlessly incorporated family, church, and schooling.

After graduating from college she pursued a diplomatic career in the United States Foreign Service. For the next thirty years, from 1955 to 1985, when she retired, she led what she summarized as a "very interesting" life, posted in succession to our embassies in Paris, Warsaw, Ankara, Stockholm, and Brussels. She recalls that she was most stimulated by Ankara during the 1970s with its mixture of ancient, traditional, and cosmopolitan, reflected in its unique visual, sensory mix. She found Stockholm during the 1960s the least interesting, describing it as "pretty, pretty, pretty, but very dull. Everybody looked alike on the street."

Spending her entire career overseas except for brief home leaves, she readily admits that she "lost touch" with what was going on in America, including the furor over *Roe vs. Wade* in 1973 and thereafter. "I might have heard about it but I didn't get personally involved or emotionally involved in many of the things going on in the United States." She volunteered that she had never married, "never had children," expressing the latter ingredient in the mixture of satisfaction and regret that we experience as we look back on our lives. "I do feel that I've missed a tremendous amount. I try not to look back . . . but I [also] feel that I have been blessed in many ways."

Mary had reached adulthood devout in her received faith and had actively maintained her relationship with the church throughout her career. She recalled that on one occasion, while posted to Warsaw in the Iron Curtain 1950s, she had gotten to know a nun who acted as the "outside liaison" for her small cloistered order located in an old part of Warsaw. The nun told her about the suffering and loss her convent had experienced during the Nazi occupation that included the slaughter of several members. Mary came to admire the woman for her personal courage, evident in the risks she took to raise financial support, obtain food, and garner other necessities under the new oppressive conditions of enforced secular communism. Referring to her own faith, she noted: "I was always a faithful Catholic, you know, but I'm much more involved in it now."

After retiring from government service in 1985, she returned to the Pioneer Valley, settling north of Springfield in the "five college" area because she thought it would be "an interesting place to live." She also "reconnected with friends [from her] childhood . . ." and through them became exposed to the right-to-life movement. Her two closest renewed friendships were with sisters, one of whom was "involved with the movement." She describes her exposure and gradually greater involvement as follows:

> She and her husband were deeply involved in the pro-life movement and bought me a ticket to the annual dinner they have. I sort of said "I don't know if I want to go." So they forced me to go and kept talking—"why don't you get involved with this?" Well I [didn't] want to. I've got other things and eventually I began to being more and more interested, and then people in the Pioneer Valley office, Massachusetts Citizens for Life, which is located in Ludlow, I began to know them. I didn't work very much with them but they said "why don't you form a chapter up here?" Well no, I wasn't going to form a chapter and that went on for several years.

In 1992, Mary relented and agreed to help organize a local chapter, doing so with eight to ten others. One year later she agreed to serve as its Chair, a position she has held ever since. Modestly referring to her role as something she simply "stuck with," she continued:

> Fortunately I say stuck, you know, because there is a lot of work, but I regard it as a very important part of my life in the sense that I feel it's a service . . . a service to God. I feel that I have been privileged [in my life] in a tremendous way . . . so I do have an obligation to give back a little, and this is one way that I can do that.

As earlier suggested, Mary's beliefs regarding the sanctity of human life appear to have been formed and have evolved within the Catholic doctrinal tradition.[30] Both her career and the church have likely fostered her ecumenical approach to activism on the right-to-life issue. Acting in the consciously informed spirit of Vatican II, which afforded " a much greater role for [lay] people to play," she emphasize that the organization "meets in a non-denominational church," in Northampton; although "most members are Catholic, and I deplore that. I think [of it] as everybody's organization." She is further concerned that "it's awfully white, too," although the group does have a black member.

The primary strategy of her organization is public persuasion. At least twice a year, they form an informational picket line on the Coolidge Bridge, the primary artery connecting Amherst and Northampton over the Connecticut River. She notes: "If we get twenty-five people we're lucky, but we stretch all the way across the bridge." They also take part in similar protests outside Bay State Medical Center in Springfield, various regional protests, and the annual mass demonstration in Washington, D.C., on the anniversary of the *Roe* decision.

Mary and her colleagues also work hard to at least limit the availability of abortion services in the Pioneer Valley. Through physicians and other supporters who work in the healthcare field, they identify and pressure hospitals and government agencies who either provide or are considering providing such services. Finally, they have done some work on college campuses helping students to organize and conduct pro-life rallies. In one such rally on the University of Massachusetts Amherst campus, she experienced the phenomenon that had made Frances Crowe somewhat uncomfortable in the mid-1980s, when students at Smith College, with her assistance, made it impossible for a State Department spokesman to be heard:

> I never went to anything like it in my life. It was so raucous and the effort to squelch and stop it and cover it up with yells and everything was, you know, it's just terrible. You think what is the University teaching? What are they teaching?

On this concern, which stands in some contrast to the greater moral complexity of the circumstances that Crowe and her colleagues had confronted, one should acknowledge the validity of her point. Tolerance, like any form of moral action, is durable only when informed both by knowledge and some form of deep, intrinsic regard for others. Further, as Frances Crowe acknowledged in her interview, there are many who are broadly active in peace and social justice causes who are informed by both concrete and abstract forms of altruistic care, including a core spiritual connection to life that has led them also to individually oppose abortion.

The interview with Mary was conducted in March 2000. At the time, she was queried about her views and possible activism on other moral concerns relating to other fundamental social and political issues. She indicated that she was interested in American foreign policy matters, as was the case throughout her career; however, now as then she generally agreed with official governmental policy, assuming its good faith correctness when she was not directly familiar with underlying facts. Further, on those occasions when she has disagreed, she has not been spurred to activism. As for domestic concerns, such as the civil rights movement, she kept aware through the international editions of the *Herald Tribune*, and held private opinions, but acted within the constraints of her career, trusting her belief in American democracy and its traditional practices of bureaucratic hierarchy and political accountability.

At the time of the interview, Mary was active only on the pro-life issue, although she volunteered that she also accepted her church's teaching on the immorality of capital punishment. More recently, however, she also got involved in a project to place a binding referendum question on the statewide ballot in Massachusetts. The proposal, since defeated by the legislature and later pre-empted by the state's highest court, called for amending the Massachusetts Constitution for the purpose of limiting civil marriage and its associated rights and privileges to heterosexual couples only. Interviewed at the state capital after the legislature's unfavorable vote, Mary was quoted as saying: "It requires a vote of the people, not these characters. It's a very serious issue for society. It can't be allowed to rest."[31]

Although Mary's activism has come later in life, and although it is informed by caring attached to ideas that are more intangibly and institutionally informed than concretely and interpersonally, it is clear that she cares deeply and ecumenically for people, likely on a level approximating the intensity of her doctrinal convictions. It is also apparent that she is greatly comforted and inspired through deep friendship and fraternal association, as were all of the core actors who were studied and interviewed, including those who for reasons of time and the other reasons offered in Chapter 1 are not expressly included.

It is further obvious that, as with all of the named and unnamed core actors herein, her affection for others is expressed in her embrace of democratic persuasive means, rather than the absolutism of violence. However, unlike the others, except for Eugene Debs and one other interviewed couple who were also involved in the pro-life cause, Mary's caring is informed by a form of knowledge that carries with it the potential to set boundaries between lives and within the continuum of life itself. Part of the problem is inherent in the institutionalization of belief within a tradition that combines moral absolutism with hierarchical formulation, pronouncement, and the sanctioning of both saints and apostates. Although much softened in the somewhat devolved practice of contemporary Catholicism, particularly in America, such knowledge continues to divide us unnecessarily. We run the institutionally enhanced risks associated with our division into believers and nonbelievers, converts and non-converts, the saved and the damned—into opposing teams of good and evil—with the risk that caring will be directed more at the preservation of an abstract doctrine, or the institution that asserts it, rather than at the broader, more inclusive truth that underlies it.

Given her broad affection for others and her concomitant support of democratic process, Mary is able to subordinate her particularized, doctrinal views concerning the sanctity of life and the nature and purpose of sexual union to a wider, more deeply held priority—upholding the sanctity of the full variety of human life. Such is the fundamental knowledge from which moral progress can be guilt in our diverse world of which America is emblematic.

NOTES

1. William James, "The Function of Cognition," from *The Meaning of Truth* (1909) in John J. McDermott, ed., *The Writings of William James*, 144–45.

2. Buber, 66.

3. Helen E. Longino, "Moral Agency and Responsibility," in *Mind and Morals: Essays on Cognitive Science and Ethics*, Larry May, Marilyn Friedman, and Andy Clark, eds. (Cambridge, MA: MIT Press, 1996), 291.

4. E. Ann Kaplan, "Women, Morality, and Social Change from a Discourse Analysis Perspective," in *Social and Moral Values: Individual and Social Perspectives*, Nancy Eisenberg, Janus Reykowski, Ervin Staub, eds. (Hillsdale, NJ: Lawrence Erlbaum Associates, 1989), 360.

5. McWilliams, 43.

6. The Buddhist practice of "mindfulness" is one such habit, similar to the idea of awareness just introduced, although it is most often a consciously acquired habit, particularly in our culture. See Thich Nhat Hanh, *The Heart of the Buddha's Teaching: Transforming Suffering into Peace, Joy, and Liberation* (1998; New York: First Broadway Books-Random House, Inc., 1999), 64–83.

7. For an interesting feminist alternative interpretation of our history, see Rosalind Miles, *Who Cooked the Last Supper? The Women's History of the World* (New York: Three Rivers Press, 2001).

8. Clarice Feinman, *Women and the Criminal Justice System*, 3rd ed. (Westport, CT: Praeger Publishing, 1994), 3–6.

9. Lawrence Kohlberg, *The Psychology of Moral Development* (San Francisco: Harper and Row, 1984), 636. Taken from his title for the sixth, or highest, stage of moral development.

10. Carol Gilligan, *In a Different Voice: Psychological Theory and Women's Development* (1982; Cambridge, MA: Harvard University Press, 1993), 18. See also quote from 1791 lecture by Founder James Wilson (Ch. 2, note 15).

11. McWilliams, 38–50; 618–24.

12. Knowledge of the Jewish historical experience, and of one's Jewish roots, was a powerful influence on Ira H., another interviewee quoted and discussed in the first chapter.

13. Pearl M. Oliner and Samuel P. Oliner, *Toward a Caring Society: Ideas into Action* (Westport, CT: Praeger Publishers, 1995), 2. The Oliners' focus is on altruistic action, which they define as "assuming personal responsibility for others' welfare."

14. Noted novelist and social critic E. L. Doctorow is the author of several books, including *Welcome to Hard Times* (1960), *Big as Life* (1966), *The Book of Daniel* (1971), and *Billy Bathgate* (1989).

15. McWilliams, 7.

16. The history of addressing the problem of battering is another microcosm of the problems of overcoming gendered perception and institutionalized gender bias in our society.

17. For a thorough discussion of battering and self-defense, see Joanne Belknap, *The Invisible Woman: Gender, Crime, and Justice*, 2nd. ed. (Wadsworth Group-Thompson Learning, 2001), ch. 8, and sources cited. See also Elizabeth Dermody Leonard, *Convicted Survivors: The Imprisonment of Battered Women Who Kill* (Albany: SUNY Press, 2002).

18. Oliner and Oliner, *Toward a Caring* Society, 2.

19. Elliot Sober and David Sloan Wilson, *Unto Others: The Evolution and Psychology of Unselfish Behavior* (Cambridge, MA: Harvard University Press, 1998), 3.

20. Sober and Wilson, 4–13. According to them, Darwin clarified his views on the mechanism of natural selection to encompass altruistic action undertaken for group benefit, as indicated in the following portion of "a famous passage" from *The Descent of Man* (1871):

> It must not be forgotten that although a high standard of morality gives but a slight or no advantage to no individual man and his children over the other men of the same tribe, yet . . . an increase in the number of well-endowed men and advancement in the standard of morality will certainly give an immense advantage to one tribe over another." Sober and Wilson, 4.

21. Sober and Wilson, 11–12. Cf. Kai Halilweg and C. A. Hooker, eds., *Issues in Evolutionary Epistemology* (Albany: SUNY Press, 1989).

22. John B. is one of two interviewees whose do not actually work or live in Western Massachusetts. Kathy K., discussed in Chapter 1, was speaking at an area church and later agreed to talk about herself from her home in Chicago. John only lived in the region for a short time when his family moved here in during his last year in high school. I learned about him from Frances Crowe and decided to interview him rather than his father, who is also an activist lawyer and practices in the Pioneer Valley. His focus is on the rights of indigenous Ecuadorians, on whose behalf he has pursued precedent setting litigation against major oil companies in U.S. federal courts.

23. From the mission statement on the group's website, http://http://nvri.org/page 6.html. The statement continues: "Through *litigation* and *public education*, the Institute aims to redefine the issue of private money in public elections as the newest voting rights barrier, and to emphasize the *constitutional rights* of *all* citizens, regardless of economic status, to participate in the entire election process on an equal and meaningful basis."

24. The account that follows has been gathered from several news accounts in the *Boston Globe* and *Berkshire Eagle*. The citizen advocates referred to include several of those interviewed, a fact that was not known in advance.

25. *Bates et al. vs. Director of the Office of Campaign and Political Finance* 436 Mass. 144 (2002).

26. Evidencing the democratic process at work within the reform coalition, the NVRI seized three parcels of state-owned land in eastern Massachusetts in early summer 2002; however, it only proceeded with the sale of one after concerns were raised

by other environmentalists and others concerning the public harm that would result if the other two were sold to private parties. Responding to pressure, the legislature released enough funds to fund the few remaining candidates who have qualified for public funding. *Boston Globe*, 22 July 2002, 18.

27. See Chapter 1, note 27.

28. Oliner and Oliner, *The Altruistic Personality*, 163–70; Monroe, 196–200.

29. See Chapter 1, note 6.

30. Her belief concerning life is consistent with church doctrine both as regards abortion and the death penalty, which she also opposes, although she has not been active on that issue.

31. Springfield, Massachusetts *Union News*, 18 July 2002, A1.

Chapter Eight

The Capacity to Learn and to Know

In effect, what seems to hold ambition and unbridled desire for power in check is some sense of a larger context of life, a recognition that something greater than the self is at stake in how one chooses to spend and be spent.

—Laurent A. Parks Daloz et al.[1]

Not all protest emerges out of clear structural positions, but often simply out of a shared vision.

—James M. Jasper[2]

I think every one of us is born with a need, an ability . . . to grow, and once we come to the realization that growth is a natural thing . . . you [can] experience it.

—Pastor B., interviewee

The rationalist's fallacy . . . is exactly like the sentimentalist's. Both extract a quality from the muddy waters of experience, and find it so pure when extracted that they must contrast it with each and all of its muddy instances as an opposite and higher nature. All the while it is *their* nature.

—William James[3]

When will we teach our children in school what they are? We should say to each of them: Do you know what you are? You are a marvel. You are unique. In all the world there is no other child exactly like you. In the millions of years that have passed there has never been another child like you. . . . You may become a Shakespeare, a Michelangelo, a Beethoven.

You have the capacity for anything. Yes, you are a marvel. And when you grow up, can you then harm another who is, like you, a marvel?

—Pablo Casals[4]

REMOVING BARRIERS

If the idea of moral progress is to become more vital in America, we must learn the actual, powerful, shareable, basic truths about ourselves, each other, and the world. Although the sources of truth to be learned from are universally available, the acquisition of the truth each offers is not. From the perspective of an isolated self, particularly one insecurely focused on its mortality, it seems more important to learn how to harness and use the world for one's own needs, rather than to learn about its profound, intrinsic nature. It is not that we are either all or entirely unaware that the latter exists, or that we are totally ignorant of the truths such knowledge reveals, although too many of us are profoundly misinformed. Treasuring our current comfort, we fear the personal consequences of learning too deeply, too intimately. We sense— correctly—that such knowing may disrupt the pattern of our lives.

As first suggested, our reluctance to look directly, openly at life has been powerfully justified by our Enlightenment heritage of human understanding from liberalism and communitarianism, and, for many still, by our belief in the last-minute availability of the undeserved grace of individual forgiveness and salvation from the temporal consequences of the original sin embedded in our nature. Overcoming such powerfully fabricated and maintained barriers that, given their apparent success as premises for a stable liberal order, are seen to have worked so well, is not easy. The task requires that we must first learn to swim against the powerful tide of our significantly unenlightened, powerfully reinforced, ontological ignorance. For many if not most of us, this means that we need to acknowledge the possibility that we have been fundamentally misinformed and, as a consequence, that we have learned to misinform ourselves.

In our time, our impoverished inheritance of moral learning—our common grasp of our own nature, that of others, and the world—has left us increasingly alone and adrift in an ersatz national community: a political world of public policy that informs us mainly with facts, trends, systemic constraints, and incremental probabilities; a political culture of increasingly narrowly construed interests and beliefs, and a national identity less maintained by the thin rhetoric of enervated political ideals than by habit and the apparent impossibility of mounting a successful challenge to our existing order; a popular culture of two dimensional, communal images, sensate dreams, and coordinated products, all produced to stimulate and satisfy consumptive behaviors that are themselves the product of previous mass images. Many of us, like Dorothy in Oz, have peeked behind the curtain, and have caught a glimpse of the ordinary wizards manning the controls.

Notwithstanding our insight, however, we feel ourselves trapped in the surrounding indifference, immense size, and complex constraints of our more well understood but still limited known world. As a result we believe that our increasingly complete isolation from others outside the private coterie of self is irremediable, at least for now.

Too many of our educated professionals, acting as the specialists of knowledge and expertise in each realm of society, are themselves caught up in the worlds that they inherited and continue to create. In growing company with the rest of us, they live paradoxical, segmented lives—one in a private world that ideally consists of affectionate, intimate relations to particular people and exclusive places. The other or "public" world lacks intimacy and the authentic disclosure of self that intimacy presupposes. It is comprised instead of instrumental, often choreographed connections to others in circumscribed relationships where structural constraints, knowledge barriers, realities of power, and undisclosed personal agendas define their boundaries. Given the fundamental disharmony of this arrangement, it is not at all surprising that so many seek relief from their existential schizophrenia in therapy, life-style adjustments, escapist adventures, spiritual comfort-seeking, and early retirement.

All the while, the external facts upon which the instrumental world is premised are shifting as its most influential operators invent, by their powerful initiating, entrepreneurial agency, new organizational and other devices to extract and control greater resources for their exclusive enjoyment, often by denying them to others. These free radicals, Ayn Rand superstars who are functionally present in any modern society and are scarcely tamed by rational morality in ours, alter the system dynamic, changing the pluralist mix by attracting a multitude of imitative actors in their wake, leaving social scientists, our rational discerners of what is, to detect each major alteration after the trend has emerged. It is no surprise, then, that so many of the latter group, upon detecting their version of Sisyphus's eternal dilemma, write articles for colleagues or go to work for those who wield the power shape the world.[5]

The foregoing is an admittedly broad and greatly oversimplified depiction of the current consequences of the take on human nature that powerfully emerged during the Enlightenment and has since grown to dominate our understanding of self and other. It is equally true that our Enlightenment legacy has enabled us to accomplish much. We live longer, and in vastly greater physical comfort, due to a myriad brilliantly conceived, life-enhancing new knowledge. We do so, however, at least somewhat aware of the growing irony of our current version of modernity. The lives we live are incredibly more factually informed and materially abundant. At the same time, they are, if anything, less profoundly satisfying than the more abbreviated ones our national forebears lived after freedom became their claim of right, but before the promise of full-time leisure and material immortality became broadly conceivable possibilities, and our social, economic, and political systems were seen to have acquired lives separate and superior to our own. We are at another moral crossroads, as important as that which helped spur the Enlightenment, and we are unable to move forward on the strength of our existing knowledge and corresponding rational means.

For many, especially those such as Frederick Douglass, whose ancestors did not experience either the status or material rewards of American freedom, and others who still do not share in the promise of opportunity, the dark portrayal of who too many of us have become, may seem patent. For others who still find themselves lacking access and material security, however, the limited potential and destructive impacts inherent in our more open system of institutionalized self-aggrandizement are often not automatically apparent. They simply want in. As Douglass understood, the effects of intentional, delusional, and innocent ignorance leading to excessive attention to self is part of our shared inheritance, unique in America only in the breadth and depth of its institutionalized legitimacy. Moreover, its individual injustices are even forgivable by the victims, especially when the fortuitous at least demonstrate that they are open to new learning and persuasion.[6] The willfully arrogant and the rigidly fearful—those who will not allow themselves to be persuaded— must be otherwise contended with, but one need not dissipate the energy necessary to overcome their narrow world-view by despising them or by employing means that only confirm that well-intentioned reformers also have much to learn.

It is not that our chronic striving to avoid death or to achieve temporal immortality is incomprehensible. Fear of death, a frequent informant of our "love of life," is chronic in our youth-obsessed culture, embedded in our notion of the driving force of evolution, whereas deep, intimate love *for* life is not. Whatever our professed fundamental beliefs, sentient life is all that too many of us have learned to know with certainty, and a greater abundance of the orgasmic, aesthetic, and lesser pleasures its extension affords is highly enticing.

We are much more than mortally insecure. Many of us are deeply aware and fundamentally ill at ease with what we have become—with our own inaction and the action that is taken in our collective national brand name. Some of us further sense that we are far from enlightened, somehow profoundly ignorant and disconnected from life, and that there is much more that we are capable of knowing and being. We have grown increasingly anxious and re-signed, searching and waiting for answers from others or awaiting some calamity that will stimulate a deeper moral response in ourselves and, per-haps, in others—passive postures that are not only dangerous, but also un-necessary. In sum, we are open to more profound learning.

The fundamental answers that we seek are, as first mentioned, already present in our common, known and knowable world, the only place where certain truth can be found, truths about ourselves, each other, and the place we severally inhabit, but seem unable to more profoundly discover and there-fore share. In order to discern these truths, we must struggle with ourselves to shed our Enlightenment-inspired core assumptions about the nature of life, including our own, and adopt new methods for learning about the full nature of who we are and all else that is, as far as we can know it.

The effort to accomplish this does not require that we deny the informative strengths of rational material discovery, nor must we automatically shed the potential vitality of received religious faith; rather, we need to add to these means of learning in order to expand and, where necessary, alter their doctri-nal insights concerning the nature and significance of ourselves, of others, and the world. Neither does the content of a more vital, profound moral framework mandate our subordination or abandonment of family, friends, and communities of others in the name of some higher principle or greater good. To do so, in fact, would not only diminish their intrinsic value, thereby sug-gesting that we have failed to learn deeply the significance of life as it is, but also would deny their *ongoing* critical role in our own moral formation, our own quest for vital truth. Their moral import lies in our robust discovery of *who* they are, derived from the authentic, intimate nature of our engagement with them, and in our own ability to broaden what we can learn from them *as* they are, not only in their formal roles, their particular setting, or from the ex-clusive perspective of our own instrumental needs.

We need to further understand that there is no cultural model, nor any cor-responding institution—political, religious, or other—that is *essential* to the initial and ongoing process of moral formation, moral discovery, or to the task of morally informed social and political change. Institutions are the product of acquired habits, patterns of thinking, learning, and doing that are initiated and sustained by human agents who precede their formation and drive their alteration. In the case of major, profound innovation or change, the locus of such actors is either outside or at the periphery of the mainstream institutions of their era. Profoundly informed core actors, the exemplars of moral learn-ing, the initiators of what may later become institutionalized, have demon-strated this phenomenon in each generation. Once formed or reformed, such institutions provide, at their highly important best, a space for vital learning, forums for moral persuasion, and other resources that extend—and limit—the potential reach of their constituents and their beliefs.

The governing agents of our institutional life are rarely comfortable, however, with core actors, their most vitally informed members, prominently located in their ranks, preferring instead to rely on the transmitted, ritualized, enhanced memory of the lives and beliefs of those who began them. As such, they are only partially reflective of our nature, especially our individual capacity to learn more deeply and to grow. We will know that we are in the process of doing so, of moving beyond the important but limited potential of our liberal and traditional communal institutional heritage, as we find ourselves discovering, caring deeply for, *and* acting with, others to build upon a broader, more inclusive image of ourselves and the world that we have, thus far, largely been unable to see with sufficient holistic clarity.

The first two parts of this project—examining our Enlightenment philosophical legacy, and introducing via a cadre of morally informed core actors a more robust, vital world-view and capacity for action—are complete. In the last chapter, the process of constructing a fuller, richer moral epistemology, a better understanding about how we become most profoundly morally informed and motivated to act, was begun. We have the capacity to care deeply for what and whom we know most intimately and profoundly. Caring deeply, we acquire the capacity or motive strength to act to our full individual and collective potential. But what is the knowledge that so powerfully informs our caring and, in turn, our action?

In this chapter an effort is made to complete this assignment, once again with the invaluable example of selected morally informed core actors. Through their assistance, we can not only discover and expand our extant capacity to learn deeply about ourselves, others, and the world, but we can also glimpse for ourselves some of the certain knowledge that they have been able to discover. They are not, however, capable of directly imparting the vitality or the certain quality that inheres in the content of their learning. At best, their example can inform us, inspire us to begin, broaden, and deepen our own direct—authentic and intimate—engagement with life in its particulars, including themselves, and thereby gain the knowledge that imparts these qualities in us. Following their example, in other words, will lead us not only to the truths they have become aware of and encountered, but also to their significance and motive strength. On the impetus of our current profound dissatisfaction, on the strength of what we perhaps suspect or have somewhat already learned, with the imperfect example and support of such actors, we must exercise our less informed wills in order to overcome our existing habits and make our own beginning.

LEARNING FROM THE PARTICULAR

Profound moral learning is inherently inductive. It begins, as first mentioned, at birth with our experience of the immediate and the particular. We enter the world unaware that it and others exist, yet carrying within us our specie's particular combination of what we already are and may hereafter become. In varied circumstances, we arrive already equipped with our mysteriously acquired, developable potential—our universal capacities to know, to care, and to act and our unique talents for doing so. It is not the mechanisms of assignment that are so mysterious; some of that is factually understood.[7] It is the wonder that it happens at all. More than any other question that expresses our profound mortal curiosity, it is the sequential, Socratic, questioning and response to the puzzle of "Why?" addressed to the fundamental matters of life that propels us to learn and potentially grow. It is not that this question can be answered, at least not in our current or foreseeable reach. Its import lies in the stimulus it provides to become more fully aware of, to directly, intimately encounter the profound nature of what is.

As has been increasingly implied and suggested, our capacities for profound learning, caring, and acting are tightly interrelated—so tightly that any effort, including this, to unwind them can be only partially successful at best. Our earliest profound childhood questioning, for example, presupposes an innate capacity for caring that is informed by our mortal curiosity and our capacity for intimate relationships. We arrive with an onboard desire to know the core "facts of life" that present themselves to us in our immediate surroundings and to comprehend ourselves in relationship to them.

The circumstances that attend our arrival are, of course, highly significant. The three general capacities we each possess are initially developed in direct relationship with and total dependence upon those who relate themselves to us by maternal and other sources of intimate, familiar love, and by the much less dependable bonds of law, custom, and rational obligation. If we are fortunate, like Frances Crowe, John B., and most of the core actors discussed thus far, we are afforded life's greatest gift apart from itself—the experience of unmediated, intrinsic or deep affection, and our capacity to extend our own authentic warmth— will mature well-nourished, robust, resilient, and contagious. We arrive curious to know, equipped to care, and anxious to act, needing only to witness, experience, and less directly learn the forms and relative strengths of each capacity.

PARTICULAR EXAMPLES

There are two additional contemporary actors who make this point well, while adding important variety. The first, Maria M-L., is the director of a community outreach agency that serves the sizeable Hispanic community in Springfield. In the spirit of Jane Addams, she is a facilitator and an organizer with others, not simply a philanthropic provider or doer for others. In her late forties when interviewed, she was in the unfortunate position of being able to share her background and insights from the vantage point of someone who was recovering from a major illness that had involved a close encounter with death. Although still weak, she was already back at work part-time and did not seem at all afraid of what she more consciously knew lay ahead.

Maria was born in a small town outside Silver City, New Mexico, one of five children of Mexican and Native American parents. In addition, there was her huge extended family of four grandparents, uncles, aunts and "many cousins." She smiled broadly and unself-consciously as she described her family, and again, more reflectively, when this was brought to her attention. "Yes, [I am]," she agreed, "because it's such a gift. It's a gift."

During the interview she told two stories that convey the role of early caring and experience with maximum effect. The first and briefest is the last event in her childhood. At eighteen, she enlisted in the Navy, thus becoming the first in her generation to leave home. Describing the culminating event in an upbringing she would only later come to appreciate, she continued:

> I remember the day I was leaving. I was getting on a bus . . . in my little hometown the bus comes like once a week or something, and I'll never forget that moment. Here comes my grandmothers and my mother and my father and siblings and some cousins and there's this large amount of people out there and they'd really come to wish me well and the little things that they gave me for the trip. My grandmother had made bean burritos and wrapped them up, you know, "in case you get hungry," and my other grandmother gave me a rolling pin, [saying] "you're going to need this."

Her leaving, as with Frances Crowe's, was motivated, in part, by a similar American version of youthful desire to explore a larger world. It was informed as well by a strong desire to escape from the harsh experiences that she underwent at home. She was introduced to a larger, often indifferent and hostile social context as Donna S. had been; however, Maria's family appeared to have learned and gained strength from their struggle. In contrast, Donna's immediate family, having moved from its traditional community locale, became more atomistic and susceptible to the damage that occurred.

Her small community and its activism was the inspiration for the 1954 movie, *Salt of the Earth*, a film that recounts the efforts of Mexican indigenous workers at the zinc mine, located in her town, but distantly owned, to unionize and bargain to obtain the same wage status and benefits that were then afforded the white or Anglo miners that they worked with. Their efforts were so unique and potentially contagious that federal government officials, at the height of the McCarthy era, pressured the film industry and at least one of its trade unions successfully to blacklist the actors and crew and suppress the film's release in America until the early 1960s.[8] Maria's father was one of the striking miners, and according to her, played himself in the film.[9]

The physical "community" that Maria grew up in was the product of externally imposed structure. The mining corporation owned the town completely, including her home and those of the other miners, Mexican and Anglo. The Anglo's homes had running water and power; whereas the Mexican homes, segregated from the Anglo's, did not. The school she attended was separated, not segregated. As she explained the arrangement,

> We would arrive to school and we would have to stand in lines, and all Mexican-Indian children would be in this line and all white kids would be in this line. We would have to be standing there waiting to come in the building, and the teacher would finally come out and the white kids would go in first and [then] we would go in. . . .

At lunch and recess it was the same, as it was for the rest of daily life that brought her family in contact with the Anglos. Maria summarized it most effectively;

> You were constantly reminded that you were different, no matter what interaction was going on. So it wasn't just that we were learning it, we were living that experience constantly. And I had [other] experiences when I was in school. Practically all my school teachers were Irish women, Irish teachers and I never knew for a long, long time why I knew so many Irish songs and so much about Irish history and why St. Patrick's was such a huge holiday when I was growing up.

Fortunately for Maria, she learned about caring and acting in particular circumstances that included her family and neighbors. It was a community maintained *in spite of* a long history of external coercive intervention, including the Conquistadors, their church, and more recent forced relocation. When asked what role formal religion had played in her moral formation the following exchange occurred:

MM-L: Well that was an important factor. I was raised as Catholic and it was reflected in everything we did in terms of . . .

Question: And did the church support the activism in your community?

MM-L: Oh very interesting.

Question: I don't mean to suggest an answer to that.

MM-L: Yeah. Actually, no. We had a priest who was . . . from Spain. Very strict. And when I was growing up all the masses and everything were in Latin and I could never really understand anything that was going on. But religion was part of the family rhythm. There was family rosary every night, [and] there was, you know, all the rituals from season to season.

It is apparent that Maria acquired her catholic spiritual perspective more from her family and its syncretic spirituality than from the institutional transmission of Catholicism. She credits her grandparents in particular:

My grandparents who were very . . . they were very humble but they were very educated about life in a lot of ways. They were farmers and great teachers and they really lived up to those beliefs in how they were and how they treated people and the way that they felt love for everyone, for everything that was living and sacred. For example, when my grandmother would send me to go get some chamomile leaf teas—*manzanilla* from the bush . . . and that's because maybe a neighbor was not feeling well. But she would say "don't forget to thank the bush for the leaves before you take [them]."

In addition to being fostered with a reverence for nature and the physical world, she had the good fortune to witness more morally informing major experiences in her childhood than most of us encounter in a lifetime. The men in her community, including her father, had been struggling unsuccessfully with the mine owners for years before she was born. When she was a toddler, the union that later co-sponsored the film sent an Anglo "outsider" to their community who assisted them in their efforts to organize and protest.

When the men were enjoined by court action from their protest outside the mine entrance, Maria witnessed her mother and others educate their male partners in their own capacity to know and act, as well as render traditional, gendered care. The women proposed that they and the older children "man" the picket line in order to circumvent the injunction, an offer the men at first staunchly refused. The women persisted, however, and moral persuasion took on a new, powerful dimension at the mine entrance soon thereafter. Demonstrating the new political dynamic introduced by their nonincremental action, the women added to the list of traditional labor demands, insisting that the owners furnish their families with electricity, running water, and more secure tenancies in their homes. Given the unique character of the protest, their cause attracted much wider attention, and the strike was ultimately resolved on terms that afforded Maria's community a measure of pragmatic success.

As a result of the women's initiative, and the men's adjustment to it, Maria grew up in a family and community whose base of moral knowledge was lastingly affected by a newly discovered sense of democratic competence. Maria's father went on to become an appointed Justice of the Peace, and, when that position was abolished, a locally elected judicial magistrate, a position he held for many years. When she got on the bus, she took with her enough moral learning to effectively inform her adult lifetime of recurring, now fulltime social and political activism.

Maria M-L. has been a core actor wherever she has lived since then, most visibly since taking over as director of the organization she now heads. She has devoted herself to observing, listening, and helping others to organize and act to enhance the quality of their lives by becoming politically literate, democratically competent, and more robustly enfranchised. Her action has reflected her early-acquired view of life itself as interconnected and sacred, and her educated awareness that her image of the world is not as broadly or deeply shared as she perceives it. This world-view, with its implicit integration of humanity as part of the whole, combined with her awareness of existential incongruity, has also furnished her life purpose:

> What's sacred [in our social and political life] is embracing each other's humanity. That's what sacredness is and that's what we've come to learn. I think that that's really what our life purpose is, to come and embrace each other's humanity and that along the way we will have many teachers and many lessons that are going to teach us how to do that.

She offers herself to us as one such teacher.

As has been already observed, the lives of both the historical and contemporary actors selected herein confirm what many already know—that the human as well as material content and consistency of our childhood and early adult moral formation does not determine our capacity to become powerful, morally informed actors in adulthood. Family and community, while highly important, are only rarely sufficient to the task. This is critical, where so much of the moral learning imparted in each venue is of the liberal and communitarian variety.

The dominant moral curriculum of conventional American cultural learning is most evident in the nurture of middle- and upper-income families that also afford the reinforcing conditions of material comfort and relative security. The lives of Elizabeth Cady Stanton, Jane Addams, Eugene Debs, and many of those interviewed suggest, however, that vital curiosity and moral learning need not end with the transition to adulthood, and need not unreflectively conform to prevailing wisdom.

Just as conventional nurture in conditions of comfort does not determine conforming outcomes, diminished nurture under harsh conditions does not inevitably starve our capacity to learn and grow. The lives of Frederick Douglass and Pastor B., one of many African American men who have been indirectly reached, informed, and inspired by Douglass's life, demonstrate that our moral capacity can be tenaciously developed against long circumstantial odds.

Pastor B., a middle-aged church minister and community activist in the predominantly African American North End of Springfield, did not begin to awaken to his now powerful moral awareness until he was almost seventeen years old. Born and raised in the Bedford-Stuyvesant minority enclave of Brooklyn, he dropped out of high school in tenth grade, angry and frustrated with the realization that he was functionally illiterate and no longer willing to accept the indignity of scant teaching and social promotion. He succinctly summarized his angry adolescence in the following: "I was functionally illiterate, I was carrying firearms and knives [at] twelve, thirteen, fourteen years old and involved in a number of different gangs in Brooklyn."

Two female African American teachers, along with his hard-working, devoted mother, were the most caring and competent of the very few "who challenged me, who encouraged me, who nurtured me, who would not give up on me despite the fact that society had caused me to see nothing in myself." He summarized his schooling in an area similar to where Gail K. had taught in the early 1960s, but from a different perspective than Gail's:

> I attended schools in particularly my early years where most of the teachers were white. Very early on there were a lot of white males who were simply dodging the draft and so really didn't care a whole lot about educating, about teaching.

Frederick Douglass was one of many external influences that helped Pastor B. transform the youthful anger implicit in the above into a much deeper intellectually informed and righteous passion. Through his hard-won literacy and our still imperiled freedom to write, publish, and read, he became thoroughly familiar with the details of Douglass's life and, equally important, his moral perspective. Further informed by his vital, mentor-introduced, social gospel form of Christian faith, he no longer focuses his anger on individual whites or on whites in general but on the particular structures and systems that their unenlightened knowledge and power have encouraged them to form. He now believes, as did Douglass and Dr. Martin Luther King, that our social, political, and economic institutions enslave whites as well as African Americans. As he directly explained it,

> Understand, you're born into a system and by virtue of the fact that you're white, living as a white person in America, you have privilege and power and I understand that. So I can be angry at the system that, unfortunately, you are part of and . . . not take out my anger directly on you. Does it mean that I disallow or just totally push aside your behavior? No, [because] I recognize that you are just as much a prisoner as I am.

The imprisonment, as he experiences and conceives it, has two dimensions. There are the systems of oppression themselves, the structured contrivances of law, belief, and practice, which still perpetuate subordination, group isolation, and exclusion from opportunity along lines of race and gender. Our criminal justice system—its drug policy is one obvious example—and our property tax supported, "community" situated, public school systems are another. The oppressive strength of these systems, apart from their reification due to systemic belief itself, is a combination of the perceptual blindness to the subtle, indirect racism of those who support them, and the wide-spread belief that the right of the majority to incorporate such "unintentional" racism in their definition of security and individual freedom trumps justice for those labeled as minority.

The irony of the second dimension of our common imprisonment, which Pastor B. has learned to personally detect, is that its walls are virtual and internal, part of one's self-definition. We are still taught to accept race, along with gender and ethnicity, as fundamental human distinctions, rather than as part of our universal human variety. From a unique black perspective, this systemically reinforced distinction leads to the devaluation of self and a corresponding lack of agency that far exceeds that of the general population. It occurs when we internalize the discrete group image of ourselves that our dominant culture so pervasively imparts, in Pastor B.'s historically assigned circumstance, a picture of inherent, color-identifiable inferiority.[10] He demonstrated the daily reality of inculcated black self-consciousness by a variety of methods, including seeing the daily reflection of his assigned inferior image with his own eyes in his own mirror. He also offered me the following simple perceptual shift, from within his church office and its racially homogeneous neighborhood surroundings: "*You* never have to think about being white . . . [except] on days like this. . . ."

Pastor B. believes that all of us have the capacity to "awaken" to a powerful understanding of self and a new, explicitly hopeful, optimistic image of the world and our relationships within it. He uses the term "awaken" much like Father Leo intended with his cave metaphor, to impart his belief "that people have fallen asleep to the possibilities of their own freedom," just as he had done. When asked how it had occurred for him, he offered the following:

> What supported my awakening [was] not one thing, one event, one person. I think it was a combination of people, a combination of events that took place in my life. I think every one of us is born with a need, an ability . . . to grow, and once we come to the realization that growth is a natural thing . . . you [can] experience it.

Judging from his eloquent, passionate discourse, his keen self-knowledge, and the number of intellectual and Biblical authorities he was able to recall and quote, Pastor B. has truly awakened to the full potential in himself, in others, and the world. He also has a profound, imaginative sense of history and of the critical role that each of us can play in its reported outcomes. He began, as with many of us who are not well-nurtured into our moral awakening but are born, like Douglass, with unusual inner strength reflected in adolescent anger, by tending to the particulars of his own. He did so, as Donna S. had also done, under the patient tutelage of the man who headed the church he now serves in. At the age of seventeen he appointed Pastor B. an assistant pastor in a Brooklyn church. Music plays a major role in its denominational liturgy, and he was encouraged to teach himself to play several instruments in what he now recognizes was in a conscious mentoring effort to impart self-mastery and competence. He also became active in the local community, in voter registration and in other areas in order gain new experience and to enlarge his world-view. As he briefly put it, "I started working, volunteering in the community at various levels."

He did so both for the sake of his own learning and, ultimately, to become capable of helping others who were still asleep. As he describes it:

> I became very aware of the fact that you have to be a part of the process. You have to learn the system. You have to understand. You don't go hunting for a lion unless you understand the nature of it.

The lion that Pastor B. was preparing himself to hunt for was the external source of the oppression, and its unique entrapment of urban African Americans and many Hispanics. He learned how to hunt for his quarry by locating it in the context of a newly discovered world where he has many allies, white and black, who, although still caught in a racial divide, are engaged in the ongoing, essential individual and small group process of revolutionary change.

Pastor B. has made himself keenly aware of the history of America before his personal awakening. He sees the revolution that he is engaged in as encompassing racial injustice and all other forms of inhumanity. He views it as a process of individual and group awakening, involving action at all levels of society. It begins with caring grassroots attention to the awakening of others, local and wider action, including direct confrontation, to bring about increased awareness and change, and throughout the entire process, moral persuasion—"a struggle that goes on within the hearts and minds of men." Speaking of its subject matter and scale of this revolt from a meta-perspective, he adds his profound understanding of the need for fraternity and sorority:

> It's a revolution which recognizes a constant struggle for development and progress. . . . It's much broader and it encompasses a variety of individuals

working from a variety of different angles who may not always be in touch with each other but that there's a spirit of commonality and a purpose.

The origins of the revolution in every generation are "people who start to do some inner growth." It is apparent that Pastor B. is well along the path of his own inner revolution. He has placed himself in a much larger context, yet is deeply, spiritually rooted in the common humanity of divine creation, and has come to understand much of the true range of his freedom—his own moral capacity—to act. His extensive community outreach work in Springfield involves persuading and assisting other African Americans from circumstances similar to his own, to experience their own awakening and to become full citizens of America and the world.

One simple, effective pedagogical technique he employs is to teach others to play chess. In The Hut, a nondenominational drop-in community center that he directs, he organizes chess clubs. He explains that before people can awaken to their full nature and capacity, they have to first learn how to think about life in greater context—how it works:

> [W]e have a theme with the chess club that is it's not about the board. It's about the players. So, for instance, the other day I put a question on the board and the question was: "What is the first step or what must black do in order to gain the advantage? What is the first step?" And naturally if you're a chess player you'll understand that when you sit down to a chess board whoever's playing white gets to go first and therefore you have an advantage.

After the group initially concludes that white moving first is simply a rule or a "given," he points to the historical, man-made source of the rule, then builds on the metaphor:

> So then, what does black have to do in order to gain the advantage to win the game? The whole concept of chess is that you will never win a game moving just one piece. It's about development, and so with every club that we have, I employ this concept of chess that it's about development. It's about putting value on your resources, knowing where things go and how things operate, knowing what's expendable, understanding that there's something I'm going to have to give up in the course of this game. Being able to anticipate or even force my opponent to move in certain ways based on my moves. It ain't about that board, it's about the players. So what we try to do is to get people to come into our space and through a process of developing relationships first, developing relationships because [they] have to understand that I'm not here to [do it for them].

Pastor B. wants his chess clubs to be self-sustaining, their members self-empowered to act effectively for themselves and for others.

It is easy to conclude that the qualities of deep, intimate caring and affectionate warmth are lacking in his approach. For those of us who have this reaction, it is likely that we are fortunate in that we lack the kind of initial formative experiences that might enable us to more readily discern the intensity of caring that is present in his blunt, direct efforts. Many may have had a similar response to the confrontational nature of Donna S.'s activism and to her candid acknowledgement of anger at the injustice she experienced as part of her motivation. Pastor B., like Donna S., and like Elizabeth Cady Stanton and Frederick Douglass before them, is attempting to enable those who have experienced generations of institutional and self-imprisonment to wake up so that they can begin the process of their own liberation. It is also likely that, like ourselves, they are not divinely ordained saints. Each of them demonstrated and at times acknowledged their occasional impatience, their intense passion, often expressed as anger—outrage at what to them was obvious injustice. Each, on occasion, also acted on those feelings, using harsh words or instrumental means that objectified and dehumanized their opponents.

Although the work of individual, social, and political awakening is frustratingly slow and progress often imperceptible in almost any setting, there is no is place more difficult to discern progress in America than from the vantage of those who labor for change within our racial urban enclaves. The immigrant population in which Jane Addams had encountered democratic competence had been economically set adrift in Europe, but not stripped of their cultural past or physical freedom and relegated to an inferior subclass of humanity upon their arrival in America. The legacy of slavery—including its justification by claims of racial superiority—persists in the acquired perceptions and habits of each generation on both sides of the continuing divide. Our self-focused concept of equality and rights has lacked the vitality to counter the competing, equally self-interested notion of liberal freedom and its protection of private communal preferences that allow our false perceptions and immoral habits to continue. One does not, as Pastor B. and so many others have done, undertake the tasks that begin and sustain further progress, or endure the frustrations and frequent failures that attend them, unless one cares deeply about others, unless one has certain knowledge of an actual, vital, inclusive, intrinsically related world, one that is populated by others who share their capacity to encounter and become aware of the world as it is, and to become competent actors within it. Our ability to be persuaded by others, such as Pastor B., is evidence not only of his nature, but of our own.

Pastor B. has also discovered the radical freedom that certain knowledge and profound caring impart. It is a freedom that lies not so much in choices but in the obligation stemming from profound knowing, deep caring, and the liberating power of profoundly informed action. Certain knowledge and the caring it instills actually narrows the range of fundamental choice—whether to act in some manner or to do nothing. This explains the common refrain from morally informed core actors who, when asked why they chose to help rescue nineteenth century slaves, or mid-twentieth century Jews, responded that they did not see how they could have done otherwise.[11]

Perhaps the rest of us can somewhat better understand the nature of the externally informed inner enslavement that Pastor B. must still regularly contend with by learning first to recognize the three hundred year plus history of our more comfortable, still growing self-confinement—our reinforced inner isolation that insures, at our intellectual best, only a fractured, inchoate grasp of what is. Lacking vital fundamental knowledge, each of us is an obstacle, in some profound manner, to moral progress—our own and someone else's. Most of us, for example, continue to own, by our ignorance and inaction, a piece of the mental and physical space Pastor B. was born into and left exposed to experience. Just as he has been able to see, with the help of others, the harsh distortions of his initial formation and, with further assistance, to overcome them, so we are capable of discovering the world not only as it is, but as it can become, and the richer content of our selves that make progress from the present possible.

To obtain this radical freedom and to use it for the social and political awakening of others, we need to answer Pastor B.'s call to revolution. To assist, he offers us his inclusive definition of revolution—a radical, transforming way of life shared by morally informed core actors and available to each of us:

> What is a revolution? It's people who start to do some inner growth and some awakening and who decide to move from the thought process to action. Jesus, one of the greatest revolutionaries . . . , taught that it starts in your heart and in your mind and then translates itself into action and the Apostle James said, "faith without work is dead and work without faith is dead."

MOVING FROM THE PARTICULAR TO THE UNIVERSAL

Just as there is no social or political action that is not motivated and informed by our caring, there is no effective moral learning that is informed by reason detached from caring, even if it is only the care of self that initially informs us. The problem with rational precepts grounded only in self-serving, however, is not simply their insular character, their inherently limited reach, and divisive potential: it is their corresponding inability to move us from the particular to the general, from the individual to the community, the polity, or beyond, except by the logic of contract or treaty, and the stimulus of external threat, common disaster, internal insecurity, and force. We have known from our national beginning that our rational political mores require too little of us, asking only for soft virtues in a legal framework of personal rights and constrained individual striving. Moreover, as the most powerful manipulators and free-riders within our enlightened political and economic architecture have long since learned, equality, reciprocity, toleration, trust, civility, and legal constraint within a rule of law are instrumentally important, but only to a self-defined point within an ever shifting circumstantial radius. Accordingly, it should not surprise us that those who benefit most from their observance by others are so often the most vociferous in their expressions of care about their preservation. Whenever stress cracks appear in the thin veneer of our rational morality, revealing the authentic underbelly of overly legitimated self-striving and implicit indifference to others, variously stationed benefactors and servants of the status quo take to their bully pulpits to issue passionate calls for repairs and restoration. "Just say no" is only one such mantra they offer to others, less powerfully fortunate than themselves.

How is it that core actors are so different in the apparent nature of their moral thought and the obvious dissimilarities of their action? The initial answer is that they are not, at least not in their basic nature. As with us, they seek to make sense of life, and, like ourselves, they attach care and significance or meaning to all that they learn.

The difference lies in the methods that they are taught or, despite their teaching, learn to rely upon, and in the particular capacities that they utilize for doing so. As a result, they are able to move from the particulars of self and the seemingly fragmented, isolated world of facts and segregated experience that we all begin with to a unified world-view—an actual image of a world that is constituted by a self that is radically free in the sense of conventional social and political constraints, yet deeply, intimately connected to other selves and things. In contrast, many of us are rationally deductive moral learners, having been taught to accept as fundamental truth some composite of the master working hypotheses of science, theories drawn from history, the principles of institutional faith, or a combination of each. Having already been furnished with the basic nature of the world, including ourselves, we are taught to attach moral significance to the learned particulars of life within these explanatory frameworks. This leaves us dependent for our derived moral precepts and their vitality upon the completeness and corresponding significance of the master explanation we have received. Even where we make alterations based on our own experience and observations, which many of us do, we too often do so within our furnished framework, abandoning science for faith, or, in many well-educated cases, the opposite.

As accounts of their lives reveal, core actors achieve their world perspective by the following interconnected means: authentic, direct or unmediated encounters with others and with the world; the critical input of intellectual framework learning that furnishes factual connections, depth, and texture to life as they encounter, experience and witness it; growing intimacy with particular others and the world resulting from recurring and new encounters; profound insights or more subtle growing awareness that includes the coalescence into simple profound truths and attachment of care to what they have directly encountered and otherwise learned; and the employment of morally rich imagination—profound inferences from what has been directly and indirectly learned—which allow them to more fully comprehend and attach deep care to the world and those within it who lie beyond their immediate reach.

What they come to learn as a result of the above processes informs, broadens, and strengthens their capacity to care, arms them with the optimism that comes from a core of certain knowledge thus obtained, and moves them to plan and act in ways that demonstrate, persuade, and awaken others to what they have learned and care about most deeply. It is not only their corresponding agenda of social and political reform that matters, but the foundational lessons or truths that they have drawn from their direct engagement with life, the manner in which they have learned to understand and vitally live, and that constitute the crux of their reform potential. They offer us not only their insights, but their examples.

EXPERIENCE AND CONVENTIONAL LEARNING

As parents, we have long since sought not only to protect our children by shielding them from certain experiences, but also to morally inform them and impart life skills through selecting and encouraging certain others. Many of us make them go to church, temple, and mosque, even as we question their doctrines and our own beliefs. We monitor their education, send them to camp, enroll them in purposeful, structured activities, limit their friendships, and attempt with varying success to control their exposure to the excesses of mass culture.

As is now apparent, the parents of core actors strive do the same. In some cases, such as that of John B., his parents, themselves powerfully informed and working to persuade others, were able to deal with the limited framework and contradictions posed by our dominant world-view by daily exposing their child to their own lives, including their authentic, caring interactions with others. In addition, there was his schooling, both in the classroom and in his crafted broad exposure to conditions of injustice and human indifference. The latter experience, most significantly, included the opportunity to know actual persons within these conditions. He further learned the value of modern means of rational thought along with their respective and overall limits.

In sum, he learned that the world was usefully understood in discrete terms by the various rational means of classification, quantification, and deconstruction. At the same time, he was exposed to the concepts *and practices* of an inclusive, integrated world-image, together with social and political ideals that were commensurate with such a world. Of greatest importance, rather than merely organizing the factual components of the world into a complex, abstract, depersonalized set of categories, processes, and systems, he was encouraged to establish relationships, to directly learn the actual identity and intrinsic worth of the wide range of others whom he directly encountered within it.

John B. was partially informed in a moral tradition—the Quaker faith—that stands in substantial opposition to our conventional cultural institutional models. He was raised in a pattern of substantial nonconformity—not simply for the sake of self-expressive liberty, but for sake of learning by direct, intimate relationships what one can only discover in that realm—the reality, as well as the social and political dynamics, of our individual and common humanity. He was nurtured into becoming an active, caring, vital citizen in a world informed not only by a critical perspective, but by demonstration and intimate exposure to life-affirming connections with a wide variety of others within it. By the time John left "home" he was already at home wherever he went. As Jane Addams had discovered as a young adult, he became more easily aware that the only reliable means of discerning the essential origins and vitality of a social or political ideal is to acquire a deep understanding of the nature and the potential of human life within its wide range of actuality.

The same cannot be said of the formative experiences of many of John's contemporaries who also came from families of abundant and ample means. In contrast to his rearing, they were lovingly and conventionally permitted to sleep to indefinitely delayed maturity in activities and structures informed by the spirit of self-discovery, self-nurture, and self-enhancement that are the paradigms of our pervasive mass culture. Those more aggressively nurtured were deprived with loving intent from their development of profound curiosity, imagination, and capacity for intimate engagement. The constraints of their choreographed preparation to dominate the competition in their generation, or, less ambitiously, to become more materially secure than their caring, overworked mentors, left little time to experience intimacy or nurture curiosity. The effect of such rearing has been to largely deny them the opportunity to become directly, intimately familiar with the immediate, concrete reality that stimulates our early spontaneous curiosity and native sympathy into progressively deep questioning, affectionate, profoundly informed mentoring, and moral growth.

For members of this generational cohort, adult awakening is likely as difficult as it is for the more conventionally life-deprived in any era. In our past, the more privileged group—those who typically become socially and political-cal influential—has required the initial intervention of harsh experience, major disturbing events, or authentic, direct confrontation by core actors, mentors, and exemplars that today are too easy to avoid.[12] Fortunately, incidental and accidental opportunities, such as those associated with other culturally endorsed activities, remain for the stimulus of perspective-expanding experience. Learning from travel, such as occurred with Jane Addams while touring in London during the 1880s, is one example. Opportunities for expanding one's vista, whether for adventure, concentrated pleasure, or instrumental enrichment, abound more widely than ever. However, seeing inhumanity, whether far away or locally, without directly encountering the actuality of common humanity that informs any truly profound image, is to experience another form of virtual reality that can be assimilated without experiencing any unmediated connection to one's own being or lifestyle. We have long since learned to travel in peer group cocoons, to blame others or the victims when they intrude in our space, and to otherwise isolate ourselves from authentic engagement as we pursue new opportunities, seek high adventure, or bask in some other luxurious escape. Those who wait upon us have also learned to dissimulate, disguising their authentic selves from our view.

John B.'s nurturing was exceptional, a model worthy of much wider emulation. From a youthful, individual perspective, however, none of us is able to order the sequence of our moral development, the breadth or depth of formative life experience. Fortunately, those of us who were more rudely introduced to the world, like some of those herein, can find, seemingly by instinct, capable mentors and further learn how to awaken themselves. They can do so on the combined strength of our human need to understand life in relation to ourselves and to our capacities to profoundly learn and deeply comprehend. In the same manner, those of us who have been induced into moral developmental slumber, or, distracted by some variant of instrumental frenzy, can also learn to wake up. Our current deep-seated unease, containing much more than mortal anxiety, is evidence of our unfocused desire and our potential to become intimately familiar and vitally engaged with life.[13]

ENCOUNTER AND AWARENESS

It is our capacity to encounter, to consciously, directly engage ourselves in mutual, authentic, intimate relationships with others, with other life and the world; it is our ability to bring to the surface and actively reflect upon our

similar, less consciously acquired awareness of such others; it is our competence to integrate in these moments what we have already experienced and
less directly learned that affords us moments of profound insight or awareness. It is to that which is realized or known in these moments that care is
most deeply attached, priorities are most readily assigned, and our capacity to
act most durably strengthened by profound motive. We awaken and further
awaken to truths that the world—life itself—offers in both the particular and
complex qualities of its being.

For some of us, insight does not occur, our awareness does not surface—
become apparent to the self—until we find ourselves in circumstances when
we feel compelled to act without our customary concern for what others are
doing, how they may react, or other evidence of our customary self-concern.
Those of us who have been more fortunately born and affectionately nurtured
by others already in profound touch with the world as it is enter adulthood already somewhat awake, in the fortunate manner of John B. and, to a lesser extent, Frances Crowe, Gail K., and Karen P. For them, such moments are more
likely to be those of recurring encounter—a deepening or enhanced awareness of the nature and congruence of self and life. For Jane Addams, it was
evident in her quest that she could only generally express at the age of eighteen: ". . . [I]f I could fix my relations to God and the universe, and so be in
perfect harmony with nature and deity, I could do almost anything."[14] Ten
years later, after experiencing both personal tragedy and the limits of moral
learning from distant, indirect sources, she determined that the only way she
could discover truth was to immerse herself in the particulars of life by active, repeated, intimate engagement with others.

Acts of new and renewed encounter and stimulation of conscious awareness
are necessary throughout one's life for three inescapable reasons: *first*, we inevitably fail to maintain by purposeful action our congruence with life, however
deeply and intentionally we have come to know it; *second*, even our most profound insights are too often fleeting and always incomplete, received in a world
where they are easily lost, along with care, in the detritus of destructive, exclusive visions, material distractions, and tragic events beyond our moral comprehension or existential grasp; *third*, given our imperfect nature, even knowledge
that eventually comes to be widely accepted as fundamental or profound is only
durable and progressive in its effects for as long as we continue in our efforts
to intentionally act, experience, reflect, imagine, and adjust our actions to better match what we have since learned. Recurrent knowing, renewed caring, and
intentional acting, each of necessity informing the other, constitute the necessary rhythm of a life lived at the full reach of human capacity.

Our variety of birth inheritance, acculturation, and particular life history is
too broad to allow for a single explanation of how the process of profound

moral knowing unfailingly occurs. The process is neither entirely intellectual nor entirely cognitive, intuitive, aesthetic, or emotional. All that can be said with any certainly is that it does happen, and that that the moral knowledge learned is simple in form, inclusive in content, certain in perception, deeply inspiring, and, when added to the unique personalities and talents of core actors, a further powerful source of encounter, awareness, and moral persuasion for others.

A NOTEWORTHY EXEMPLAR

Jean Grossholtz, introduced in the first chapter, offers a rich version of the above epistemological composite. Of the contemporary core actors interviewed, her broad moral methodology was the most extensive and seemingly incongruous. Her intellectual nature, her patent brilliance, is easy for anyone schooled in the high cultural tier of the Enlightenment tradition to comprehend. Yet she is a rare combination of gifted scholar and wide-ranging peace, social justice, and environmental activist—a powerful gadfly with brilliant, multi-hued, epistemological wings, and an arrest record as long as her arm.

Her academic intellectual-direct action anomaly is heightened by her elemental descriptions and expressions of the moral and the good. It should be noted that "moral" is not a word that she is comfortable with. She associates it with institutional religions and their common tendency to reach out into the world from an inward doctrinal stance, and then only when changing values in the broader society threaten institutional authority.[15] Jean's preferred terms are "right" and "wrong," "makes sense" and "makes no sense," and, occasionally, "what I want" and "what I don't want." One suspects that she rarely couches her social and political views in the enervating comfort of "that depends."

The anomaly disappears when one recognizes that she has discovered a coherent world of vital interconnection, a world that contains "the natural harmony" of place and of "people living together." Widely informed and keenly mindful of existential reality, she further explained her world in its teleological form: ". . . the kind of world I want to live in . . . If I say 'This is the kind of world I want to live in' . . . it is a world where no baby is born unwanted, no baby is ever without food, clothing, shelter, healthcare. I want to live in a world like that." For her it is also a *present world*, one that she and others—past and present—have struggled to enlarge, in the midst of contradiction, by their words and actions. It is a world informed by fundamental, profound, simple, and certain truths. It is a world of hope that consists of life vitally comprehended and congruently lived in the present.

Jean's apparent existential incongruity—her nonconformity with conventional expectations in the world as conceived and acted upon by others—is also the partial product of actual life circumstance. Growing up as one of eight siblings in a small rural farm community in northeastern Pennsylvania, her youthful, intensely curious mind craved information. Like her activist colleague Gail K., she is "a reading addict." Referring to her sizeable office, where the interview took place, she described the origins of her habit: "In the town I grew up in, the library was not much bigger than this room. I started at 'A' and read it all . . . Some of the stuff I never understood. I mean, I [would] tell people, when I was talking about my life, that I loved this book called 'Less Miserable.'" Summing up her reasons for reading, she added a further explanation for her identification with Victor Hugo's novel, however its title is spelled or pronounced: "So I read a lot, and [as a result] I had some understanding of different worlds that I could live in because my world was so miserable all the time."

As mentioned in Chapter 1, there was much for Jean to be miserable about. They were poor. Her father, a dreamer with a sensitive, compassionate nature, felt himself unable to provide adequately for his large family ("He did his best"), leaving them with a small farm, their first crop unharvested, to enlist in the merchant marine.[16] She was then thirteen, the oldest of three siblings still at home. When her mother had a breakdown in the stressful aftermath, Jean learned to care for all of them, including speaking for the family in court where she "lied about her age [and said she] had a job" to keep her younger sister from being removed from their family. She was enabled in this formidable task by the fact that her own capacity to care had already been nurtured in a family that, although far from idyllic, was full of knowledge, concern, and affection not only for and about each other, but also strangers and their children. It was a knowing concern that was to be acted upon, not simply expressed.

After high school, she worked locally for a while, helping to support her family until the two younger children had further matured, and her mother had regained her health and remarried. At that point, she broadened her horizons beyond her home and the contents of its library by enlisting in the Army, thinking that she would advance her education, although she was not eligible for the G.I. bill when she signed up. Elaborating on her military experience, she explained:

> Despite all the other things that people say about the Army, it was a good experience for me. I learned a lot. I learned how to take care of myself. I learned how to have respect for people, how to have people have respect for me. I learned discipline, I learned order, *I learned a lot.*

Jean also demonstrated that she had already learned a great deal at home. At one point she was assigned to teach short classes on current events to sister recruits:

> They gave you a piece of paper containing what you were supposed to teach. So I kind of started then. We would have discussions about the ownership of property, about trade unionism and stuff. The Army didn't like that much, so they [removed her from the assignment]. They actually interviewed me to see if I was a communist, which in some ways I probably was. . . .

What she had not yet explained was that her youthful reading had included such authors as Dos Passos and Steinbeck. By imaginative reflection on their narrative contexts and characters, and comparing them to her own experience, she found herself mentally and emotionally connected to a larger world and with an expanded grasp of just and unjust, humane and inhumane.

THE TOOL OF MORAL IMAGINATION

Imagination, as Jean learned early on, is one means available to all of us to extend all other forms of our knowledge beyond their immediate source and context. It is much more than detached, freely floating dreaming or cerebral ideation, although such forms or thought are valuable and potentially informative. Moral imagination—extending the potential significance and reach of what can only be intimately and directly learned—is an important means in the process of knowing and caring, a further conjoining of our own hearts and minds with others and portions of the world not personally known or familiar.[17] It is important because the world is simply too large or too complex to fully experience, adequately witness, and completely organize, let alone become deeply known in relationship with ourselves.

Encounter and awareness, the source of our most profound, certain knowledge, can occur only in intimate, particular, direct relationships. Further, the knowledge thus obtained, however universal and potentially unifying its content, is perceived only by the self. The profound learning experience itself is both relational and individual, inner and variable, not of any necessity visible or apparent to or in others, even when we are in close proximity to each other and a common relational source—listening to the same authentic, inspiring speech or viewing the same sunset from the same vantage point on the rim of the Grand Canyon. While the truths so acquired, and, to a lesser extent, our varied experience of their acquisition can be significantly, supportively shared in the comfort of affectionate relationships of family, fraternity, and sorority, their knowing remains undeniably personal and mystical.

As with other forms of knowledge, our profound insight becomes effective in the world—socially and politically vital—only to the extent that we act on it. The means employed and the results obtained, given the human condition, are typically imperfect, incomplete experiments with truth that we can, at our best, only partially comprehend, and which others may not grasp at all. Equipped with truth and other useful forms of knowledge, however, our imaginations can not only enlarge the dimensions of our profoundly known world beyond the context of our immediate learning, but can also give us valuable insight concerning the potential reach of our own informed action.

Imagination informs us that our own profound knowledge, although unique to us in the circumstances of its acquisition, is already known, shared, and acted upon by others, past and present. The origins of our high ideals of human equality and freedom have there ancient roots in actions too anonymous in locale and remote in time to be captured, in the most meaningful sense, by anything but imagination. The end of slavery's institutional reign in America likely began long before the institution—or America—was established, with individual acts of quiet dignity and moral opposition witnessed by at least one other, or merely demonstrated to the perpetrator by someone of certain conviction.

In addition to connecting us over time and space, our imagination lends assurance that we are not alone in our knowledge of truth, or in our consequent caring. It further informs us will we likely not be alone, except perhaps in our immediate setting, when we answer the implicit call of truth to act. Many others have already encountered and become deeply aware of the same truths, and more will likely do so, inspired by our example or via direct relationship with ourselves.

By the employment of imagination we are able to form vital hypotheses about the world beyond our intimate view or grasp, on the basis of certain knowledge and profound caring already in the possession of the self. When we read, for example, some description of physically distant facts of calamity or human injustice, and of courageous moral action in response, we can imagine the actors learning, knowing, and caring for each other, or for some particular of their nearby world *in the same manner, informed to the same extent* as we have learned to care and act locally. We are able to take in the description of their caring and associated action, compare it to our own knowledge, feelings, and aspirations, and comprehend that because the latter are actual, the former are as well. If, however, the latter lack vitality, so will our imagination and, accordingly, our grasp of what is possible.

With more reflective effort, we can even learn to discern concrete human or other life consequences in nonemotive, impersonally presented, and otherwise abstract data. In our imagining, we are able to attach at least some greater value to the place and to the actors within it, seeing them as part of a common process of striving to live enjoyably and well in a world that becomes both larger and smaller in the process. Imagination enables us to at least know life more broadly and stimulates our capacity for direct encounter and deepening awareness. As such, it is an indispensable means of moral learning.[18]

Imagination is the process that allowed Jean Grossholtz to enlarge her world before she left home. She had read about the black experience in America from Richard Wright and others but had little contact with African Americans. Accordingly, she welcomed the opportunity to do so in Truman's newly integrating Army. While stationed in Virginia, she went with two black female enlisted friends at her post to their house for dinner:

> And the next morning, my commanding officer called me in and said I was never to do that again . . . not in Virginia. . . . And I was ready to go AWOL [until her CO] talked to the [two] women, and they talked to me. They said "look, we could have all gotten killed. We didn't think." And that was it, but it was hard for me. . . .

As she continued, she expressed more fully the extent to which her knowledge and caring acquired through encounter, experience, learning, reflection, growing awareness, and imagination has affected the course of her life: "You see, my problem has always been, when people say to me, 'how can you live your life like this [as an activist], how can you spend so much of your time doing these [things]?' My answer to them is 'How can I not?'" Jean has clearly discovered a world that is vital in its actuality—in its initial furnishing and confirmation of certain truths, and in her own extensive efforts to awaken the rest of us to comprehend and help achieve what she and too few others have so well learned. What appears to others as exceptional, nonconforming action is, for her, living her life in the world as she has come to know it.

CERTAINTY AND TRUTH

Two important questions remain to be discussed. First, assuming that the process of moral learning is as varied, subjective, and mystical as described, how are we able to discern the quality of certain truth in the knowledge that is obtained? Finally, within the limited scope of what can be profoundly learned, what are these truths?

Most of us have already obtained some glimpses of profound truth. Notwithstanding the flaws in our dominant ontological frameworks, the fundamental truth about the nature of life and the world still lies all around us, making at least the beginnings of deep awareness readily available, in fact difficult to avoid. Most of us have come to love, to care deeply for at least one other concrete being, both accepting and reacting with wonder to their intimate revelations of who or what they are. Many have also felt a sense of familiar, yet mysterious, belonging, relationship, or connection to at least one place that is more than an expression of our desire for security and comfort. Still others have at least sensed some hint of the universal and interrelated quality of the knowledge acquired in the growing variety of their particular learning encounters. It is from these ordinary beginnings that our profound knowledge originates and potentially grows.

Encounter is the most deeply informing ability of our general capacity to know, yet it is an event or occurrence that we often do not consciously discern until after it has happened and we are called by what we have learned to act. As noted in the first chapter, some bush does not burst into a flame of brilliant insight for most of us, particularly in our customary isolated mindset and constrained instrumental settings. Like a physicist testing in the world of matter for some invisible form of energy, for proof that it exists, the realization that something profound in our state of knowing has happened can also become apparent to us when we reflect on, contemplate, or simply become aware of its results in the self. We recognize a changed attitude; a deeper, more informed caring; an awakened sense of intrinsic relationship to the world, to others, or both; a more complete, integrated understanding of life. We may also note that we are prepared to act differently, or, belatedly, that we have already done so.

The certainty associated with profound knowledge arises by virtue of repeated and expanded intimate or unmediated encounters with its sources, in as much variety as our circumstances permit. As we do so, we learn, as the core actors herein demonstrate, that life can be understood deeply and with certainty only to the extent that we engage ourselves with it actively, concretely, directly, authentically, intimately, and broadly.

To live our lives in the above vital manner has major implications. Profound knowledge, and the deep caring that attends it, have existential consequences. We must inevitably confront the social and political realities that result from our own prior inaction—or wrongly informed action—and the ongoing actions of those who are otherwise informed. Having learned what we can, we feel ourselves obligated to insert our understanding of truth into the organized world by the most effective means that we can become more fully aware of it ourselves, namely, by offering ourselves as imperfect exemplars of a better, more congruent way to live. In doing so, we become authentic subjects, actively related to the world, and available for encounter by others. In the absence of such vigorous existential assertion, as theologian

Paul Tillich observed, our certainty will remain only personal or private and unshared, lasting only as long as we look directly at its content.[19] Fortunately, as core actors so amply affirm, a life of profoundly informed action, with the certain knowledge it uniquely affords, and its demonstrated potential to instantiate profound changes in our society, is possible.

To the extent that we are able to accept a discernible coherence within a generation and over time to the actions of a diverse group of morally informed core actors, and further detect a shared set of certain beliefs that inform their capacity to care and to act, that fusion should be enough to open the mental door for our own conscious encounters. This persuasive but indirect knowledge, alongside our own existing base of learning and experience, and our resonance with at least some core actors themselves, should encourage us to deepen and expand our own grasp of truth and its implications for our time and setting.

Taken together, the actors that have been discussed and their similarly informed efforts suggest the existence of a uniquely powerful means of knowing the nature and significance of the self, of others, and the world, and the intrinsic relationship of all three. To be fully sharable, any truths that such a form of knowing may afford must, as argued by William James, be directly evident and commonly accessible at their source — in the concrete world of life itself.[20] There are no certain, readily apparent answers or explanations for the "why" of the human life that lays within the humanly knowable world.[21] There is, however, profound knowledge in the nature and significance of being or "what is." It is the only knowledge that we are capable of learning, and, although it can only be individually acquired, its contents can be powerfully demonstrated, learned by others, and thereby shared.

An encounter can be further thought of as a process that reveals fundamental truth, a proposition, an image, or a sense, which is *self-evident* in its presentation, *inclusive* in its subject matter, and *universal* in its applicability. One cannot discover the reality of genuine love or deep friendship—let alone their qualities as universal goods—except in an authentic, unmediated relationship. Our common capacity to encounter is the highest stage of moral induction: we become aware of something in a moment that contains our self *and* some it, our self *and* some other, a moment that briefly identifies both as related within some larger existing whole. It is the experience of an unmediated relationship in the local and the particular that informs the self, over time and changing circumstance, of a larger, more encompassing reality.

The occurrence of encounter differs from an intellectual breakthrough leading to some higher level of abstraction or a mental inspiration that leads to new invention or discovery, although it can happen in the context of either. It is also not merely the overwhelming emotional rush of some new or renewed passion, whatever its form and however concretely of diffusely informed. It is a state or condition of profound awareness—of *certain knowing*—that the world and our worlds, your life and mine, are separate yet alike, part of some vital common enterprise, existing in a realm of unified explanation, or possessing the same essential quality of life. The core actors in our midst and our past inform us to ask ourselves and each other the following: why else would someone, anyone, act beyond impulse to rescue a stranger from some powerfully organized campaign of extermination or a runaway slave from re-enslavement, or initiate some other risk-laden, other regarding, nonconforming, authentic, and ongoing social or political action, unless they had encountered some profound truth that somehow trumped the ordinary magnitude of one's own life or well-being?

Although not fully explicable, an encounter with truth is not an out-of-body or otherworldly occurrence, although when we realize what we have learned, we react with wonder, awe, amazement, humility, and other expressions of deep caring. We also experience the obligation to act, having obtained a powerful motivation to do so. It is no wonder that in our culture, as in most others, the experiences of encounter are effectively banned from public social and political discourse, authoritatively labeled as subjective, emotive, or exceptional. Shareable or common truth in our society, we have been taught, is predicated upon the human condition of mortality and mortal needs, and associated passions that are reliably civilized only by institutions of inculcation and coercion. Yet encounters occur, awareness deepens, and the profound truths they reveal are of critical import, but only if they can be shared by action, so that others are awakened, invited, and encouraged to encounter truth for themselves.

As Martin Buber observed, "Those who [only] experience [life] do not participate in the world. For the experience is 'in them' and not between them and the world."[22] We can only encounter truth—detect the actual nature of the world of things and others by reciprocal, active, authentic engagement—by actively taking in the living, physical world in all of its known aspects, accepting them as they are in relation to each other and our selves. We further this process by presenting our most informed, genuinely disclosed selves to others, and accepting the same from them. It should not surprise us that morally informed action and persuasion, at their profound best, have the same qualities as an encounter with truth.

TWO EXAMPLES OF ENCOUNTERING TRUTH

Although the historical and contemporary core actors that are relied upon in this project were chosen for other reasons, they demonstrate a variety of forms of encounter and express a common, expandable core of certain truth. They confirm Buber's observation of three realms of relationship in which encounters occur: in life with nature, life with others, and life with "spiritual beings."[23] He did not suggest that the world is organized in this manner, only that we have mentally arranged it this way in Western culture. If there is a God or a single creative, purposive explanation for ourselves and the world, he believes that the answer, to the limited extent that we can discern it, lies within our capacity to encounter truth in relationships within any realm. The discovery of certain truth, as already suggested, does not present itself to passers-by, but, as in the subrealm of politics, only to those who place themselves, as a necessary expression of their discovered freedom, into the public arena where they must relate authentically and reciprocally with others if they are to experience truth in action and instantiate it by demonstrating its content to others.[24]

Jean Grossholtz is fortunate to have experienced life and to have discerned truth in both nature and society. As a result she is attached intimately to life in its broad particulars. As mentioned in the first chapter, she seeks to encounter life daily in nature, going for walks in the woods with her dog. She brings life with her, and relates there to life as it offers itself back to her, harmoniously, relating with no need for conscious effort, apart from her attentiveness, on the part of either. What she has encountered invites her into a relationship that is more entire than what she directly perceives—the suggestion of an organically related whole to which she is somehow intimately related. It seems to her that this is the natural relation of humankind to the world, given what she has learned elsewhere about herself, other people, and the world more broadly. She is aware that death is inevitable in both realms, but that man has learned to kill beyond the needs of the physical self, as opposed to the behavior of those she observes in their "lesser" nature. She cares deeply about the sanctity of life and the plethora of evidence that demonstrates our alienation from nature. Her regular encounters both inform and sustain her current substantial efforts to do something about it.

Upon returning to "her estate," which she owns alone but has lived in with between twenty and thirty other women for many years since she reluctantly accepted the contradictory practice of ownership, she re-enters the realm of human interrelationship. Her household is part her intentional effort, as with Jane Addams, to add to the human sphere the actual experience of authentic democratic encounter. Unlike the realm of nature she just left, it is often in much greater visible disarray, due entirely to the nonessential nature of its occupants. Jean reflected on this in the following:

People say, well "How can you do that? You have all these different people. . . ." Over the years, I think we've had two people I've had to ask to leave because they didn't fit in. There was no way we could do it. But what I've had to do is learn how to live with different people. And we all have to. We have to figure out every time something changes in the house, . . . the new dynamic, what makes sense, and how to work with it. So we do. And it's a logical, practical way of living together in community. We can't set up a model that will go through time. Each time we get different personalities and we've got to work with it. I guess there are certain basic principles—sort of morals, I guess—that have to be there. People have to be kind to each other; they have to be caring for each other . . . respectful of each other. . . . So there are certain standards, but to me, it's a practical thing. It's practical and it's logical.

Her sororal living arrangement and her sororal and fraternal relationships in her activism and professional life are each the product of and part of the process by which she has encountered truth in the social and political realms. It is apparent that she is keenly aware of human nature—her own and others'. As she, Douglass, Stanton, Debs, and Addams each expressed, we are flawed, far from perfect, and therefore carry within us the potential for evil as well as for good.[25] Most of us have an abiding, ontologically rooted preference for the latter and profoundly wish to live in a world where our predilection for good prevails. Such a world, she understands with Buber, can be created only in an actual context where authentic relationships are difficult to establish and must coexist with instrumental ones, and where truth must be demonstrated in action that constitutes an integral part of a life that is never entirely free of contradiction.

Her intimate relation with nature, the "special sense of belonging" that she experiences in diverse locations, her extensive network of deep friendships, together with her rich acquired learning, imagination, and deep caring, inform her that the concrete world she has not yet been in and others whom she can not reach and directly engage with are part of a common reality. Just as with Stanton, Douglass, and Addams, she confronts but cares for those who disagree with her, or who are willing, as with many of her faculty colleagues, to only privately express their admiration and respect.

Learning in our time the truths that are so evident and palpable to Jean and most of those interviewed can most effectively happen through the initiatory action of those, like her, who have already discovered their content and motive strength. Given the nature of the truths she has derived from her daily, recurring encounters, one thing is abundantly clear: she will not risk the world or life itself in order to save it. Thus, morally informed core actors can typically be seen at work, from a conventional "realist's" perspective, with one hand tied behind their backs—the hand of violent coercion. Persuasive confrontation, with its potential for violence by others, is quite a different thing.

Many core actors derive their truths largely or entirely from the sphere of human relationship. This is true, for example, of Ira H., the physician activist introduced with Jean Grossholtz in the first chapter. Ira has spent his life caught up in the realm of human interaction. Accordingly, it is apparent from his extensive, lengthy, ongoing efforts to confront Americans, Russians, and others with the magnitude of risks and consequences—the moral evil—of nuclear weapons, that he is motivated by truth derived from encounters with others, and only secondarily by the natural world. He has learned to care most deeply, to relate most profoundly with people. It is not that he is ignorant concerning the natural world or unconcerned for its welfare. It is rather that his deepest, most familiar experiences have been with others. Like Gail K., his Jewish heritage and knowledge of the Jewish historical experience has strongly informed his world-view and caring, along with intimate, loving relationships within family and among a few intimate friends. Formal religious institutions, however, did not appear to pay a major, direct, formative role in his moral education, or in the lives of the clear majority of the historical or the contemporary core actors. Further, where their role was apparent, it was as a departure point for the individual's own quest for truth, and in the case of at least three, the influences were described by them as more negative than affirming.

In particular, Ira H. demonstrates that encounters with others do not lead to the inevitable discovery of joyful, centripetal truth; in fact, they often do not. Along with the realization of common humanity comes the awareness of stupendous evil, behavior rendered more horrific by its sheer magnitude, and the banality of its perpetration.[26] As described in the introductory chapter, his first encounter with this truth occurred in the setting of a loving relationship with his father, a Holocaust survivor. Since establishing this intimate, affectionate connection with evil he has worked to understand, confront, and overcome it ever since.

He has most powerfully learned the nature of modern evil—the willful, routine ordering of society and the state into systems whose ordinary participants are capable of performing their assigned portions of otherwise unimaginable horror, all as part their daily routine. He further learned that he is potentially implicated, capable in his own evolved nature and in America, his country of birth, of "being a good German," or permitting one's self to live in the midst of inhuman contradiction—unless he acts to ameliorate it. Ira H. is powerfully awake to our capacity for evil, as well as its Enlightenment and older historical legitimations. Yet he shares, detectably within his reserved, carefully measured words, the assessment of Jean Grossholtz, and almost all of those interviewed, of our general essential goodness:

> I do think that human character is at least significantly determined by our evolution [or] history. People clearly have important needs that need to be satisfied and the satisfaction of those needs often puts them in conflict with other people,

and the competitiveness to get ahead, to stay alive, to feed yourself, to have that piece of land which will let you and your family live well—I think that stuff is very deeply ingrained in people too. But most people, I think, in trying to meet those needs, are capable of behaving humanely and with consideration to the people around them. . . . For most people the initial response to other people is positive.

In common with many men, especially those with his rigorous intellectual and scientific training, Ira H. does not speak easily and fluently to strangers about matters of caring or the heart. Neither did James M. or John B. However, he clearly knows, as do they, that people are capable of experiencing and encountering each other, and growing in their understanding of truth through love, intimate friendship, and the sometimes uncomfortable, awkward, agonistic practice of fraternal and sororal democratic relationship.

It is this further awareness, that not only he but most of us can experience such intimacy and acquire profound knowledge in the process, melding self-care with morally congruent action and candid, powerful, humbling self-knowledge, which further informs, sustains, and renews him. His work has enabled him to profoundly relate with others across national, cultural, and ideological borders in the common international project of nuclear disarmament. As first quoted, his core value, his highest integrating truth, is: "Human life is good. That is what it is all about." Finally, given his intimate awareness of the banal causes and consequences of nuclear war, he is cognizant of the most fundamentally realizable truth of modernity: There is but one earth and a single, common humanity within it. He only hopes that he can help deepen this awareness in others before it is too late.

SIMPLE TRUTHS AND ESSENTIAL INFERENCES

Each of us starts life outside the womb, in America or elsewhere in the world, with a varied genetic reservoir of learned human experience. We are the products of still dimly understood evolution, a process of ongoing creation that we are unable to grasp at all without a belief in some kind of beginning.

By definition, we cannot imagine, let alone live or achieve progress in, a world whose core organizing principle is the isolated, atomistic self. Such a world, like a cosmos seen only as infinity or chaos, holds no durable shared meaning, and no possibility of substantial common endeavor. Fortunately, infinity and chaos are the province of only a few minds seeking existential truth by nonexistential means—pure reason employed from an inherently unachievable omni-perspective. So it is with the rational possibility of non-being. As a truth it has no verifiable reality within the only place where its existence can be known—in intimate relationship with life itself. In fact, such empirical evidence as exists suggests the dynamic presence of some organic entirety of being, although we continue to despair at the prospect of our own, inevitable, personal, post-communicative, organic transformation.

As a metaphor for the post-death unknown, nonbeing serves mostly to remind us of our mortal anxiety and encourages us to lean on an external God—one we cannot intimately, concretely know—or upon the rare courage of an immutably isolated self that we cannot always depend upon to safely assign its own meaning. If there is a comprehensive purpose or meaning that can potentially be known, its content is knowable only in the conditions of our existence and by the means of our capacity to learn and to know, attaching moral significance to what we learn by caring and acting—spreading and instilling the word by seeking justice and decrying injustice, and by living the truths we have learned, even as we continue our efforts to expand our learning.

Our acquired birth legacy serves as further evidence that we have become and developed as a species on the strength of what we have learned from experience, abstracted learning, from intended purposive action, and from our intimate, direct engagement with life.[27] In its primal, inherited forms such learning is evident in our physical features, our instinctive behaviors, and in our cognition—the things that pediatricians assess when we are born and monitor as we progress toward adulthood. There is also evidence of much that we are constantly in the process of unlearning: our reactive tempers, our tail bones, our tendencies to fight or flight, and other vestigial behavioral and atavistic evidence that reminds us that our evolution is irregular and ongoing.

We are fortunate to live in a country and a culture where so much of our specie's recent learning and unlearning has occurred. Enlightenment Man is indeed an improvement over the previous, still evident, vertically segmented social and political model, and modern Communitarian Man has a less localized heart than his still evident traditional forebears. Most of the time, each harbors a gentle disposition that is predisposed to see the basic good in most others, and to include some of those formerly excluded from the country and the neighborhood, the workplace and the state.

We are now, in general, further able to somewhat deduce that those in other categories of humanity—national, ethnic, racial, and gender—are entirely human and significantly interdependent, although we are still getting used to the assertive presence of those who have arrived here more recently (or much earlier) than ourselves. We are also are familiar with the physics, chemistry, and biology of other living things, the material world, and their overall instrumental as well as sentimental importance to our lives. Our public policy concerns and our polling data confirm our growing factual awareness that the world with ourselves, other humans, other life-forms, and resources within it are all part of a common rational puzzle whose many parts somehow constitute a unified, interdependent, integrated picture. We still await conclusive proof, however, not realizing, perhaps, that our species, and the planet itself, will not likely survive what goes on in the perennial meantime.

What remains largely unchanged, apart form the vastly greater amount of factual and practical knowledge we have acquired and variously stored, is our undying fear of death and our consequential need to protect, comfort, and enhance the self. As already discussed in a number of ways, our mortal self-absorption, and our related false-static comprehension of our natural, fallen condition, have combined to effectively block the possibility of our garnering from each other and from life the profound knowledge, the simple core truths that rationalism, thus informed, can only weakly identify.

We are blessed to have morally informed core actors in our midst. We surely need more of them, widely known and local alike. It is not that they are flawless prophets, apostles, or certain architects of our evolution—of our promise as a species. What they have demonstrated for us in our past, what they exhibit in our midst, is a fuller, richer, more robust version of ourselves, both alone and in social and political concert. Their actions stir us from our sleep, attract us from our distraction, and confront us with their open invitation to relate with them and to encounter for ourselves what they already know:

- The world and life within it reveals itself—its inherent nature—to us, in all its particulars and assemblages as an interrelated, somehow unified, still mysterious, precious, and wonderful whole;
- In the process of self- and world-discovery we can further detect the inherent good in the actual and potential nature of ourselves and others, including our ability to add to the knowledge that informs our improvable nature, all the while realizing that we each likewise possess at least some of the capacity to intend, tolerate, and commit both lesser harms and catastrophic evils;
- Neither others, nor the self, nor the world can be adequately experienced and known, let alone lived in, by rational means that are premised on unbridgeable self-isolation or utter social dependence;
- Profound social and political knowing, and caring for what we thereby learn, can only come from authentic, direct, democratic engagement with others, including our engagement in fraternity and sorority with those whom we are affectively drawn to and who can most intimately inform us;
- To undertake such learning, we have to go out into the world authentically, with an open heart and mind, as demonstrated by Addams and others, and otherwise learn and imagine what we cannot directly experience or encounter;

- Discernible moral progress, whenever and wherever it most durably occurs, is begun and sustained by authentic, direct social and political action that is informed by the above truths, and motivated by the deep caring that attends them;
- Authentic action can be initiated and maintained more readily in the liberal realm that it has critically helped to produce and advance; moreover, when focused on specific tasks, it has succeeded, and can succeed again. It can do so not only on the strength of the initiating efforts of core actors, but because the knowledge and caring that inform and support their acts are generally accessible, shareable, and powerfully persuasive;
- Knowing, caring, and acting in the manner that morally informed core actors demonstrate is possible, is the way of life that all of us must aspire to adopt to the full extent of our varied talents and potential, so that we can lend our full measure of insight and strength to the task of persuading still others to see more clearly.

As Jean Grossholtz said in an address to a graduating class at her college, "It always starts this way, with one or two, this fight for justice, for equality." She concluded, as does this effort, with the following: "I can tell you this, there is joy in the struggle, in putting your whole self behind your deepest passions, in marching with [others] for justice. But let that struggle be your own [as well]. Resist compromise, and don't take anything lying down." It takes that kind of informed passion, and the strength of the action it informs, to ultimately persuade and move others to reverently, humbly, and courageously participate in the ongoing creation of both America and the world. It is a world that, by its very nature, informs us to do no less.

NOTES

1. Laurent A. Parks Daloz, Cheryl H. Keen, James P. Keen, and Sharon Daloz Parks, *Common Fire: Leading Lives of Commitment in a Complex World* (Boston: Beacon Press, 1996), 181.

2. Jasper, 89.

3. William James, "Pragmatism's Conception of Truth," in *Pragmatism: A New Name for Some Old Ways of Thinking* (1909; New York: Longman's Green and Co., 1947), 197–236; taken here from *The Writings of William James*, John, J. McDermott, ed., 441.

4. Pablo Casals, *Joys and Sorrows: A Reflection*, narrator, Albert E. Kahn (New York: Simon and Schuster, 1970), 295.

5. According to Albert Camus, Sisyphus was condemned by the gods of Greek mythology "to ceaselessly roll a rock to the top of a mountain, whence the stone

would fall back of its own weight." *The Myth of Sisyphus and Other Legends*, trans. Justin O'Brien (New York: Vintage Books, 1955).

6. Too often such openness comes at the end of life, when our need for meaning prompts us to reflect more deeply. In 1888 Douglass met with his former owner, Thomas Auld, then in his late eighties and dying. At Auld's request, Douglass visited him at the same plantation where he had gone through "some of the saddest experiences of [his] slave life." As he recalled the visit, "I was not only willing to meet him, but very glad to do so. The conditions were favorable for the remembrance of all his good deeds, and generous extenuation of all his evil ones. He was to me no longer a slaveholder in fact or in spirit, and I regarded him as I did myself, a victim of the circumstances of birth, education, law, and custom." Douglass (1892), 440–41.

7. Edward O. Wilson provides a rich, accessible account of our genetic and cultural inheritance in *Consilience: The Unity of Knowledge* (New York: Vintage Books, 1999).

8. *Salt of the Earth*, dir. Herman J. Biberman, produced by Independent Productions Company and International Union of Miners, Mill, and Smelter Workers, 1954 (Available in VHS and DVD formats). The film's director, one of the blacklisted "Hollywood Ten," was stripped of his membership in the Director's Guild of America in 1950 in the aftermath of his jailing for contempt of Congress. He had refused to testify before the House Committee on un-American Activities concerning the influence of the American Communist Party in the Hollywood film industry. His membership was posthumously restored in 1997. See "DGA to Restore Membership Posthumously to Biberman," *Studio Brief*, 24 Oct. 1997, http://us.imdb.com/SB?19971023. Cf. Herman J. Biberman, *Salt of the Earth: The Story of a Film* (Boston: Beacon Press, 1965).

9. The cast credits show two actors with the same last name as her father; however, the first names do not match and her assertion can not be confirmed.

10. Derrick Bell, *Faces at the Bottom of the Well* (New York: Basic Books, 1992). Bell illustrates well the terrible power of racism taken into the self and how it helps to perpetuate the myth of white superiority in our society:

> Victimized themselves by an uncaring society, some young blacks vent their rage on victims like themselves, thereby perpetuating the terror that whites once had to invoke directly. We should not be surprised that a society that once legalized slavery and authorized pursuit of fugitive slaves with little concern about the kidnapping of free blacks, now views black-on-black crime as basically a problem for its victims and their communities (196).

11. According to Oliner and Oliner, this was the common refrain of those who rescued Jews in Nazi occupied Europe during World War II. *The Altruistic Personality*, 163–70; 269.

12. The "public square," as Robert Dahl observed, has vastly shrunk in our era, often privatized from existence in its traditional locales and institutional forms. Robert A. Dahl, After the Revolution? 2nd ed. (New Haven: Yale University Press, 1990). Cf. Richard John Neuhaus, *The Naked Public Square: Religion and Democracy in Amer-*

ica, 2nd ed. (1984; Grand Rapids, MI: W.B. Erdman Pub. Co., 1986). Both prior to and following the terrorist attacks on September 11, 2001, newly sophisticated tactics of protest preemption and public isolation have emerged. The public ether of electronic and other technologically created space is also at risk of commercial and coercive political closure. As Hannah Arendt powerfully reminds us, all such political space is created and maintained, in the first and last instance, by nonconforming action. (See note 24, following.)

13. In Chapter 2, somewhat dated survey data gathered by McCloskey and Zaller was used to demonstrate that liberal values, although dominant in America, are not universally accepted. More recently, our ambivalence with our corporate-driven economy and political system is again evident. For a good source, summary, and analysis of more current polling data, see Ruy Teixeira, "Is the Big-Business Era Over?" *The American Prospect* 13, no.12 (26 August 2002): 12–13.

14. Letter from Jane Addams to Ellen Gates Starr, Nov. 22, 1879, quoted in Addams, *Democracy and Social Ethics*, intro. by Anne Fior Scott, ed. (Cambridge, MA: Belknap-Harvard University Press, 1964), xx.

15. As Richard John Neuhaus observes, our churches reflect society and are therefore prone to the same forms of mendacity and corruption that we see in politics and business. Their critical social and political importance lies in the fact that they are at least structured by different "ordering principles." This is highly significant, as are the "ordering principles" of our liberal regime, where each provides some legitimate opening for core actors to challenge corrupt practices, as well as silence or neutral stances, on matters of matters of social and political justice, and to garner conventional support. Richard John Neuhaus, *America Against Itself: Moral Vision and the Public Order* (Notre Dame, IN: University of Notre Dame Press, 1992), 17–18.

16. After reviewing what had been written about her father, she added the following:

> My father, dreamer though he certainly was, did his best to provide for his family. . . . [A]ll his varied projects raised money for the family and during them all he kept his fulltime job at the electric company and moved up that ladder. . . . Finally, his desire for a different life got the best of him; he had always appreciated his days in the Navy and that's where he finally found his escape. I found out later that he died in some remote village in Tennessee where he was making stringed instruments.

17. Philosopher Mark Johnson uses the term "moral imagination" to describe part of the process of moral deliberation. It involves "projecting possible actions to determine their probable results, taking up the part of other people who may be affected, and reading with sensitivity the relevant dimensions of a particular situation. . . ." Although he speaks in terms of moral reasoning, he concludes his discussion of imagination with the following: "My point is that moral reasoning is a much richer, more complex, and more flexible capacity than it has been conceived to be in traditional Enlightenment accounts of practical reason." Mark L. Johnson, "How Moral Psychology Changes Moral Theory," in Larry May et al., eds., *Mind and Morals: Essays on Ethics and Cognitive Science* (Cambridge, MA: MIT Press, 1996), 66.

18. Walter Kaufmann, intro. to Martin Buber, *I and Thou*. In his introduction, philosopher Walter Kaufmann gives one of the most apt accounts of how one morally imagines through books:

> We must learn to feel addressed by a book, by the human being behind it, as if a person spoke directly to us. A good book of essays or poems is not primarily an object to be put to use, or an object of experience: it is the voice of You speaking to me, requiring a response (39).

One can assume that he was not referring to the products of committees or hired writers.

19. Paul Tillich, *The New Being* (New York: Charles Scribner's Sons, 1955), Chap. 9.

20. William James, "The Sentiment of Rationality," in *The Writings of William James*, John J. McDermott, ed., 317–45. James's idea of radical empiricism informs this notion, and to some extent, the overall project. Cf. William James, "Pragmatism's Conception of Truth," in McDermott, ed., 428–41. His related effort to understand the mystical perception of truth through the lens of his brilliant insights on empirical knowledge is helpful; however, he ultimately leaves the source of the truth, whose contents and practical impacts he so keenly appreciates, located in the sub-conscious, for reasons that are neither clear nor necessary. William James, *The Varieties of Religious Experience: A Study in Human Nature* (New York: Random House, Inc., 1994).

21. Paul Tillich, *The Courage to Be* (1955; New Haven: Yale University Press, 1968), 44–50.

22. Buber, 56. It is his account of encounter that has been relied upon extensively herein, although his assertion of our capacity to encounter God directly has not.

23. Buber, 56–57.

24. Hannah Arendt, "'What Remains?' The Language Remains: A Conversation with Günter Gaus," in, *Essays in Understanding: 1930–1954*, Jerome Kohn, ed., 22–23.

25. Stanton, for example, although she devoted her entire adult life to the cause of women, did not harbor any romantic illusions concerning their insightful strength, any more than men. In an 1865 letter apparently written to console her colleague and dearest friend, Susan B. Anthony, for a recent bout of personal criticism she had received from women opposed to her uncompromising calls for female equality alongside African American men, she wrote:

> Well, the human family is affording you abundant experience in the degradation of women; their littleness and meanness are the result of their abject dependence, their utter want of self-respect. But this must needs be so until they reach a higher development. Poor things!

Elizabeth Cady Stanton, "To Susan B. Anthony," Sept. 10, 1865, in *Elizabeth Cady Stanton*, vol. 2, Theodore Stanton and Harriet Stanton Blatch. eds., 107–8.

26. Hannah Arendt, *Eichmann in Jerusalem: A Report of the Banality of Evil* (1963; New York: Penguin Books, 1994).

27. Hopefully, we are in the process of rediscovering that we are not born as "*tabula rasa*—scraped tablet." This view, still held by many social scientists, "is often attributed to . . . John Locke, who wrote that the mind is 'white paper void of all characters.' " Steven Pinker, "The Blank Slate," *Discover*, 23, no. 10 (Oct. 2002): 35.

Bibliography

BOOKS, ARTICLES, PAPERS

Addams, Jane. "A Modern Lear." In *The Social Thought of Jane Addams*, edited by Christopher Lasch. Indianapolis: Bobbs-Merrill Co., Inc., 1965.

——. *Democracy and Social Ethics*. Edited and introduced by Anne Fior Scott. Cambridge, MA: Belknap-Harvard University Press, 1964.

——. *Newer Ideals of Peace*. Edited by Richard T. Ely. New York: MacMillan Co, 1907.

——. *Peace and Bread in Time of War*. New York: MacMillan Co, 1922.

——. "Trade Unions and Public Duty." *American Journal of Sociology* 4 (1899): 448–62.

Arendt, Hannah. *Crisis of the Republic*. New York: Harcourt Brace Jovanovich, 1972.

——. *Eichmann in Jerusalem: A Report of the Banality of Evil* (1963). New York: Penguin Books, 1994.

——. *Essays in Understanding: 1930–1954*. Edited and introduced by Jerome Kohn. New York: Harcourt Brace, 1994.

——. *The Human Condition*. Chicago: University of Chicago Press, 1958; New York: Doubleday-Anchor Books, 1959.

Bailyn, Bernard. *The Ideological Origins of the American Revolution*. Cambridge, MA: Belknap-Harvard University Press, 1992.

Beatty, Jack. "The Case for and Against Incorporation." In *Colossus: How the Business Corporation Changed America*, edited by Jack Beatty. New York: Broadway Books, 2001.

Belknap, Joanne. *The Invisible Woman: Gender, Crime, and Justice*. 2nd ed. Wadsworth Group-Thompson Learning, 2001.

Bell, Derrick. *Faces at the Bottom of the Well*. New York: Basic Books, 1992.

Bellah, Robert N., et al. *The Good Society*. New York: Alfred A. Knopf, 1991.

——. *Habits of the Heart: Individualism and Commitment in American Life*. Berkeley and Los Angeles: University of California Press, 1985; 1996.

Bennett, William, John J. DiUlio, Jr., and John P. Walters, *Body Count: Moral Poverty and How to Win America's War Against Crime and Drugs*. New York: Simon & Schuster, 1996.

Berlin, Isaiah. *Four Essays on Liberty*. New York: Oxford University Press, 1969.

Biberman, Herman J. *Salt of the Earth: The Story of a Film*. Boston: Beacon Press, 1965.

Blatch, Theodore Stanton, and Harriot Stanton Blatch, eds. *Elizabeth Cady Stanton as Revealed in her Letters, Diary, and Reminiscences*. Vol. 2 (1922). Chicago: Arno Press, Inc., 1969.

Brooks, David. *Bobos in Paradise: The New Upper Class and How They Got There*. New York: Simon & Schuster, 2000.

Buber, Martin. *I and Thou*. Translated and introduced by Walter Kaufmann. New York: Charles Scribner's Sons, 1970.

Camus, Albert. *The Myth of Sisyphus and Other Legends*. Translated by Justin O'Brien. New York: Vintage Books, 1955.

Carter, Stephen L. *Civility: Manners, Morals, and the Etiquette of Democracy*. New York: Harper Perennial-HarperCollins, 1998.

——. *The Culture of Disbelief: How American Law and Politics Trivialize Religious Devotion*. New York: Anchor Books-Doubleday, 1993.

Casals, Pablo. *Joys and Sorrows: A Reflection*. Narrated by Albert E. Kahn. New York: Simon and Schuster, 1970.

Chesebrough, David B. *Frederick Douglass: Oratory from Slavery*. Westport, CT: Greenwood Press, 1998.

Cobban, Helena. "Boost US Foreign Aid, Big-time." *Christian Science Monitor*. 13 Dec. 2001.

Coleman, McAlister. *Eugene V. Debs: A Man Unafraid*. New York: Greenberg, 1930; Ann Arbor, MI: University Microfilms, Inc., 1966.

Constantine, J. Robert, ed. *Letters of Eugene V. Debs*. 3 vols. Urbana: University of Illinois Press, 1990.

Costin, Lela B. *Two Sisters for Social Justice: A Biography of Grace and Edith Abbott*. Urbana: University of Illinois Press, 1983.

Connolly, William E. "The Challenge to Pluralist Theory." In *The Bias of Pluralism*, edited by William E. Connolly. New York: Atherton Press, 1969.

Cooney, Robert, and Helen Michalowski, eds. *The Power of the People: Active Nonviolence in the United States*. Culver City, CA: Peace Press, 1977.

Croly, Herbert. *The Promise of American Life* (1909). edited by Arthur M. Schlesinger, Jr. Cambridge, MA: Harvard University Press, 1965.

——. *Progressive Democracy* (1914). New Brunswick, NJ: Transaction Press, 1998.

Currie, Harold W. *Eugene V. Debs*. Boston: Twayne Publishers, 1976.

Dahl, Robert A. *After the Revolution?* 2nd ed. New Haven: Yale University Press, 1990.

——. *Dilemmas of Pluralist Democracy: Autonomy versus Control*. New Haven: Yale University Press, 1982.

Daloz, Laurent A., Cheryl H. Parks, James P. Keen, and Sharon Daloz Parks. *Common Fire: Leading Lives of Commitment in a Complex World*. Boston: Beacon Press, 1996.

Dalton, Russel J., and Manfred Kuechler, eds. *Challenging the Political Order: Social Movements in Western Democracies*. New York: Oxford University Press, 1990.

Davis, Mike. *City of Quartz: Escavating the Future in Los Angeles*. New York: Vintage Books, 1992.

Day, Dorothy. *On Pilgrimage: The Sixties*. New York: HarperCollins, 1972.

DeMott, Benjamin. "Seduced by Civility: Political Manners and the Crisis of Democratic Values." *The Nation*. 9 Dec. 1996: 11–19.

Dewey, John. *The Public and its Problems* (1927). Athens, OH: Swallow Press-Ohio University Press, 1997.

Diggins, John P. *The Lost Soul of American Politics: Virtue, Self-interest, and the Foundations of Liberalism* (1984). Chicago: University of Chicago Press, 1986.

Diliberto, Gioia. *A Useful Woman: The Early Life of Jane Addams*. New York: Lisa Drew-Scribner, 1999.

Diskin, Martin. "El Salvador: Reform Prevents Change." In *Searching for Agrarian Reform in Latin America*, edited by William C. Thiesenhusen. Winchester, MA: Unwin Hyman, Inc., 1989.

Douglass, Frederick. *My Bondage and My Freedom* (1855). Introduced by James M'-Cune Smith. New York: Dover Publications, 1969.

———. *Life and Times of Frederick Douglass* (1892). London: Collier-Macmillan Ltd., 1962.

Dryzek, John S. *Democracy in Capitalist Times: Ideals, Limits, and Struggles*. New York and Oxford: Oxford University Press, 1996.

DuBois, Ellen Carol, ed. *The Elizabeth Cady Stanton – Susan B. Anthony Reader*. Boston: Northeastern University Press, 1992.

Dunn, Richard S. *Sugar and Slaves: The Rise of the Planter Class in the English Indies, 1624–1713*. New York: W. W. Norton, 1972.

Durkheim, Emile. *On Morality and Society: Selected Writings*. Edited and introduced by Robert N. Bellah. Chicago: University of Chicago Press, 1973.

Eisenach, Eldon J. *The Lost Promise of Progressivism*. Lawrence: University of Kansas Press, 1994.

Etzioni, Amitai. *The New Golden Rule: Community and Morality in a Democratic Society*. New York: Basic Books, 1996.

Farrell, Jonh C. *Beloved Lady: A History of Jane Addams Ideas on Reform and Peace*. Baltimore: Johns Hopkins University Press, 1967.

Feinman, Clarice. *Women and the Criminal Justice System*. 3rd ed. Westport, CT: Praeger Publishing. 1994.

Festinger, Leon. *A Theory of Cognitive Dissonance*. Evanston, IL: Row, Peterson, 1957.

Foner, Philip S. *Frederick Douglass: A Biography*. New York: Citadel Press, 1964.

Fox, Matthew. *Original Blessing*. Santa Fe, NM: Bear & Company, 1983.

Gandhi, Mohandas K. *An Autobiography: The Story of My Experiments with Truth*. Translated by Mahadev Desai. Boston: Beacon Press, 1957; 1993.

Gilligan, Carol. *In a Different Voice: Psychological Theory and Women's Development*, (1982). Cambridge, MA: Harvard University Press, 1993.

Glendon, Mary Ann. *Rights Talk: The Impoverishment of Political Discourse*. New York: Free Press-Macmillan, Inc, 1991.

Green, Donald P., and Ian Shapiro. *Pathologies of Rational Choice Theory: A Critique of Applications in Political Science*. New Haven: Yale University Press, 1994.

Griffith, Elizabeth. *In Her Own Right: The Life of Elizabeth Cady Stanton*. New York: Oxford University Press, 1984.

Guigni, Marco, Doug McAdam, and Charles Tilly, eds. *How Social Movements Matter: Social Movements, Protest, and Contention Series*. Vol. 10. Foreword by Sidney Tarrow. Minneapolis: University of Minnnesota Press, 1999.

Hahlweg, Kai, and C. A. Hooker. "Evolutionary Epistemology and Philosophy of Science." In *Issues in Evolutionary Epistemology*. edited and introduced by Kai Hahlweg and C. A. Hooker. Albany, NY: SUNY Press, 1989.

Hanh, Thich Nhat. *The Heart of the Buddha's Teaching: Transforming Suffering into Peace, Joy, and Liberation*. New York: First Broadway Books-Random House, Inc, 1999.

Hawking, Stephen W. *A Brief History of Time: From the Big Bang to Black Holes*. New York: Bantam Books, 1988.

Himmelfarb, Gertrude. *Poverty and Compassion: The Moral Imagination of the Victorians*. New York: Knopf, 1991.

Hobbes, Thomas. *Leviathan*, Chap. 13: *The English Philosophers from Bacon to Mill*, edited by Edwin A. Burt. New York: Random House, 1939.

Holifield, E. Brooks. *Era of Persuasion: American Thought and Culture 1521–1680*. Boston: Twayne Publishers, 1989.

Holstein, James A., and Jaber B Gubrium. *The Active Interview*. Qualitative Research Methods Series (vol. 37). Thousand Oaks, CA: Sage Publications, 1995.

Hume, David. *An Inquiry Concerning the Principles of Morals* (1751). Edited and introduced by Charles W. Hendel. Indianapolis, IN: Bobbs-Merrill, 1957.

Huntington, Samuel P. *American Politics: The Promise of Disharmony*. Cambridge, MA: Belknap Press of Harvard University, 1981.

Irons, Peter. *A People's History of the Supreme Court*. New York: Penguin Putnam Inc, 1999.

James, William. *Pragmatism: A New Name for Some Old Ways of Thinking* (1909). New York: Longman's Green and Co., 1947.

——. *The Writings of William James: A Comprehensive Edition*. Edited by John J. McDermott Chicago: University of Chicago Press, 1967; 1977.

——. *The Varieties of Religious Experience: A Study in Human Nature* (1902). New York: Random House, Inc., 1994.

Jasper, James M. *The Art of Moral Protest: Biography and Creativity in Social Movements*. Chicago: University of Chicago Press, 1997.

Johnson, Mark L. "How Moral Psychology Changes Moral Theory." In *Mind and Morals: Essays on Ethics and Cognitive Science*, edited by Larry May, Marilyn Friedman, and Andy Clark. Cambridge, MA: MIT Press, 1996.

Kaplan, E. Ann . "Women, Morality, and Social Change from a Discourse Analysis Perspective." In *Social and Moral Values: Individual and Social Perspectives*, edited by Nancy Eisenberg, Janus Reykowski, and Ervin Staub. Hillsdale, NJ: Lawrence Erlbaum Associates, 1989.

Katz, Claudio J. "Syndicalist Liberalism: The New Republic of Herbert Croly." Paper presented at the annual meeting of the American Association of Political Science, Boston, MA, August, 1998.

Keller, Morton. *Regulating a New Economy: Public Policy and Economic Change, 1900–1933*. Cambridge, MA: Harvard University Press, 1994.

Kennedy, Lawrence W. *Planning the City Upon a Hill: Boston Since 1630*. Amherst, MA: University of Massachusetts Press, 1992.

King, Martin Luther, Jr. *A Testament of Hope: The Essential Writings and Speeches of Martin Luther King, Jr.* Edited by James M. Washington. New York: Harper-Collins, 1986.

Kohlberg, Lawrence. *The Psychology of Moral Development*. San Francisco: Harper and Row, 1984.

Kozol, Jonathan. *Amazing Grace: The Lives of Children and the Conscience of a Nation*. New York: Crown Publishers, 1995.

Lasch, Christopher. *The Revolt of the Elites and the Betrayal of Democracy*. New York: W. W. Norton, 1995.

Lefko, Claudia. "Conscientious Objector." *Hampshire Life Magazine* in *Daily Hampshire Gazette*. 18 Dec. 1998.

Leonard, Elizabeth Dermody. *Convicted Survivors: The Imprisonment of Battered Women Who Kill*. Albany: SUNY Press, 2002.

Linn, James Weber. *Jane Addams: A Biography*. New York: D. Appleton-Century Co., 1935.

Lippmann, Walter. *The Good Society*. Boston: Little-Brown, 1937.

Locke, John. *Two Treatises on Government* (1688). Edited and introduced by Peter Laslett. New York: Mentor-New American Library, 1965.

Longino, Helen E. "Moral Agency and Responsibility." In *Mind and Morals: Essays on Cognitive Science and Ethics*, edited by Larry May, Marilyn Friedman, and Andy Clark. Cambridge, MA: MIT Press, 1996.

Lovejoy, David S. *The Glorious Revolution in America*. New York: Harper and Row, 1972.

Lynd, Staughton, and Alice Lynd, eds. *Nonviolence in America: A Documentary History*. Maryknoll, NY: Orbis Books, 1995.

Machiavelli, Niccolò. *The Prince*. Translated by Luigi Ricci, In *The Prince and the Discourses*. Edited and introduced by Max Lerner. New York: Random House-Modern Library, 1950.

MacIntyre, Alasdair C. *After Virtue: A Study in Moral Theory*. Notre Dame, IN: University of Notre Dame Press, 1981; 1984.

MacPherson, C. B. *The Political Theory of Possessive Individualism: Hobbes to Locke*. Oxford: Oxford University Press, 1962.

Madison, James. *Notes of Debates in the Federal Convention of 1787*. Introduced by Adrienne Koch. New York: W. W. Norton, 1987.

Madison, James, et al. *The Federalist Papers*. Edited and introduced by Clinton Rossiter. New York: Penguin-Mentor, 1961.

Mansfield, Harvey C., Jr. *Taming the Prince: The Ambivalence of Modern Executive Power*. Baltimore: The Johns Hopkins University Press, 1989; 1993.

Marchand, Roland. *Creating the Corporate Soul: The Rise of Public Relations and Corporate Imagery in American Big Business*. Berkeley and Los Angeles: University of California Press, 1998.

Marsh, Charles. *God's Long, Hot Summer: Stories of Faith and Civil Rights*. Princeton: Princeton University Press, 1997.

Martin, Waldo E. *The Mind of Frederick Douglass*. Chapel Hill: University of North Carolina Press, 1984.

May, Larry, Marilyn Friedman, and Andy Clark eds. *Mind and Morals: Essays on Ethics and Cognitive Science*. Cambridge, MA: MIT Press, 1996.

McCloskey, Herbert and John Zaller. *The American Ethos: Public Attitudes toward Capitalism and Democracy*. Cambridge, MA: Harvard University Press, 1984.

McGrory, Mary. "Their Passion Was Politics." *Washington Post*. 12 Feb. 1991: A2.

McWilliams, Wilson Carey. *The Idea of Fraternity in America*. Berkeley: University of California Press, 1973.

Miles, Rosalind. *Who Cooked the Last Supper? A Women's History of the World*. New York: Three Rivers Press, 2001.

Mill, John Stuart. *On Liberty* (1859). Edited by Elizabeth Rapaport. Indianapolis, IN: Hackett Publishing, 1978.

Monroe, Kristen Renwick. *The Heart of Altruism: Perceptions of a Common Humanity*. Princeton: Princeton University Press, 1996.

Montesquieu. *Spirit of the Laws* (1748). Translated and edited by Anne M. Cohler. Cambridge, UK: Cambridge University Press, 1989.

Morgan, H. Wayne. *Eugene V. Debs: Socialist for President*. Syracuse: Syracuse University Press, 1962.

Morris, Aldon D. *The Origins of the Civil Rights Movement: Black Communities Organizing for Change*. New York: Macmillan, Inc.-Free Press, 1984.

Nash, Gary B. *The Urban Crucible: The Northern Seaports and the Origins of the American Revolution*. Cambridge, MA: Harvard University Press, 1986.

Neuhaus, Richard John. *America Against Itself: Moral Vision and the Public Order*. Notre Dame: University of Notre Dame Press, 1992.

———. *The Naked Public Square: Religion and Democracy in America*. 2nd ed. Grand Rapids, MI: W. B. Erdman Publishing Co., 1986.

Niebuhr, Reinhold. *Moral Man, Immoral Society: A Study in Ethics and Politics*. New York: Charles Scribner's Sons, 1932; 1960.

———. *The Children of Light and the Children of Darkness: A Vindication of Democracy and a Critique of its Traditional Defense*. London: Nisbit, 1945; New York: Charles Scribner's Sons, 1960.

Oakeshott, Michael. *Rationalism in Politics, and Other Essays*. New York: Basic Books, 1962.

Oakley, Mary Ann B. *Elizabeth Cady Stanton*. Westbury, NY: Feminist Press/State University of New York Press, 1972.

Oates, Stephen B. *Let the Trumpet Sound: A Life of Martin Luther King, Jr.* New York: Harper and Row, 1982; New York: HarperCollins/Harper Perennial, 1994.

Oliner, Samuel P., and Pearl M. Oliner. *The Altruistic Personality: Rescuers of Jews in Nazi Europe*. New York: The Free Press, 1988.

———. *Toward a Caring Society: Ideas into Action*. Westport, CT: Praeger Publishers, 1995.

Pangle, Thomas L. *The Enobling of Democracy: The Challenge of the Postmodern Age*. Baltimore: Johns Hopkins University Press, 1992.

———. *The Spirit of Modern Republicanism: The Moral Vision of the American Founders and the Philosophy of John Locke*. Chicago: University of Chicago Press, 1988; 1990.

Pateman, Carole. *The Problem of Political Obligation: A Critique of Liberal Theory*. Berkeley and Los Angeles: University of California Press, 1985.

Pinker, Steven. "The Blank Slate." *Discover* 23, no.10 (Oct 2002): 35-40.

Putnam, Robert D. *Bowling Alone: The Collapse and Revival of American Community* New York: Simon & Schuster, 2000.

———, et al. *Making Democracy Work: Civic Traditions in Modern Italy*. Princeton: Princeton University Press, 1993.

Radosh, Ronald, ed. *Great Lives Observed: Debs*. Englewood Cliffs, NJ: Prentice-Hall, 1971.

Rauschenbusch, Walter. *Christianity and the Social Crisis* (1907). Foreword by Douglas F. Ottati. Louisville, KY: Westminster-John Knox Press, 1991.

Rochon, Thomas R., and David S. Meyer, eds *Coalitions and Social Movements: The Lessons of the Nuclear Freeze*. Boulder, CO: Lynne Rienner Publishers. 1997.

Roy, William G. *Socializing Capital: The Rise of the Large Industrial Corporation in America*. Princeton: Princeton University Press, 1997.

Rudé, George. *The Crowd in History: A Study of Popular Disturbances in France and England, 1730–1848*. New York: John Wiley & Sons, 1964.

Salvatore, Nick. *Eugene V. Debs: Citizen and Socialist*. Urbana: University of Illinois Press, 1982.

Sandel, Michael J. *Democracy's Discontent: America in Search of a Public Philosophy*. Cambridge, MA: Belknap-Harvard University Press, 1996.

Schattschneider, E. E. *The Semi-Sovereign People: A Realist's View of Democracy in America*. Hinsdale, IL: Dryden Press, 1960.

Schweitzer, Albert. *The Philosophy of Civilization*. Translated and introduced by C. T. Campion. New York: Macmillan, 1950.

Sen, Amartya K. "Rational Fools: A Critique of the Behavioral Foundations of Economic Theory." *Philosophy and Public Affairs* 6, no. 4 (Summer 1977): 317–44.

Shanahan, Edward K. "Tracking is Attorney's Latest Cause." *Daily Hampshire Gazette*. 24 May 1997.

Shapiro, Ian, and Donald P. Green. *Pathologies of Rational Choice Theory: A Critique of Applications in Political Science*. New Haven: Yale University Press, 1994.

Siedman, I. E. *Interviewing as Qualitative Research*. New York: Teachers College Press, 1991.

Skocpol, Theda. *Protecting Soldiers and Mothers: The Political Origins of Social Policy in the United States*. Cambridge, MA: Belknap Press, 1992.

Skowronek, Stephen. *Building a New American State: The Expansion of National Administrative Capacities, 1877–1920.* Cambridge, UK: Cambridge University Press, 1982.

Sober, Elliot, and David Sloan Wilson. *Unto Others: The Evolution and Psychology of Unselfish Behavior.* Cambridge, MA: Harvard University Press, 1998.

Stanton, Elizabeth Cady. *Eighty Years and More: Reminiscences 1815–1897* (1898). Introduced by Ellen Carol DuBois. Boston: Northeastern University Press, 1993.

Stout, Harry S. *The New England Soul: Preaching and Religious Culture in Colonial New England.* New York and Oxford: Oxford University Press, 1986.

Strauss, Leo. *Natural Right and History.* Chicago: University of Chicago Press, 1953.

Tarrow, Sidney. Foreword to *How Social Movements Matter: Social Movements, Protest, and Contention Series.* Vol. 10. Edited by Marco Guigni, Doug McAdam, and Charles Tilly. Minneapolis: University of Minnnesota Press, 1999.

Teixeira, Ruy. "Is the Big-Business Era Over?" *The American Prospect* 13, no. 12 (26 August 2002).

Tillich, Paul. *The Courage to Be* (1955). New Haven, CT: Yale University Press, 1968.

Tocqueville, Alexis de. *Democracy in America.* Translated by George Lawrence, and edited by J. P. Mayer. New York: Harper & Row, 1966; New York: Harper Perennial-HarperCollins, 1988.

True, Michael. *An Energy Field More Intense Than War: The Non-Violent Tradition in American Literature.* Syracuse: Syracuse University Press, 1995.

Tussman, Joseph. *Obligation and the Body Politic.* New York: Oxford University Press, 1960.

von Hayek, Friedrich A. *The Road to Serfdom* (1944). Chicago: University of Chicago Press, 1994.

Walters, Ronald G. *American Reformers, 1815–1860.* New York: Hill and Wang, 1978.

Walzer, Michael. *Obligations: Essays on Disobedience, War, and Citizenship.* Cambridge, MA: Harvard University Press, 1970.

———. "The Problem of Dirty Hands." *Philosophy and Public Affairs* 2 (Winter 1973): 160–80.

———. *Spheres of Justice.* New York: Basic Books, 1983.

Weber, Max. *The Protestant Ethic and the Spirit of Capitalism.* Translated by Talcott Parsons, New York: Charles Scribner's Sons, 1958.

West, Darrell M., Diane Heath, and Chris Goodwin. "Harry and Louise Go to Washington: Political Advertising and Health Care Reform." *Journal of Health Politics, Policy, and Law* 21, no. 1 (Spring 1996): 35–68.

Wilson, James. *The Works of James Wilson.* 2 vols. Edited by Robert Green McCloskey. Cambridge, MA: Harvard University Press, 1967.

Wilson, James Q. *The Moral Sense.* New York: The Free Press-Macmillan, Inc., 1993.

Wilson, Woodrow. *The New Freedom: A Call for the Emancipation of the Generous Energies of a People* (1914). Englewood Cliffs, NJ: Prentice-Hall, 1961.

Wolfe, Alan. *One Nation After All.* New York: Penguin Group, 1998.

Zinn, Howard. *Declarations of Independence: Cross-Examining American Ideology.* New York: HarperCollins, 1990.

———. *A People's History of the United States: 1492 – Present.* New York: Harper Perennial, 1995.

INTERNET REFERENCES

American Association of Fundraising Counsel/AAFRC Trust for Philanthropic Giving. *Philanthropy News Digest.* 6, no. 21 (23 May 2000). http://www.aafrc.org/.

The Idea Logic Company, Inc. "BaseballLibrary.com." http://www.pubdim.net/baseball library/.

Independent Television News Service. "The Democratic Promise: Saul Alinsky and His Legacy." http://www.itvs.org/democraticpromise/alinsky1.html.

The Internet Movie Database. "DGA to Restore Membership Posthumously to Biberman." *Studio Briefing.* 24 Oct. 1997. www.us.imdb.com/SB?19971024#5.

National Voting Rights Institute. "Mission Statement." http://nvri.org/page 6.html.

Physicians for Social Responsibility. Home page. http://www.psrus.org.

School of the America's Watch. Home page. http://www.soaw.org.

U.S. Census Bureau. Data set: Census 2000 Redistricting Data (P. L. 94-171). Summary File, Connecticut Matrices. http://quickfacts.census.gov/cql-bln/state.

FILMS

Salt of the Earth. Herman J. Biberman, dir. Produced by Independent Productions Company and International Union of Miners, Mill, and Smelter Workers. 1954.

Index

abolition, 8. *See also* Douglass, Frederick; Stanton, Elizabeth Cady
academia, emergence of, 44; Jane Addams as early product of, 110
ACLU, Kantian purists in, 37
action, interpersonal, social, and political: authenticity of, 83–84, 100n7, 166; backed by power, efficacy of, 86; care and (*see* care); confrontational, 141, 151; congruence with belief, 85, 139–40; context of, 84 (*see also* current context; *accounts of individual core actors*); of core actors, 81–83 (*see also* core actors: initiatory action by); demonstrative nature of, 81, 84, 96, 230; disclosing nature of, 79, 81, 178–79, 184; emotion as motive force of, 118–19; as "experiments with Truth," 112, 184–85; habit contrasted with, 79–80; heroic, 119; initiatory, 8–9, 81–82, 89, 231; instrumental, 82, 86; intentional nature of, 82; moral beliefs, relationship to, 81–82; moral knowledge and (*see* moral knowledge); persuasive, 82; political ideals, relationship to, 14, 114; political and social vitality of, 92,
220; speech, publication, and organization as, 83, 92–97; and will, 80–81, 168; words, artificial distinction from, 100n4
activism *See* action; core actors
Addams, Jane, 21–22, 79, 107; background and context, 107–8, 110; Catt, Carrie Chapman, 120; Chicago, University of, School of Social Work, 122; comparison with Elizabeth Cady Stanton, 110, 118, 119; *Democracy and Social Ethics*, 117; democratic engagement, experience, and immersion, 112–13, 115, 117–18; Dewey, John, 118, 121; early life, 110, 216; growing unease, 110–11; Hull House, 112–13, 115, 117, 121, 122, 128n54; on industrial philanthropy, 116; influence of William James, 128n62; Lloyd, Henry Demarest, 115, 116; moral pragmatism, 119, 121–22; Nobel Peace Prize, 122; persistence, 122; as pacifist, 118–21; Pullman, George, as King Lear, 116; Pullman Strike of 1894, 114, 115–17 (*see also* Debs, Eugene V.); Rockford Seminary for Women, 110; role of action, 121; scope of activism, 112–13, 115–16,